The Book of
MOUSE

Other Books by Jim Korkis

The Vault of Walt: Volume 3 (Theme Park Press, 2014)

Animation Anecdotes (Theme Park Press, 2014)

Who's the Leader of the Club?
Walt Disney's Leadership Lessons (Theme Park Press, 2014)

The Vault of Walt: Volume 2 (Theme Park Press, 2013)

The Book of Mouse (Theme Park Press, 2013)

The Revised Vault of Walt (Theme Park Press, 2012)

Who's Afraid of the Song of the South? (Theme Park Press, 2012)

The Book of Mouse

A CELEBRATION OF
WALT DISNEY'S MICKEY MOUSE

Jim Korkis

Foreword by
Don "Ducky" Williams
Senior Disney Character Artist

Theme Park Press

Contents

Foreword

At the age of ten, I first wrote to Walt Disney for a job as an artist. I even got a letter back from Walt himself that I still have! It is one of the treasures in my collection. It basically said that he had no openings for a ten-year-old artist at the time but to keep drawing.

And I did. For years and years and years.

I worked at a bank and I decorated the walls at Christmas with my paintings of Disney characters, including Mickey Mouse. That caught the attention of a local television news show and eventually caught the attention of the Disney Company. They told me there were no openings in California for an artist but there might be in Florida.

From seven o'clock in the evening until two o'clock in the morning each night after work, I spent one week finishing one hundred Disney drawings to send to the person in charge in Florida. I sent another hundred drawings the second week. I sent another hundred drawings the third week. I continued to do that amount of drawings every week for two years.

I was afraid that if I cut back, they would think I was losing interest.

Finally, I just quit my job at the bank and moved to Florida. I wanted a mouse, Mickey Mouse, on my paycheck.

The art department at the time was underneath the Magic Kingdom in the Utilidors. I would go down there constantly until, finally, there was a temporary opening to increase the staff.

To convince the manager of the department that I was the guy for the job, the boxes and boxes of artwork that I had sent were brought in. It was over ten thousand drawings. So I was loaned out to the Art Department for thirty days.

The first week I did nothing but practice drawing Mickey from all angles and with every possible expression. Eight hours a day.

Within the first few weeks after I was hired to be a Disney character artist, I discovered that it wasn't going to be the dream come true I thought it would be.

And it was all because of Mickey Mouse!

I'd already been drawing Mickey for years. My ability to draw him — and dozens of other Disney characters — was what (I thought) qualified me to get this job after years of waiting, wishing, and drawing.

Two outstanding Disney character artists — Russell Schroeder and Harry Gladstone — were assigned to supervise my work. So, I'd sit down and draw Mickey.

Russell would look at it, lay tracing tissue over it, and show me what lines needed adjusting. That was fine, easy to fix, no problem.

Later, Harry would visit, check out the same drawing and show me a different approach with other line treatments.

This would go on and on, back and forth, day after day. I thought I would never be able to get Mickey right. Both of them couldn't be wrong, right?

There weren't wrong. Russell had a specific way of drawing Mickey. His was a more mature Mickey. Harry's Mickey was a little more youthful.

Every artist who draws Mickey Mouse puts a bit of himself into the character no matter how closely they try to follow the approved model sheet. A model sheet was a reference developed for animation at Disney so that multiple artists would draw the character the same way. It shows how the character is constructed, how tall he is, hints about the placement of details, and more.

The general public just sees Mickey Mouse if all the right elements are there.

Trained artists, however, can pick out a Freddy Moore Mickey in '40s cartoons, a Floyd Gottfredson Mickey in '50s comics, a Mark Henn '80s Mickey in *Mickey's Christmas Carol*, and so on.

They are all Mickey Mouse, every one of them. None of these depictions of Mickey are what we call "off model" (a term for a character drawing that doesn't match the approved set of poses created for reference).

Drawing the characters is more than a job for me. It's a way of life. Like many people, I have been infatuated with the characters since childhood. The characters are more than drawings to me. They are living, breathing personalities, and you've got to get that personality into your drawing. And the only way you can really project that personality of the characters is to really know the characters.

I know their films inside and out. I have studied the studio and the animators. If you show me a Mickey Mouse cartoon from 1934, I can tell you which animators animated which scene. That's a Milt Kahl Mickey. That's a Frank Thomas. I am that close to it. All of this study is to help me make the characters like Mickey come to life on the page.

When it came time to build Mickey Mouse's house in Mickey's Birthdayland at the Magic Kingdom to celebrate Mickey's 60th birthday in 1988, Disney came to Russell Schroeder and myself because we knew the Mouse so well. Russell even wrote a book about Mickey's life story in 1997.

We were amazed how little they knew about Mickey and how he lived.

"What does his house look like inside?" they asked. Russell and I just looked at each other and thought, "Just look at the cartoons. That's what the inside of Mickey's house looks like."

The house had to be designed and built in three months, and so time was of the essence. I guess that's why they came to us because we already knew. Russell and I designed all the furniture. We went to Home Depot to pick out carpeting and wallpaper. Mickey had a den and they had no props so I brought in my own: a snow globe of WDW, my Disneyland records, Disney books, etc., to decorate the Mouse's domicile. Guests loved it.

When Mickey's Toontown Fair opened years later in 1996, they had much more time and did a nice job redesigning the entire house with curved cartoony lines and wonderful little details.

Russell and I even illustrated together a Little Golden Book with Mickey, *Mickey's Prince and the Pauper*, that first appeared in December 1990.

Over the decades, I have drawn Mickey Mouse on all sorts of merchandise and lithographs and I even taught singer Michael Jackson how to draw Mickey because he was so eager to learn. I have done seventy-five Disney Cruises and the guests always want to see me draw Mickey.

The more I get to know Mickey, through my drawings and through the ways I see how he affects so many people, from the simplest sketch to his appearances in Walt Disney World, the more aspects I discover about his personality, his emotional range, and his worldwide appeal.

And the Mickey Mouse I draw and paint is a little different from the others. After over 30 years now as senior character artist for Walt Disney Parks and Resorts, I must have been doing something right about drawing Mickey because they keep asking me to do it.

With all I've learned, I know I can always learn more, which is why I am grateful that my friend Jim Korkis has put together this book with all this wonderful information about Mickey Mouse. I intend to keep it handy.

Jim has a knack for uncovering new facts and setting the record straight on myths, and I know his book will give me a new perspective on Mickey.

Oh, by the way, I do wear an official Disney cast member nametag that says "Ducky". It was a nickname my mother called me. I know that Clarence Nash's nickname was also "Ducky" and he did a terrific job providing Donald Duck's voice for decades.

In 1984, I met Clarence Nash in person. Along with Bill Justice and artist Russell Schroeder, we were to tour the country as part of the publicity campaign for Donald Duck's 50th birthday. Clarence and I became friends and I have photos and things signed by him "To Ducky from Ducky". Thank heavens, he had no problem letting me keep the nickname.

We were both ducks that loved the Mouse.

I know you'll enjoy this book as much as I do! See ya real soon!

Don "Ducky" Williams
Senior Disney Character Artist
September 2013

Introduction

Mickey Mouse cannot be trapped between the covers of a book.

The little fellow has been involved with just too many different things over eight decades and all of them were significant in one way or another. However, I felt that I might be able to produce a book that would gather important information in one location that would save endless hours searching through hundreds of other books and magazines, countless websites and dozens of films and videos.

I have tried to write a book that can be used by the casual fan to track down information on their favorite cartoon or to learn more about some of the people involved with Mickey's life and career.

I also wanted a book that the more knowledgeable fan could utilize as a reliable reference and to get a deeper appreciation of Mickey with rarely revealed stories and appropriate documentation.

More significantly, I wanted to clarify some of the many Mickey Mouse myths that have been told and re-told for decades.

"Mickey Mouse" was not the code word to launch the D-Day invasion but it was connected to that event. Mickey's first words were not "Hot Dogs!" plural as it is authoritatively posted so many places but "Hot Dog!" singular. Walt Disney and Mickey Mouse were not given a special award in 1935 from the League of Nations. The stories behind those stories are in this book along with hundreds of others.

Over the decades, many fine authors have tried to chronicle the complete tale of Walt's alter ego, but the elusive mouse easily slips away, leaving behind huge holes in the narrative like a wheel of Swiss Cheese.

I admit that I am as frustrated as some readers picking up this book to see some of those same missing pieces in this attempt.

Where is the story about Mickey's long career in comic books? Where is the listing of Mickey in videogames? Where is the complete story of Mickey's European merchandise?

I can only helplessly point to the many stacks of pages containing some of those tales surrounding my feet like so many crumbs of discarded cheese. Despite my best efforts, these stories could not be crammed into the limited confines of this book or they needed more access to certain research before they could be properly documented.

Even though I have included many additional pages of quotes and anecdotes as well as extra notes in the filmography to try and fill a few of those holes, it is clear that there is still enough information about Mickey Mouse left over for another book at least.

However, there is plenty of material to enjoy in the following pages of this book that has never been set down in print before or, at least, never with this particular perspective and documentation.

The book is subtitled "A Celebration of Walt Disney's Mickey Mouse" for a specific reason. Arguably, Mickey Mouse was Walt's finest achievement. Most definitely, the early Mickey Mouse, in particular, was a reflection and extension of Walt Disney. Most of the stories in this book center on that special time that Walt and Mickey shared together.

Walt Disney still lives on today in the character of Mickey Mouse and I felt it appropriate that the final chapter is composed of Walt talking about Mickey.

Writing is hard. It can get lonely. It can get frustrating. It can even get scary when you stare at the blank whiteness of a page and have no clue where to start.

However, every day I worked on this book I loved it. It was always fun to research Mickey Mouse, re-watch all the cartoons, re-read the books and magazines, correspond with other authorities, and literally surround myself with stacks and stacks of Mickey material as if they were treasures in Uncle Scrooge's Money Bin. I hope that readers will find some of that same joy when they stumble across some of the things they discover in this book.

As always, I have tried to convey the information in bite-size tasty appetizers rather than a heavy multi-course meal. I am not telling Mickey's story in a chronological fashion so feel free to scamper to those topics that interest you without feeling the need to read the whole book from beginning to end.

I have done my best to verify and re-verify the information included in this book but there is always more to be discovered about the story and some of those items will probably only be uncovered after this book is in print.

I hope that we never forget what Walt Disney once memorably said on October 27, 1954: "it was all started by a mouse".

Or more accurately, a man and his mouse. This is their story.

Jim Korkis
Disney Historian
September 2013

Mouse-ce-llaneous

Disney's copyrighted character Mickey Mouse is perhaps the most universally known and loved cartoon character in the world. For generations, children and adults alike have been entertained by Mickey Mouse, who has appeared in hundreds of Disney animated motion pictures, television shows, video cassettes, comics, books, and in various other media. Indeed, the Mickey Mouse character identifies and symbolizes Disney itself.

—How the Disney Company described its star, Mickey Mouse, for the copyright infringement case *Walt Disney Company v. Transatlantic Video Inc., U.S.D.C.*, Central District of Ca., Case No. CV-91-0429 (1991).

Who Is Mickey Mouse?

Mickey Mouse is a universally recognized character and icon who has represented Walt Disney and the Disney Company for over eight decades.

While he physically resembles a three-foot-tall black mouse, spiritually he is a clever and appealing young boy created by Walt Disney in 1928.

Mickey's instantaneous popularity was due to numerous factors, including the artistic skill of Ub Iwerks, the storytelling ability of Walt Disney, the novelty of sound on film, and the perfect timing of his appearance as a scrappy "everyman" whose indomitable spirit and good humor overcame all challenges at the beginning of the Great Depression.

In addition to being a popular animated cartoon star both in films and on television, Mickey was a significant part of a multitude of different areas from merchandise to music to theme parks to comics to just about everything imaginable. He is a unique pop culture phenomenon embraced by audiences of all ages around the world.

Mickey Mouse was very much a direct reflection of his creator. They both shared the same philosophy of life and transitioned at the same time from a rural background into a more sophisticated Hollywood environment. Walt was the original voice for the character and the acknowledged "keeper of the Mouse" when it came to decisions about him.

Mickey Mouse celebrated his 85th birthday on November 18, 2013.

How Was Mickey Mouse Created?

The exact details about the creation of Mickey Mouse have always been unclear because Walt Disney told different versions of how it happened. The most common is some variation on this story:

Walt Disney went to New York to renew his contract and ask his film distributor, Charles Mintz, for more money to produce the second series of Oswald the Lucky Rabbit cartoons that had become very popular.

Mintz offered less money because he was setting up his own animation studio to produce the cartoons cheaper using Walt's own staff, whom he had secretly hired away. Only animator Ub Iwerks and two apprentice animators refused Mintz's tempting offer.

Walt had no recourse. The Oswald character and animated cartoons were copyrighted by Universal Pictures and they had hired Mintz to oversee the series. Contrary to stories that the character was "stolen" from Walt even though he had created the design for the character, wrote the stories, and produced the animation, Walt was aware he had no legal rights, only an ethical commitment he felt was being dishonored.

Walt telegraphed his anxious brother Roy back in Hollywood that everything was fine and that Walt would explain when he arrived back in Los Angeles.

He boarded the train to Los Angeles on March 13, 1928.

In an interview with Tony Thomas in 1959, Walt said:

> So I had to get a new character. And I was coming back after this meeting in New York, and Mrs. Disney was with me, and it was on the train — in those days, you know, it was three days over, three days from New York... well, I'd fooled around a lot with little mice, and they were always cute characters, and they hadn't been overdone in the picture field. They'd been used but never featured. So, well, I decided it would be a mouse... Well, that's how it came about... I had [his name] "Mortimer" first and my wife shook her head, and then I tried "Mickey" and she nodded the other way and that was it.

Walt's wife Lillian told Don Eddy in the August 1955 issue of *The American Magazine*:

> He was a raging lion on the train coming home... All he could say, over and over, was that he'd never work for anyone again as long as he lived. He'd be his own boss... I was in a state of shock, scared to death. He read the script [for *Plane Crazy*] to me, but I couldn't focus on it. I was too upset. The only thing that got through to me was that horrible name, Mortimer.

> Horrible for a mouse, at least. [Lillian actually told Walt it was a "sissy" name.] When I blew up, Walt calmed down. After a while, he asked quietly, "What would you think of Mickey? Mickey Mouse?" I said it sounded better than "Mortimer" and that's how Mickey was born.

Later, Walt would embellish the tale with the apocryphal story of him befriending a mouse in his Kansas City studio, sketching him, training him, and then letting him go "in the best neighborhood I could find" before he made his trip to Hollywood to seek his fortune.

Walt's nephew Roy E. Disney, in an interview with Bob Thomas in 1988, remarked:

> [The train story] has been told so many times that you don't know what's true. The name part I'm sure of. I often heard my father and Walt say, "Thank God we didn't name him Mortimer!"

Walt's daughter, Diane Disney Miller told me that she believed her father did indeed come up with the original Mickey Mouse on the train ride:

> I knew my father and traveled with him and he always had to be busy doing something. He couldn't relax on a trip. Especially with the fate of his studio at stake, it just seems obvious to me that he played around with paper and pencil trying to come up with a solution like he usually did. He liked seeing things visually, not in the abstract. He wouldn't have just sat there on the train worrying. He probably drew a sketch of a cartoon mouse.

In the March 1931 issue of *The American Magazine*, Walt explained:

> I can't say just how the idea came. We wanted another animal. We had had a cat; a mouse naturally came to mind. We felt that the

public — especially children — like animals that are "cute" and little. I think we were rather indebted to Charlie Chaplin for the idea. We wanted something appealing and we thought of a tiny bit of a mouse that would have something of the wistfulness of Chaplin...a little fellow trying to do the best he could.

Did I realize that I had hit upon an idea that would go round the world? Well, we always thought every new idea was a world-beater. And usually found out that it wasn't. We were enthusiastic over the idea of Mickey Mouse, but we had been just as enthusiastic over Alice.

The first Disney animated series was the *Alice Comedies*, featuring a live-action little girl interacting with animated characters including a black cat named Julius.

In a 1959 interview with David Griffiths, Walt elaborated:

We had to create a new character in a hurry to survive. And find a market for it. We canvassed all the animal characters we thought suitable for the movie fable fashion of the time. All the good ones — the ones that would have instant appeal and would be comparatively easy to draw — seemed to have been pre-empted by the other companies in the cartoon animal field. Finally, a mouse was suggested, debated and put on the drawing boards as the best bet. That was Mickey.

There had been plenty of mice in the *Alice Comedies* and even in the Oswald the Rabbit cartoons. The *Aesop's Film Fables* series produced by the Van Beuren cartoon studio that Walt originally set as his standard to meet in animation, had cartoon mice, including a pair named Milton and Rita who were later re-designed to more closely resemble Mickey and Minnie by making them several feet tall and dressing them in clothes.

In 1926, Walt drew a birthday card for his father, Elias, that featured three black mice without gloves or shoes and who looked a lot like an early version of Mickey Mouse but skinnier and with longer snouts. And when Walt moved into the new Hyperion Studio, animator Hugh Harman drew a publicity poster of cartoon mice around Walt's photo.

While Walt may have thought of a mouse character and a possible storyline on that three-day train trip, it is more likely that once he arrived in Los Angeles, he spent time with his brother, his wife, and Ub Iwerks coming up with the character.

Otto Messmer, the animator of Felix the Cat, told animation historian John Culhane that:

Walt designed a mouse but it wasn't any good. He was long and skinny.

Flipping through humor magazines like *Life* and *Judge*, according to Iwerks, they ran across some cute mice in the drawings of cartoonist Clifton Meek. In fact, the sheet of paper with Iwerks' earliest drawings of what Mickey would look like has the "little Lord Fauntleroy" version of Mickey in the upper-left corner, with the character attired in similar fashion to the Meek mice with a frilly white shirt and black knickers.

Essentially, Mickey Mouse was a "mouse-ified" version of Oswald the Rabbit (designed by Iwerks), with mouse ears replacing rabbit ears and with a mouse tail replacing Oswald's small rabbit tail. Even the shorts remained the same. As Iwerks told author John Culhane:

> Pear shaped body, ball on top, couple of thin legs. You gave it long ears and it was a rabbit. Short ears, it was a cat. Ears hanging down, a dog... With an elongated nose, it became a mouse.

Iwerks later told his sons, who had asked him whether he resented not getting enough credit for designing Mickey Mouse:

> It was what Walt *did* with Mickey that was important, not who created him.

Disney Legend Frank Thomas, one of Walt's fabled "Nine Old Men", put it this way:

> Ub Iwerks was responsible for the drawing of Mickey, but it was Walt Disney who supplied the soul. The way Mickey reacted to his predicaments, how he tried to extricate himself from a situation he could not control, never giving up and eventually finding a solution. That was all Walt.

Where Does Mickey Mouse Live?

According to the Disney Company, Mickey Mouse lives in Mouseton (a variation on "Houston").

The real answer, however, is much more complicated.

In the earliest animated cartoons, Mickey lived in a rural area with farms, wide-open spaces, rustic devices, and barnyards filled with a variety of animals. In the early Mickey Mouse comic strips drawn by Floyd Gottfredson, Mickey's hometown was called Silo Center, although this name was never used in the animated cartoons.

In 1939, Gottfredson used the name Mouseville for the urban city where Mickey now lived and worked. He used it again in several Mickey Mouse comic strip stories in the 1950s. Disney Publishing used that name in the comics it produced for foreign markets from the 1960s through the 1980s.

The general public assumed that Mickey Mouse lived either in Burbank, California (home of the Disney Studio), or in Hollywood (home of the movie stars).

Mr. Mouse Takes a Trip (1940) had Mickey departing from the Burbank train station. *Mickey's Kangaroo* (1935) had Mickey receiving a crate addressed simply to "Mickey Mouse Hollywood".

When Mickey fills out his tax form on the cover of the March 14, 1942, issue of *Liberty* magazine, he lists his address as Hollywood, California, and his only dependent as Walt Disney.

American Magazine (March 1931) reported that:

Mickey Mouse receives great stacks of fan mail. Some of the letters are just addressed to Mickey Mouse — Hollywood.

With the opening of Disneyland in 1955, the company stated that Mickey lived there in his own clubhouse (which originally was planned for Tom Sawyer's Island). The walk-around costumed characters reinforced the idea that Mickey and Minnie were living at some undisclosed location at the park, and not just visiting.

In 1988, with the opening of Mickey's Birthdayland at the Magic Kingdom in Florida, Mickey and Minnie's houses were on the outskirts of Duckburg, home of Donald Duck and his relatives.

With the release of *Who Framed Roger Rabbit* in 1989 and the opening of Mickey's Toontown at Disneyland in 1993, Mickey had moved to Toontown.

Examining the early comic strips, books and theatrical cartoons, however, it was clear that Mickey did not live in a city where mailboxes talked or where cartoon animals were segregated from humans, so even though Disney Parks promoted that concept for years, it was not used outside the theme parks in comics, animated cartoons, stories, or in any other format.

In 1990, starting with the stories in the Disney comic books, the Disney Company established that Mickey lived in Mouseton, and that is his official residence today. (Mouseton, by the way, is not far from Duckburg, Donald Duck's hometown, which accounts in part for their close friendship.)

Either writer Michael T. Gilbert or one of the editors, David Seidman or David Cody Weiss, came up with Mouseton. The town was going to be called Mouseville, but at that time on Saturday morning television there was a *Mighty Mouse* cartoon series produced by animator Ralph Bakshi who had Mighty Mouse living in Mouseville. To avoid confusion, Disney wanted a new name for the town — a unique name that it could own — and so Mouseton was created.

How Tall Is Mickey Mouse?

In the animated cartoons, Mickey is about three feet tall. In the Disney theme parks, he is about five feet tall. Actually, animation model sheets indicate Mickey is "three heads high," meaning that whatever the size of his head, his remaining body height is twice that size. Over the years, Mickey has sometimes been drawn to be almost four feet tall.

Animator Frank Thomas, remembering a recording session for the Mickey Mouse short *The Pointer* (1939), recalled:

When he recorded the voice, [Walt] couldn't help but feel like Mickey and he added all these little gestures that were spontaneous with him. At one point, he put out his hand like this (roughly waist high to indicate that Mickey was about three feet tall). It was the only time we knew how big Walt thought Mickey was.

In the July 1930 edition of the *Standard Casting Directory for Talking*

Pictures and Stage, which included almost 300 pages of headshots, contact information, and brief resumes of working Hollywood actors looking for more work, there was a half-page devoted to Mickey Mouse, who was described as "two feet three inches tall and weighs eighteen pounds." (Later entries put his weight at 23 pounds.) Mickey's agent was listed as Walt Disney at the Hyperion Studio in Los Angeles.

In *When The Cat's Away* (1929), Mickey and Minnie were portrayed as roughly the size of real mice but audiences did not find that size appealing. Instead of sitting on a stool and playing a piano, Mickey and Minnie were so small that they danced on the keys to make music.

Arguably, Mickey was also mouse-sized in *The Barnyard Battle* (1929), where he fought an army of cats, though his size fluctuates wildly in the film. In one scene he is small enough to ride on a mousetrap, while in another he is roughly the size of a child standing next to an upright piano.

In the January 1964 issue of *LOOK* magazine, Walt told interviewer Hooper Fowler:

> I had him as a mouse. And it wasn't well received. The distributor wrote to me and said, 'You've done something to Mickey; we've lost him". And it's because we brought him down and we thought of him as a mouse. Then I went back and thought of him as I originally did (as a young boy) and we went on from there. He was a little fellow is what he actually was, a little fellow.

In a 1956 interview, Ub Iwerks stated:

> I don't recall any special meetings or discussions on how Mickey should look... We decided to make Mickey the size of a little boy. We couldn't have him mouse-sized because of scale proportions (in terms of being seen clearly on the screen with objects). We asked ourselves "What are people going to think?" The size must have been right — people accepted him as a symbolic character, and though he looked like a mouse he was accepted as dashing and heroic.

Disney Legend Ward Kimball elaborated upon the height issue in comments made during Mickey's 40th birthday in 1968:

> In the old days of cartooning, the characters didn't have much relationship to reality. You could put almost anything into animation and the public accepted it. But whoever heard of a four foot tall mouse? That was the problem.

> Donald Duck, Goofy, Pluto, Clarabelle Cow and all the rest were drawn to scale. They were believable because they were of a relative size. Then along comes a mouse as big as they are and it stopped working.

> The more we got into reality, the more Mickey became an abstraction. When our pictures began to use psychology and realistic stories, Mickey Mouse became an outcast.

In the March 1931 issue of *American Magazine*, Walt Disney said:

In the beginning we thought we had to make the mouse very small in order to win the sympathy of the audiences. We have learned that we can make him as big as a horse. Sometimes we do.

And in a September 21, 1947, interview with the *New York Times Magazine*, Walt told Frank Nugent:

[Mickey was] three quarters the size of The Goof, about a head taller than The Duck and a third bigger than Pluto. He stands exactly level with Minnie.

During the first decade of Disneyland, there were no size limitations, and sometimes Mickey could be as tall as six feet. Since 1964, however, the Mickey found in the Disney theme parks stands about five feet tall.

Why Does Mickey Mouse Wear Big Shoes?

Mickey first wore shoes in *Gallopin' Gaucho* (1928). In 1957, Walt told interviewer Bob Thomas:

[Mickey's] legs were pipe stems, and we stuck them in big shoes to give him the look of a kid wearing his father's shoes.

From an artistic perspective, that approach made Mickey's feet more definitive against the background of a scene, and it also hid Mickey's real feet so that he appeared more human and less animal.

It's also the reason why Minnie's high-heel shoes looked so big in the early cartoons.

Why Does Mickey Mouse Wear White Gloves with Only Four Fingers?

Walt told Bob Thomas:

We didn't want him to have mouse hands, because he was supposed to be more human. So we gave him gloves. Five fingers seemed like too much on such a little figure, so we took away one. That was just one less finger to animate.

Every time Mickey's gloveless black hand moved across his solid black torso, his hand just disappeared, so white gloves made it easier for audiences to see the animation and gave Mickey more expressiveness with his hands.

The three black lines that sometime appear on the backs of Mickey's gloves represent darts in the fabric extending from between the digits of the hand, typical of the design style of a child's glove from the 1930s.

Mickey first wore his white gloves on screen in *The Opry House* (1929), the fifth Mickey cartoon. Mickey starts without gloves, but about three minutes into the film, he dons white gloves to perform for an audience and has rarely removed his gloves since.

In an August 1933 interview with the *Minneapolis Star* newspaper, Walt recalled:

> I evolved him (Mickey) out of circles. They were simple and easy to handle. Leaving the finger off was a great asset artistically and financially. Artistically, five digits are too many for a mouse. His hand would look like a bunch of bananas. Financially, not having an extra finger in each of 45,000 drawings that make up a six-and-one-half-minute short has saved the Studio millions.

"No one seemed to notice," affirmed Walt in *Collier's Magazine* (April 9, 1949).

Why Did Mickey Mouse's Eyes Change?

In *Disney Animation: The Illusion of Life* (Disney Editions, 1995), Disney Legends Frank Thomas and Ollie Johnston stated:

> Mickey's eyes were a special problem. They had started as black pupils in large eyes that looked more like googles than an eye shape. Since the whole figure was stock cartoon formula for the time, the eyes worked well.

As Mickey quickly developed, the rims of his eyes got so large that they seemed to resemble eyebrows with two mirrored, curved lines near the top of the head. The pupil of his eye also got bigger and was considered by the audience Mickey's actual eye, much like a solid black eye on a doll. While this image was appealing, it became almost impossible to draw Mickey looking in any direction other than directly in front of his face.

In print appearances, a flesh-colored hue sometimes would be added to the bottom of Mickey's face to better delineate that the large white area was indeed an eye with a black pupil.

Mickey's head had to be raised to make him look up or turned to look toward the side.

When staging a scene in one of the shorts, it was sometimes necessary for Mickey to look to either side without his entire head moving, as in *The Band Concert* (1935). This motion often presented a challenge because it would appear as if Mickey's eyes were not moving as an entire unit but that just the black dots were floating or drifting toward the side of his face. As a result, when seen on a large screen, Mickey would sometimes have an unappealing or odd expression. Although the skilled Disney animators were able to partially hide this oddness from the audience, the few people who focused on it would feel queasy, and so such staging was often avoided even though it limited the artistic possibilities for a scene.

For Mickey's appearances in print, including film posters, it was necessary for a viewer to be able to tell where Mickey was looking. The solution was the "pie-eye", in which a white triangular section would be drawn on the black oval eye to represent the highlight from a light source. This section, in appearance much like a slice cut from a whole pie, would indicate where Mickey was looking.

In a 1975 interview with *Crimmer's* magazine, Marc Davis said:

> I think it is intriguing that the interest now is in the Mickey of that early period, with the pie-shaped highlight that doesn't look like a (real) highlight.

This technique was primarily used on print images and merchandising in the 1930s, but it had first appeared in the animated Mickey short *The Karnival Kid* (1929).

The first use of the now familiar eyes in the white area of Mickey Mouse's face was an illustration done by animator Ward Kimball for the cover of the party program for Walt's Field Day, a staff party held on June 4, 1938, to celebrate the completion of *Snow White*. Mickey is attired in a golf outfit getting ready to take a swing at a golf ball. Kimball remembered:

> In order to have Mickey's head addressing the ball and at the same time smiling at the audience, I said, "What the hell, I'll use our regular eyes... we're using on the Dwarfs, Snow White, Goofy, Pluto... and put black pupils in them." This really caused a riot. Fred Moore agreed that it gave Mickey more personality... [and] Walt bought it.

Disney Legend Ollie Johnston stated:

> When some animators were pressuring Walt to let them change Mickey's eyes so that more delicate expression could be handled, Walt asked Don [Graham, Chouinard art instructor teaching at the Disney Studio] to bring it up in his class to see what all of the fellows thought.
>
> It was a difficult night for Don [as he] found himself trying to control a spirited discussion between authorities of varied opinions and even more varied personalities. Some felt the audience would never accept the new design and would wonder what was wrong. Others claimed that people would never notice. Some felt it would be all right to try it for just one picture and see what happened.
>
> As the talk became more heated, one man [animator Bill Tytla] quipped, "Why don't we just change one eye at a time?"

Society Dog Show (1939) was the last short to feature Mickey's "dot" eyes. Officially, *The Pointer* (1939) was the first short released with Mickey having his now familiar pupils. (When that short started production, the original model sheets had Mickey with the older style eyes but they were soon changed.) However, a commercial short, *Mickey's Surprise Party*, created for Nabisco and released months earlier for the 1939 New York's World Fair and the San Francisco Golden Gate International Exposition, featured Mickey with the new eyes, predating *The Pointer*.

In a 1975 interview with Disney archivist Dave Smith, Mickey Mouse comic-strip artist Floyd Gottfredson said:

When I first saw the pupils in Mickey's eyes in model sheets in 1938, I liked it immediately although it was hard for me to do for a while until I got used to it. I'm sure that Fred Moore had more to do with developing it than anybody else.

With the release of *Fantasia* (1940), Mickey's new eyes be-came the accepted standard, and audiences had no difficulty accepting them.

Why Does Mickey Mouse Sometimes Wear Green Shorts?

Green shorts for Mickey Mouse were an alternate coloring variation in the early 1930s. Since Mickey Mouse was portrayed in black-and-white, it had never occurred to Walt Disney what color to make the shorts.

In fact, some of the early title cards for Mickey Mouse films had Mickey occasionally wearing striped shorts or checkered shorts, although he never wore them in the cartoon itself.

Mickey wore shorts as a boy, not an adult, would wear them. In 1928, when Mickey was created, young boys wore shorts (sometimes referred to as "knee-length trousers") made with three buttons and no zipper. One unseen button secured the waist band. The other two secured a flap. When a boy had to urinate, he'd unbutton the flap rather than take off his shorts. A boy's shorts usually only had these three buttons.

Mickey's buttons originally started almost as high as his waist band, just like a child's shorts, but they have gotten larger and been moved lower over the decades as the inspiration for their original placement was forgotten.

Some have suggested that the buttons were meant for use with sus-penders, but Mickey almost never wore suspenders, not even in his earliest rural outings. On the rare occasions when he did wear them, it was clearly with a different set of clothes.

With no official color guide, some of the earliest George Borgfeldt mer-chandise had Mickey with green shorts (and green shoes). The *McCall's* pattern for making a Mickey Mouse doll also had green shorts as the preferred color choice. In fact, the Charlotte Clark Mickey Mouse doll, the Steiff Mickey Mouse doll, and the Dean's Rag Book (from England) Mickey Mouse doll were all produced with green shorts. Some of these stuffed dolls, such as the ones by Charlotte Clark, also featured red shorts.

When Walt first produced a color version of Mickey Mouse in the special short *Parade of the Award Nominees* (1932), he put Mickey in green shorts to contrast with the red drum major jacket. Walt did the same thing in the first official Mickey color cartoon, *The Band Concert* (1935). Mickey wears green shorts to contrast with his oversized red band-leader jacket.

Some items like the Mickey Mouse figural Bisque Toothbrush Holder came in versions with Mickey in green shorts and Mickey in red shorts.

Despite all the merchandise with Mickey in green shorts, he was also appearing more frequently and more prominently in red shorts in the early 1931 Mickey Mouse David McKay storybooks as well as a multitude of toys.

The most common 1932 "stock" United Artists movie poster advertising a Mickey Mouse cartoon had Mickey in red shorts (and green shoes). When individualized posters for specific Mickey Mouse cartoons were released in 1932, such as those for *Mickey's Nightmare*, *The Wayward Canary*, and *The Mad Dog* (in which Mickey has red shoes), Mickey wore red shorts.

Around 1933, Kay Kamen, newly in charge of merchandising for Disney, helped establish that Mickey's shorts would always be the now familiar red when Mickey was portrayed in color, just in time for the first Mickey Mouse Technicolor animated cartoons.

Kamen's 1934 *Mickey Mouse Merchandise* catalog as well as his Christmas Promotion 1934 spiral-bound booklet featured Mickey in red shorts (and yellow shoes) on the covers to emphasize to those using Mickey's image for merchandise and display that he officially wore red shorts and yellow shoes.

In *Designing Disney* (Disney Editions, 2003), John Hench remembered when Walt asked him to paint Mickey's official 25th birthday portrait in 1953:

> I wanted to change his short pants. I said [to Walt], "Look, he's the richest mouse in the world, the best known, and so forth. Why is he still in those short pants?" Walt said, "I'll tell you why — because I like those little short pants." So that's what I painted.

When interviewed in 1975 by Disney Archivist Dave Smith, Floyd Gottfredson said:

> As far as [Mickey's appearance], dropping the short pants and so on... we have always felt that that wasn't too great a change in that Mickey has always been an actor in the films so he adopted the costume of whatever part he was playing at the time whether he was a bandmaster, a fireman or a brave little tailor or whatever. As time went on and as they began to put him in suits and long pants in the pictures, we just went along [in the newspaper comic strip].

Why Does Mickey Mouse's Tail Sometimes Disappear?

Officially, Mickey Mouse always has a tail, but depending on the role he is playing or on the occasion, he tucks it in to his pants.

Around 1940, Mickey's tail disappeared for a period of time simply because of the labor of adding it to so many drawings when budgets were limited at the Disney Studio during the War Years. In *One of Walt's Boys*, (Tytle 1997), Disney producer Harry Tytle wrote:

> Walt disliked the Mickeys drawn without tails (he called them "bobtailed") but capitulated because he knew how much easier (and faster) this rendered the animation.

The tail is missing in cartoons like *Lend a Paw* (1941), *The Nifty Nineties* (1941), *Mickey and the Seal* (1948), and others, as well as in the popular comic strip during this same time period.

Mickey's tail was not just a squiggly line behind him; in the early Mickey Mouse cartoons, it reacted to Mickey's moods just like Pluto's tail reacted to Pluto's moods, and required a great deal of time and effort to get right.

In *Walt Disney: An American Original* (Simon and Schuster 1978), Bob Thomas recounted the story of Walt describing a fight sequence for a Mickey Mouse short and acting out all the parts for director Wilfred Jackson, who did many of the early Mickey Mouse shorts. Jackson was confident that he could capture what Walt wanted.

> When Walt saw the animation, he complained, "You've got the tail all wrong. Look — Mickey's mad all over. His tail is tense, not a limp thing hanging there. What's the matter, Jack — didn't we talk this over?"

In the earliest black-and-white cartoons, Mickey often mimicked cartoon superstar Felix the Cat by using his tail to do things like grab a mallet or help reel himself up the side of a building. These type of antics disappeared in 1929 when the tail became just an appendage not a tool.

In his 1975 interview with Dave Smith, Floyd Gottfredson said:

> The tail was dropped briefly during the war. As I understand this, it was because of the limited number of animation personnel [at the Disney Studio]. They felt that it just would save some time in animation. The tail was a thing that always had to be drawn to move pretty gracefully, so it required a little attention.
>
> Then, after the war, they decided to bring it back on again and Walt asked [the comic strip department] to reinstate the tail on Mickey, and we've had it with us ever since. I don't know whether anyone ever noticed, but as far as I know, we've never had any fan mail or comments on it.

Today, Mickey proudly displays his ever-expressive appendage.

Are Mickey Mouse and Minnie Mouse Married?

Officially, the Disney Company firmly states that Mickey and Minnie are not married. Being married is an adult thing to do, and Mickey and Minnie are not officially adults.

Yet, Mickey and Minnie are capable of driving cars, owning homes, having jobs, and pursuing other activities only adults would do. In 1933, Walt told the British publication *Film Pictorial* that:

> What it amounts to is that Minnie is, for screen purposes, his leading lady. If the story calls for a romantic courtship, then Minnie is the girl; but when the story requires a married couple, then they

appear as man and wife. In the studio, we have decided that they are married really.

Being a conservative, moral man, it is doubtful that Walt would tolerate his alter ego dating a girlfriend for decades with no marriage plans. It is more likely that Walt considered Mickey and Minnie to be just like George Burns and Gracie Allen, Jack Benny and Mary Livingstone, and other popular performing couples in the 1930s who were married in real life but who on the radio and on the screen often appeared to be single.

There are definite indications in the early 1930s that Walt was not adverse to the two characters marrying.

One such example is "The Wedding Party of Mickey Mouse" (1931), with music by Robert Bagar and lyrics by Milt Coleman and James Cavanaugh, and published by Bibo-Lang Incorporated (which held a merchandise license with the Disney Studio from 1930-1932). Bibo-Lang published the first Mickey Mouse storybook. Later reprints of the sheet music were done by Stasny up through 1936.

The sheet music cover, with its prominent Walt Disney Productions copyright notice, features Mickey in a tuxedo coat but wearing his two-button shorts. Minnie wears a veil and is followed by Horace Horsecollar, Clarabelle Cow, and a half dozen other cheering animals.

"The Wedding of Mister Mickey Mouse" (1933), a novelty fox trot, with music by Franz Vienna and lyrics by Edward Pola, shows a happy Mickey Mouse outfitted in a tuxedo leading Minnie Mouse, also happy and covered with a veil, down the carpet with best-man Horace Horsecollar and maid-of-honor Clarabelle Cow cheering them on.

The sheet music was from Keith Prowse & Co. and the cover has the phrase "By special permission of Walt Disney — the creator of the popular Mickey Mouse." The cover artwork was by Wilfred Haughton, a British cartoonist responsible for much of the artwork in early Disney comics and in annuals published in the United Kingdom. In the song, even "Peg-leg Pete calls a truce" for the wedding ceremony.

In *Mickey's Nightmare* (1932), Mickey dreams of getting married to Minnie and the bliss it will bring. However, borrowing a plot device from an Oswald the Rabbit cartoon, *Poor Papa* (1928), Mickey is so inundated with a never-ending stream of baby mice and their many demands that the dream becomes a nightmare.

Walt told writer Louise Morgan of the *News Chronicle* (June 1935) that "there's no marriage in the land of make-believe. Mickey and Minnie must live happily ever after."

In 1934, British novelist E.M. Forster wrote:

> It seems likely that they have married one another, since it is unlikely that they have married anyone else, since there is nobody else for them to marry.

A Mickey Mouse short abandoned in 1941, entitled *Mickey's Elopement*, has

Mickey trying to get Minnie to an all-night wedding chapel.

Actress Russi Taylor, who provided the voice of Minnie Mouse starting in 1986, was married to late voice actor Wayne Allwine, who did the voice of Mickey Mouse. So, for a while, it was true that Mickey and Minnie were happily married in real life.

As Taylor stated in an interview with *Disney Magazine* (Spring 1997):

> The characters aren't going to get married, because children relate to Mickey and Minnie at their own levels. They don't know how old Mickey and Minnie are, but if they were to get married, they would become adults and spoil the illusion.

How Old Is Mickey Mouse?

Mickey will have been around for 85 years as of November 2013.

The Disney Company, however, no longer celebrates Mickey's birthday for fear that his real age will seem too old for new, young audiences.

At a birthday celebration for Mickey, Disney Legend Frank Thomas said:

> I think Walt saw Mickey as having the spirit of a nine-year-old boy with the capability of a fourteen year old. But he also thought of him as ageless.

Walt Disney told *American Cinematographer* magazine in 1932:

> In some pictures, [Mickey] has a touch of Fred Astaire; in others, Charlie Chaplin and some of Douglas Fairbanks but in all of these should be some of a young boy.

In 1988, Disney Legend Ollie Johnston stated:

> Mickey reflected Walt's boyhood personality and did a lot of the things Walt had wanted to do as a boy himself — rescuing princesses, beating up bullies, putting on variety shows.

Disney storyman Ted Sears, while lecturing in 1939 to a group of animators at the Disney Studio, had this to say about how Mickey should be portrayed:

> Mickey is not a clown... he is neither stupid nor idiotic. His comedy is subordinate to the situation in which he finds himself. His age varies according to the situation; sometimes his character is the one of a young boy, whereas at other times, particularly in the adventure films, he acts like an adult.

When Is Mickey Mouse's Birthday?

Officially, Mickey Mouse's birthday is November 18, 1928, which is the official birthday of Minnie Mouse as well.

Of the Fab Five, only Mickey, Minnie, and Donald Duck have official birthdays. Pluto and Goofy evolved through several cartoons, so it is difficult to credit a particular cartoon with their emergence.

Disney archivist Dave Smith determined through a program from the Colony Theater in New York that Mickey's first truly public appearance was in *Steamboat Willie* on November 18, 1928. For Mickey's 50th birthday celebration in 1978, that date became his official birthday.

In 1988, Dave Smith told Disney historian Jim Fanning why an official birth date for Mickey Mouse had to be established:

> The Walt Disney Company is now reaching a point in its history where there are many significant anniversaries to celebrate, and the company has come to realize that these celebrations can be very useful marketing tools.

For the previous fifty years, the Disney Company had selected any date from September through late November as Mickey Mouse's birthday primarily as a merchandising tool to encourage theaters to rent Mickey Mouse cartoons and to do special promotions like parties.

On October 25, 1931, the *Los Angeles Times*, after contacting the Disney Studio, affirmed that Mickey Mouse's birthday was October 24, and that was when he had celebrated his third birthday.

In 1932, Mickey's fourth birthday was announced as October 1, although the celebration lasted for several days. A "Mickey Mouse Birthday Party of the Air" was broadcast on NBC radio the night of September 29. The next morning, internationally known restaurateur George Rector went on WJZ and NBC to announce, in honor of Mickey's birthday, a special cheese sandwich that would be featured in all A&P stores.

On October 1, W.T. Grant department stores unveiled special displays by the Candy Institute of America, Inc., whose members produced a large share of the confections sold in the United States, with the slogan: "Celebrate Mickey Mouse's Birthday with Candy".

United Artists, distributors of the Mickey Mouse films, announced a "mouse-warming" at the Rivoli theater in New York.

On October 4, George Olsen and his orchestra hosted a Mickey Mouse birthday party at the Hotel New Yorker that began at 11:00 p.m. and was broadcast live from midnight to 12:30 a.m. on a nationwide hookup over the National Broadcasting System. It featured several Mickey Mouse songs including "What? No Mickey Mouse? What Kind of a Party Is This?". Invited guests included actors Paul Muni, Paulette Goddard, and Edmund Lowe, as well as such celebrities as boxer Jack Dempsey.

The October 7, 1932, issue of *San Antonio Light* reported that one of Mickey Mouse's birthday parties (celebrated that year on October 1) was held at the prestigious Coconut Grove nightclub in the Ambassador Hotel in Los Angeles, with "Walt Disney cutting Mickey's birthday cake."

Mickey's fifth birthday was celebrated on September 30, 1933, with a Hollywood testimonial party featuring speakers like Charlie Chaplin, Mary Pickford, and Will Rogers.

Yet, in the September 1933 issue of *Film Pictorial* magazine, Walt Disney was quoted as saying:

> Mickey Mouse will be five years old on Sunday. He was born on October 1, 1928. That was the date on which his first picture was started so we have allowed him to claim this day as his birthday.

Actually, Ub Iwerks had animated a test scene from *Steamboat Willie* as early as July 1928 so that Walt could practice synchronizing the sound to the scene, but that date was never claimed as Mickey's birth.

Iwerks began work on Mickey Mouse's first cartoon appearance, *Plane Crazy* (1928), during the last week of April 1928. That date was never used in publicity as Mickey's official birth date because its Spring time period wouldn't have significantly increased theater bookings for a Mickey Mouse short. A Fall date like September or October, when theater attendance usually dipped before the holiday season, was a better time for theaters to celebrate Mickey's birthday by hosting a party and screening Disney shorts.

Mickey's seventh birthday was celebrated on September 28, 1935, with movie theaters encouraged to book entire programs of *Mickey Mouse* and *Silly Symphony* cartoons as part of the celebration, which Disney called "Mickey's Lucky Seventh Birthday".

In fact, every print of every available Disney animated cartoon was in use during this celebration. The theaters in Chicago alone booked more than 450 reels. Theater celebrations included birthday cake and costume parties, and some theaters offered free admission to anyone dressed as a Disney character. Guy Lombardo and his orchestra even recorded a special fox trot, "Mickey Mouse's Birthday Trot", for the occasion.

Floyd Gottfredson drew a birthday-themed installment of the Mickey Mouse comic strip.

Disney and United Artists contacted thousands of businesses and institutions to join in the celebration with special parties.

For Mickey's eighth birthday, Radio City Music Hall hosted a week-long salute with three Disney cartoons as part of every show.

Other theaters had smaller celebrations with prizes for Disney costumes, and coloring and essay contests. The prizes? Mickey Mouse and Donald Duck dolls from Charlotte Clark, personally autographed by Walt Disney!

The Disney Studio even produced two animated shorts, *The Birthday Party* (1931, in black-and-white) and *Mickey's Birthday Party* (1942, in Technicolor), as the centerpiece for a collection of Disney cartoons to be shown in theaters.

In 1938, Mickey's birthday was celebrated on September 27.

In 1949, to celebrate Mickey's 21st birthday, Ingersoll produced a Mickey Mouse alarm clock packaged in a birthday box in the shape of a cake "with real candles that light" and which included a "sterling silver ring" and a bright red ballpoint pen with a decal of Mickey on it. It sold for eight dollars.

At Walt Disney's request, the first official birthday portrait of Mickey Mouse was done this year by Disney Legend John Hench for the April issue of *Collier's* magazine. It featured Mickey leaning against a globe of the earth with blue curtains behind him. Walt liked it so much that Hench became the official portrait artist for the Mouse and four years later did the much more famous 25th birthday painting with Mickey in Walt's office. In the background of that painting, the hi-fi equipment and bookcase were from Hench's own house. Walt hung the original painting in his office where it stayed until his death. Hench later painted other official Mickey Mouse portraits, including those for the character's 50th (1978), 60th (1988), and 75th (2003) birthdays.

In 1953, the entire month of September was considered Mickey's "birthday month."

Capitol Records produced a "record-reader" entitled *Mickey Mouse's Birthday Party* (DBX 3165) to celebrate Mickey's Silver Anniversary of being twenty-five years young.

A record-reader was a two-record set accompanied by a storybook and some cue, like the sound of a bell or a horn, to let a child know when to turn the page so that the sounds on the record would match the story in the book (in this case, Mickey Mouse coaxed Donald Duck to give the signal to turn the page).

The voice of Mickey Mouse was provided by Stan Freberg. In 1996, Freberg told me:

> Walt Disney was always the voice of Mickey, when he was alive, but when he was too busy, his sound effects wizard Jimmy MacDonald did it. Once, when Capitol Records was recording a children's album called *Mickey Mouse's Birthday Party* and both Walt and Jimmy were busy, Walt asked me to record Mickey's voice: [imitating the falsetto] "Hi, Minnie, Hi Pluto, Happy Birthday! Ha-ha, ha-ha, ha-ha!".

In September, Dell Comics printed a special one-hundred-page comic book "giant", *Mickey Mouse Birthday Party*, with a Dick Moores cover of Mickey Mouse by a birthday cake where the candles were actually Disney characters. The interior included reprints from several Dell Four Color issues (#181, #27, and #79) as well as some reformatted Mickey Mouse comic strips from 1941 by Floyd Gottfredson and Bill Wright.

Magazines such as *Child's Life* ran articles about Mickey's Silver Anniversary throughout the month.

According to a 1968 issue of *Disney News*, Mickey's 40th birthday was to be officially celebrated September 27, 1968. This event was featured on Disney's weekly television program in an episode entitled "Mickey Mouse Anniversary Show" (December 22, 1968) with host Dean Jones joined by the original Mouseketeers.

On October 16, 1975, cartoonist Floyd Gottfredson drew another commemorative version of Mickey's daily newspaper comic strip to celebrate the character's 47th birthday.

Mickey's 50th birthday in 1978 was a year-long celebration that generated not only an official "Happy Birthday, Mickey" logo but a variety of commemorative merchandise. It was the first official celebration of Mickey's birthday as being November 18.

Retrospective screenings of Mickey's cartoons were shown at venues such as the New York Metropolitan Museum of Modern Art, the American Film Institute, and the Chicago Film Festival.

Animator Ward Kimball accompanied Mickey on a special Amtrak train for a cross-country, fifty-seven city Birthday Express tour. The tour ended at the Broadway Theater (formerly the Colony Theater, where *Steamboat Willie* premiered), where a plaque designating the theater as the official birthplace of Mickey Mouse was installed. Kimball later recalled one of his experiences on the tour:

> The time of day that we stopped at a town didn't matter a bit. Even at two or three o'clock in the morning, there were hundreds of people out there holding their kids up high just to get a glimpse of Mickey as he stepped from the train or waved to them from the platform of the observation car. I have never gotten over that and realized then the power that Mickey Mouse has as a symbol.

> Sometimes the press of people was so great, even after Mickey had gone inside that it was impossible to move the train out of the station without the danger of hurting someone. I devised a method that solved that problem in most places. We had cartons of little yellow pin-back buttons that said 'Happy Birthday, Mickey" on them and I would stand on the rear platform and toss those buttons far to the rear of the train. As the people scrambled to pick up the buttons, the train was able to slowly pull out of the station. Interestingly enough, those buttons have become very attractive to collectors today.

Seven huge scrapbooks in the Disney Archives are filled with newspaper clippings from the year-long birthday event.

In addition, Mickey received his star on the Hollywood Walk of Fame, making him the first cartoon character ever to do so.

People were singing a specially written song, "The Whole World Wants to Wish You Happy Birthday, Mickey Mouse."

And finally, a parade was held in his honor at both Disneyland and Walt Disney World during that year.

For Mickey's 50th birthday in 1978, a special episode of *The Wonderful World of Disney* weekly television show ("Mickey's 50") aired on November 19. It featured celebrities like Johnny Carson and Jonathan Winters honoring Walt's mouse.

For Mickey's 60th birthday in 1988, another special episode of *The Wonderful World of Disney* ("Mickey's 60") aired on November 13. It featured Mickey fooling with a sorcerer's hat and disappearing, forcing Roger Rabbit to find him while "news reporter" John Ritter gave commentary and updates.

From summer 1988 through spring 1990 at Walt Disney World, Mickey's birthday was celebrated at a new temporary area of the park near Fantasyland called Mickey's Birthdayland. Guests could tour Mickey's house and then meet him in the Movie Barn next door. Mickey cartoons were shown continuously in the queue area.

Disney produced a 68-page slick magazine, *Mickey is Sixty*, with a special edition "cel" of Mickey as the Sorcerer's Apprentice. Excerpts from this magazine appeared in *Time*, *Life*, *People*, and elsewhere. Sharp-eyed readers found that at the bottom of page 35, instead of "Mickey is Sixty," someone had cleverly snuck in "Mickey is Sexy" — much to the embarrassment of the Disney Company.

Ear Force One, a hot air balloon in the shape of Mickey's head, toured the United States.

The Disney Company planted a 520-acre cornfield in Sheffield, Iowa, in the shape of Mickey Mouse's head. When the field was seen from overhead in an airplane, it looked like a birthday card for Mickey from Minnie. (This idea was the brainchild of Disney Legend Jack Lindquist, who was then Disney's Vice-President for Creative Marketing.)

In addition, Disney created another special Mickey Mouse birthday logo as well as a flood of nicely done commemorative merchandise honoring both the classic Mickey and the modern Mickey.

For Mickey's 70th birthday, Walt Disney Art Classics, the art and collectibles division of the Disney Company, commissioned Imagineer John Hench to render Mickey in an official portrait. which was published as a limited edition print in December 1998. It was an instant sell-out.

Today, the Disney Company does not officially celebrate a year for Mickey's birthday for fear that children might think Mickey is too old. In a statement from 2003, Chris Curtin of Disney Synergy and Special Projects wrote:

> We particularly worry about this when it comes to children, whose understanding and appreciation of our characters can be undermined by suggesting they have real-world ages. As a company, we feel our characters are timeless and therefore don't mark the passage of time.

So, that is why the Disney Company did not celebrate Mickey Mouse's 75th birthday in 2003, but in a smaller fashion celebrated "75 Years WITH Mickey".

On November 18, 2003, in a private media ceremony, Michael Eisner unveiled 75 Mickey Mouse statues each standing six feet tall and weighing 700 pounds. They were designed by a mix of celebrities including Tom Hanks, John Travolta, Ben Affleck, Susan Lucci, and others. Those who participated in the design created the Mickey Mouse statues to fit one of six themes: heritage, adventure, magic and fantasy, fun and laughter, friendship, and the future.

The statues were displayed in various locations at Walt Disney World through April 2004, after which they were exhibited in 12 U.S. cities on an 18-month tour sponsored by The Coca-Cola Company. After the tour, the statues were auctioned off with the proceeds benefiting a charity of each artist's choice.

The Disney Company did not officially celebrate Mickey's 85th birthday in 2013.

Who Does Mickey Mouse's Voice?

The original voice of Mickey Mouse was Walt Disney.

Currently, Bret Iwan is the official voice of Mickey Mouse, although Chris Diamantopoulos voiced the character in a series of 19 Disney Channel shorts released beginning in 2013. Before Iwan got the job, the Disney Company officially recognized only three performers in this role:

- Mickey's creator Walt Disney spoke for the little fellow from 1928 to 1947. He also supplied Mickey's voice for animated portions of the original *Mickey Mouse Club* television show in 1955.
- Disney sound-effects genius Jimmy MacDonald took over from Walt in 1947 and continued until 1977.
- Wayne Allwine performed the famous vocalizations from 1977 to 2009.

Over the years, many other people have voiced the famous falsetto of Mickey Mouse for a variety of projects.

- J. Donald Wilson once did it on radio, as did Joe Twerp, who supplied the voice for 17 episodes of *Mickey Mouse Theater of the Air* in 1938.
- Comedian and writer Stan Freberg supplied the voice on a 1955 children's record, *Mickey Mouse's Birthday Party*.
- Jack Wagner, the voice of Disneyland, often did Mickey's voice for various theme park-related events like parades and announcements. Pete Renoudet filled in after Wagner passed away performing these same duties.
- Carl Stalling and Clarence "Ducky" Nash stepped in during the early cartoons to cover a line or two. Nash also did Mickey's voice for television commercials in 1955.
- Les Perkins did the voice of Mickey in the 1987 television special *Down and Out With Donald Duck* as well as in *DTV Valentine* in 1986.
- Quinton Flynn did Mickey's voice in some episodes of the 1999 television series *Mickey Mouse Works*.

That incomplete list doesn't include the many foreign voice artists who supplied Mickey's voice in German, Japanese, Italian, Bulgarian, Chinese, Spanish, Swedish, and other languages over the decades.

A talented and humorous natural performer, Walt Disney was the very first person to supply voices for Disney animated cartoons. He used his theatrical skills to bring an extra dimension to Mickey's personality. As Walt told interviewer Tony Thomas in 1959:

> We were foolin' around and tryin' to get a voice for a mouse. And we didn't know what a mouse would sound like, so I said, "It's kind of like this." And the guys said "Well, why don't you do it?" And I knew I'd always be on the payroll so [laughs] I did it.

Walt's vocal characterization of Mickey is the only existing evidence of his remarkable acting ability, which was usually witnessed only by his artists at the lively story meetings held at the Disney Studio. Playful Walt would often ad-lib dialog for lovable Mickey in that well-known voice resulting in appreciative laughter from his listeners.

Walt told an interviewer:

> He [Mickey Mouse] still speaks for me and I still speak for him. In *Steamboat Willie* (1928), in addition to speaking for Mickey, I also supplied a few sound effects for Minnie, his girlfriend, as well as the sarcastic squawking dialogue of Captain Pete's annoying parrot.

While *Steamboat Willie* has Mickey vocalizing his many feelings, the character's first words were not uttered until *The Karnival Kid* (1929). That historic moment showcased carnival hot dog vendor Mickey gleefully shouting "Hot dog! Hot dog!" (Not "hot dogs!" plural, as many others have claimed.)

At one point, Walt felt his Midwestern twang and lack of professional acting experience might hamper Mickey Mouse's success, so he spent a week auditioning professional actors to take over the part. Despite Walt's impassioned coaching and the best efforts of these performers, no one was able to capture Mickey's intrepid optimism and pluck as deftly as Walt himself. He told others that he preferred his unique vocal interpretation because "there is more pathos in it."

Disney Legend Les Clark said:

> Walt was Mickey and Mickey was Walt. Even Mickey's gestures were copied from Walt when he performed Mickey.

Bob Thomas, author of *Walt Disney: An American Original*, explained:

> It was no easy matter to get color into such an unnatural, limited voice, but Walt managed. No one else could capture the gulping, ingenuous, half-brave quality. Walt's depiction of Mickey was so accurate, so inspired, that animators wished they could capture the Disney facial expressions and movements to help them with animating Mickey.

A famous clip from *The Pointer* (1939) features a frightened Mickey as a hunter who is overshadowed by a growling, threatening bear. Mickey tries to calm the situation by nervously stuttering: "Well, I'm, uh, Mickey Mouse. You know? Mickey Mouse? I hope you've heard of me, I hope."

There is a wonderful story behind that short clip of dialog. Animator Frank Thomas had finally convinced Walt to be filmed for a short sequence to help the animators, who were having challenges coming up with appropriate actions for surprised hunter Mickey as he confronted an angry bear. Thomas recalled:

> Walt didn't want to be in front of a camera when he was doing the voice of Mickey Mouse. Finally, he told me, "If you're way back in the booth over there and I can't see you, well, I guess so." When he recorded the voice he couldn't help but feel like Mickey and he added all these little gestures that were spontaneous with him. At one point [when he said, "you know? Mickey Mouse?"], he put out his hand like this [to indicate that Mickey was three feet tall], it was the only time we knew how big Walt thought Mickey was.

While that memorable piece of live-action film no longer exists, film restoration expert Scott McQueen discovered a clip over a decade ago in the dusty Disney vaults that shows Walt and voice artist Billy Bletcher (also known for the gruff tones of the Big Bad Wolf) doing several takes for a sequence of Mickey Mouse being interrogated by the villainous Pete on a train for *Mr. Mouse Takes a Trip* (1940). The film records Walt professionally performing the flustery falsetto and shy giggle for multiple takes of the dialog. (It's also fun to see Walt's lips moving as he reads Bletcher's lines silently to himself.)

It was almost impossible to imagine anyone else supplying the distinctive dialog for Walt's alter ego. However, as the Disney Studio expanded, it became harder and harder for busy Walt to schedule time to go to the soundstage to record the vocal tracks and the changes in dialog as a film was in production. Disney producer Harry Tytle explained:

> Part of Walt's preference for sparing use of dialog [with Mickey Mouse] could have been that it was less time consuming for him, for as most Disney buffs are aware, Walt was the original voice of Mickey Mouse. In later years, others did the voice, but we also had a film library of Walt's Mickey Mouse lines to fall back on. Walt was generally so involved in other work that he was not available on short notice. Then, too, the falsetto voice was not an easy thing for him to do in later years.

Wayne Allwine, one of the official voices for Mickey Mouse, concurred:

> Walt was a high baritone. His constant smoking dried out his vocal chords over time so it brought down the pitch and you could hear the difference.

In 1934, Jimmy MacDonald was playing drums and percussion in a jazz band that was used by the Disney Studio to record music for a Mickey Mouse short. After the recording was over, Walt Disney was so impressed with MacDonald's versatility that he hired him to form a sound effects department.

MacDonald invented many of the Disney sound effects himself, building the necessary contraptions in his home workshop. He built more than five hundred different devices from scratch. MacDonald said:

> I was never onstage very much when Walt was doing Mickey. He might come down while I was doing effects, and they suddenly needed some Mickey [dialog], and maybe it was the only time he had.

Often, animators would be delayed in their work because they didn't have Walt's voice track to animate, but Walt was becoming busier and busier with the many responsibilities of running his studio. In addition, Walt's chain smoking was giving his Mickey voice a harshness not appropriate for the young character and requiring more takes to capture just the right tone.

Jimmy MacDonald remembered:

> Being on staff, you were asked to do bits of everything. For instance, on *Cinderella* (1950), I did the two mice, Jaq and Gus. It was something that I'd never tried before; we just thought we'd try it because I was on staff, and if I could do it, it would save having to pay actors to come in. Storyman Winston Hibler had written a lot of strange jargon — he called it "Mouse Latin", an unintelligible language. The one mouse we had to speed up a bit, and the other one we slowed down. When that was cut into a rough cut, and shown to the people here, everybody loved the picture, and they loved the mice.

MacDonald was also the voice of another mouse, the dormouse in *Alice in Wonderland* (1951), for which he recorded his voice at double speed and then played it back.

While MacDonald invented the voices for those mice, he inherited the most important mouse voice for the Big Cheese himself when Walt finally was too overwhelmed with other work.

Walt originally recorded Mickey's dialog for *Mickey and the Beanstalk* in May 1940, but production on the film was continually delayed for five years and the story frequently rewritten, which meant that Walt had to return to the sound stage over the years to record the new lines. Jimmy MacDonald recalled how this led to his opportunity of a lifetime:

> When I started doing Mickey's voice we were doing 'Mickey and the Beanstalk' [a segment from *Fun and Fancy Free* (1947)], and the animators and the director in charge of the sequences that needed Walt's voice on Mickey approached him and said, "Walt, we need you on the stage; we want to go ahead with this." He said, "'I'm too busy, I just can't do it. Call Jim up here."
>
> They said, "Walt wants to see you," and I thought, "What have I done now?" He said, "Have you ever tried to do Mickey?" I said, "No, Walt." You wouldn't try to do that, because it was always Walt's voice; there was no reason ever to try it. So he said, "Do it. Just say something." So I said (in Mickey's voice), "Hi, Walt, how are you?" You know, Mickey always had that little identifiable giggle.

A test recording was done of MacDonald trying to match the vocal track Walt had done five years earlier. When the tracks were compared, Walt was pleased that MacDonald had captured Mickey's spirit and limited vocal range. As MacDonald remembered:

> Walt said, "'That's fine." He told the directors, "'Have Jim do it, in the future. He can do it fine." But, he told me, "Don't let them give you long speeches. Because you have that falsetto, and you have a couple of inches of area for inflection, and it'd be terrible to have a long speech in falsetto voice. You don't have much room for inflection; you're already up there. And if you get too low, you start to yodel, and yodel right out of it." So it was always best, he said, to have short speeches.

Harry Tytle said:

> While supplying the voice for Mickey Mouse could give one "bragging rights" within the studio, it carried little prestige. Jimmy [MacDonald], while certainly talented, and who performed the voice well, was primarily called upon because he was already on salary, and his voice didn't add to the film's cost.

MacDonald fondly remembered:

> One day I was doing something and Walt came on the dialog stage. As he turned to leave, he turned around to the fellow at the soundboard and said, "Hey, don't forget I do Mickey's voice, too."

In fact, in the mid-1950s, Walt stepped in and recorded Mickey's voice for the daily introductions on the *Mickey Mouse Club* television show — almost a decade after he had officially stopped doing the voice.

MacDonald only provided Mickey's voice in less than a dozen cartoons for theaters before the final theatrically released Mickey Mouse short, *The Simple Things* (1953). He had to convey the more sedate fatherly tones of a mature, suburban Mickey in cartoons like *Mickey and the Seal* (1948) and *Pluto's Christmas Tree* (1952). Fortunately, there were many other opportunities, including the Disney television shows, commercials, records, and special projects that required MacDonald to use his skills in vocalizing Mickey.

However, MacDonald always felt that his main job was running the sound effects department.

Just a few months before Walt Disney died in 1966, twenty-year-old Wayne Allwine was hired for a job in the mail room at The Walt Disney Studios. From there, he worked briefly in Wardrobe, then moved to Audio Post Production and eventually began a seven-and-a-half year apprenticeship under MacDonald, where he won awards for his sound-effects editing. Allwine sometimes referred to himself as the "Sorcerer's Apprentice".

When MacDonald decided to retire in 1976, the Disney Studio searched for a replacement to provide Mickey's voice. Allwine recalled:

> They were re-voicing Mickey in 1977. Somebody missed their audition appointment. So they called the Music Department where I worked

and said, "Send the kid down if it's okay. We have a space here, and we want to put a name on the list." I'd never done anything like that before and didn't expect to ever do it again. A couple of months later, Disney executive Lou Debney stopped me on Mickey Avenue on the studio lot and said, "You've got to join the Screen Actors Guild, kid. They're going to use you."

Besides working with MacDonald for so many years, Allwine had strong memories of the voice of Mickey from the original *Mickey Mouse Club* television show that he had watched avidly as a youngster. He easily got the part and made his vocal debut on *The New Mickey Mouse Club* (1977–1978), and went on to provide Mickey's voice for Disney theme parks, movies, television specials, records, and video games for over three decades.

"Just remember, kid," Jimmy Macdonald told Allwine with a smile, "you're only filling in for the boss."

Allwine's premiere theatrical vocal appearance as Mickey Mouse was in *Mickey's Christmas Carol* (1983), the first new Mickey Mouse animated cartoon released to movie theaters in thirty years. In that film, Allwine not only had to recreate Mickey's distinctive voice but also convey Mickey's acting skills as Bob Crachit, the browbeaten clerk of the stingy Mr. Scrooge.

Over the years, Allwine continued to expand Mickey's dramatic repertoire by singing in *The Prince and the Pauper* (1990) and performing as an enormous monster in *Runaway Brain* (1995).

Allwine was heard constantly as Mickey in everything from new cartoon shorts for the television series *Mickey Mouse Works* (1999) and *Disney's House of Mouse* (2001) to popular video games like the *Kingdom Hearts* series that began in 2002.

Wayne Allwine died on May 18, 2009. The last Disney product to feature his voice work, *Kingdom Hearts 358/2 Days*, has a dedication to his memory.

Allwine said:

> Mickey is an actor and he's capable of doing whatever he's given to do — provided it's kept in context of what Mickey would and wouldn't do. Walt always has been very much alive in Mickey Mouse and we try to direct him more toward Walt's version of Mickey who was an actor, forever young and forever optimistic. Mickey is Walt's. I'm just filling in for the boss, too. Mickey's the star. I get to take this wonderful American icon and keep it alive until the next Mickey comes along. That is what is heart-breaking about this job. I am "Number Three" so it means that someday there will be a "Number Four".

The Disney Company was already looking for an understudy to provide Mickey's instantly recognizable voice. The man selected was Bret Iwan, who won the role after a nationwide search.

Born September 10, 1982, Iwan graduated from the Ringling College of Art and Design in Sarasota, Florida, and began his career as an illustrator for Hallmark in Kansas City where he worked for five years after graduation.

In a final audition, Russi Taylor, the voice of Minnie Mouse and the widow of Wayne Allwine, helped in choosing Iwan, who took over the role just two weeks after Allwine's death. Iwan said:

> The audition was basically a voice match. They provided an MP3 of clips from a couple of Walt's cartoons and a couple of Wayne's cartoons. And the audition was to do the best you could to match those voices.

Iwan has done the voice of Mickey in videogames like the *Epic Mickey* series, television shows like *Mickey Mouse Clubhouse*, and toys like "Dance Star Mickey", and has recorded Mickey's dialogue for the new musical stage show at Disneyland, *Mickey and the Magical Map*, that opened May 2013.

However, for the 19 new Mickey Mouse cartoons that aired on the Disney Channel in 2013, Executive Producer Paul Rudish wanted an "edgier" tone to Mickey's voice and used actor Chris Diamantopoulos instead of Iwan to supply the voice.

In June 2013, Diamantopoulos wrote:

> I'm so proud to be the voice of Mickey in these [cartoons].

Who Was Ub Iwerks?

Ubbe Eert Iwwerks (who officially shortened his Dutch name to Ub Iwerks in the 1920s) was a legendary animator and inventor who worked with Walt Disney for much of his life. He was a shy, sometimes inarticulate, serious fellow whose talent amazed everyone.

Iwerks was born March 14, 1901, and passed away July 7, 1971. Iwerks was Mickey Mouse's second father and has been called "the hand behind the mouse". He was the best draftsman at the Disney Studio, able to turn out more footage than anyone else. Iwerks could do 600–700 usable drawings a day, or roughly one drawing a minute during a 10-hour day.

Walt and Iwerks became friends as teenagers. Iwerks started working for Walt in 1922 at the Laugh-O-Gram Studio and continued through the *Alice Comedies* and the Oswald the Rabbit cartoon series at the Disney Studio in California. He was the only animator who remained loyal to Walt when Disney lost the Oswald series. It was Iwerks who came up with the final design of Mickey Mouse based on Walt's ideas, and it was Iwerks who animated virtually all of the first three Mickey Mouse films by himself.

Iwerks' son Dave said in an interview published in the November 12, 1978, issue of *Family Weekly*:

> Mickey was not born on that [train] ride, as per legend. He was created at a drawing board in Los Angeles. Father drew many characters, one of which was a mouse. Whether Walt suggested [draw a mouse] is in doubt.

> It's quite possible the mouse was just one of the many characters Dad churned out. He never spoke of Mickey or regaled us with stories

of those early days. Once he accomplished something — no matter what — he forgot all about it and moved on to other things. He wasn't one to boast "Look what I did!" It was all in his day's work.

Dad did everything on the first three Mickey cartoons from the first stroke on the drawing board to the finished cartoon. Proof of Dad's importance to Walt lies in the fact that in 1930, Dad earned $150 a week. Walt collected $75. Reason Dad got twice as much as Walt was because Walt wanted to keep Dad there at all costs. He understood his value.

Iwerks also did the lion's share of the animation work, including backgrounds, on the next two 1929 Mickey shorts, *The Barn Dance* and *The Opry House*. In addition, he illustrated the first few weeks of the Mickey Mouse comic strip as well as many promotional items featuring Mickey Mouse such as a giveaway phenakistoscope of Mickey walking forward.

Disney animator and director Ben Sharpsteen affirmed:

If there ever was a right-hand man to Walt, it was Ub.

For a variety of reasons, including some personal disagreements with Walt, Iwerks left the Disney Studio in January 1930 to start his own animation studio. He returned to the Disney Studio in 1940 but not as an animator; instead, he developed the Special Process Laboratory that handled photographic processes such as special effects both for animation and live action.

Iwerks was awarded two special Oscars for these achievements. In 1959, he was given an Academy Award for the design of an improved optical printer for special effects and matte shots, and in 1965 he was awarded again for advancements in the traveling matte system used in *Mary Poppins* (1965) to combine live action and animation. In addition, Iwerks contributed many other technical improvements to the Disney Company, including the use of Xerox in producing cel animation and the continuous loop projection system used for films at the Disney theme parks.

Ub Iwerks was inducted as a Disney Legend in 1989.

Who Was Fred Moore?

Robert Fred Moore, born September 7, 1911, and often referred to as "Freddy" or "Freddie", was a legendary animator whose work is still studied today for Moore's ability to instill "appeal" in his characters. Moore died November 23, 1952.

Disney Legend Marc Davis, one of Walt's "Nine Old Men", said:

Fred Moore *was* Disney drawing. That was the basis of what Disney stood for. It was certainly the springboard for everything that came after.

Moore is credited with the appealing re-design of Mickey Mouse in the mid-1930s, including the pear-shaped body, cheeks, and the effective addition of pupils to Mickey's eyes.

When he first showed these changes to Walt in a "sweatbox" session (where preliminary work was reviewed), Moore was nervous, especially knowing Walt's deep connection to Mickey Mouse. Walt reran the scene several times without saying a word. Then, Walt lifted his eyebrow, turned to Moore and said: "Now that's the way I want Mickey to be drawn from now on!"

Disney Legend Ward Kimball remembered his friend:

> Fred was just right for the time. He decided to make Mickey's cheeks move with his mouth, which they had never done before because you drew everything inside the circle.

When he was hired at the Disney Studio, Moore became an assistant to Disney Legend Les Clark, a former assistant to Ub Iwerks and the resident Mickey Mouse specialist at the time. Soon, it was Moore who was considered the Mickey specialist.

Unlike Iwerks, Moore was the charming life of the party with a cocky innocence that often showed itself in prankish behavior. Coordinated and athletic, his body awareness transferred to his animation, giving his characters a fluidity lacking in the animation of others.

In the late 1930s, though no later than 1938, Moore gave an illustrated presentation to the Disney animators about how to approach the character of Mickey Mouse. Entitled "Analysis of Mickey Mouse", it was part of a series of lectures given by top Disney animators like Art Babbitt, Norm Ferguson, and Fred Spencer on the characters of Goofy, Pluto, and Donald Duck. From Moore's lecture:

> Mickey seems to be the average young boy of no particular age; living in a small town, clean living, fun loving, bashful around girls, polite and clever as he must be for the particular story. In some pictures he has a touch of Fred Astaire; in others of Charlie Chaplin, and some of Douglas Fairbanks, but in all of these there should be some of the young boy.

Moore went on to talk about the construction of the figure:

> The legs are better drawn tapering from the pant leg to the shoe, that is, larger at the shoe with the knee coming low on the leg. This also applies to the arms; the hands being fairly large.

He also discussed handling Mickey in animation:

> The ears are better kept far back on the head and often act as a balance for the figure. However, do not shift them around on the head just to balance.

The lecture included Moore's commentary about Minnie Mouse:

> Minnie seems cuter with the skirts high on her body — showing a large expanse of her lace panties. This skirt should be starched and not hang limp.

Unfortunately, Moore developed an alcohol problem that escalated in severity during the late 1940s. He was inducted as a Disney Legend in 1995.

Mickey Mouse Myths

The 1935 League of Nations Medal

For nearly eighty years, both the Disney Company and the world press believed as absolute fact that in June 1935 Mickey Mouse received a special gold medallion from the prestigious League of Nations as "an international symbol of Good Will".

That it would have been the only such special award ever given out by the organization during its entire existence should have aroused some suspicions.

The story of the award was first reported in the June 18, 1935, edition of *The Times* of London. News organizations around the world picked up on the item and shared it as well. Roughly a week later, even Edna Disney, Walt's sister-in-law, wrote in her personal diary: "Walt was presented with a League of Nations medal."

The award was proudly displayed at the Disney Studio for decades. Merchandising guru Kay Kamen used a photo of the medal front and center on the cover of the 1935 *Mickey Mouse Merchandise Catalog* along with pictures of almost a dozen other awards won by Disney within the last twelve months.

But as Disney historian Didier Ghez discovered while researching *Disney's Grand Tour* (Theme Park Press 2013), it was all just a misunderstanding.

Summarizing Ghez's groundbreaking research, The League of Nations did not present a special award to Walt Disney and Mickey Mouse.

The award was actually given by an organization called Comité International pour la Diffusion Artistique et Littéraire par le Cinématographe (C.I.D.A.L.C.), or in English, the International Committee for the Diffusion of Arts and Literature through the Cinema. At the gala event where the award was presented on the morning of June 25, 1935, attendees were shown eight Disney animated shorts and watched live-action performances by several French entertainers.

Then, Walt was formally presented with a gold medal from Mlle. Hélène Vacaresco, President of C.I.D.A.L.C.

Everything seemed to support the notion that C.I.D.A.L.C. was an official sub-committee of the League of Nations. Mlle. Vacaresco, its president, was the Romanian League of Nations delegate; M. Nicolas Pillat, Permanent General Secretary of C.I.D.A.L.C., was the economic counselor of the Romanian delegation. The members of the Executive Committee of the organization included Brazilian and Italian ambassadors, ministers, and famous writers. C.I.D.A.L.C. also claimed to act "in the spirit of the League of Nations".

Everyone, from Walt Disney and his family to the press, was convinced that C.I.D.A.L.C. was acting on behalf of the League. Because of all this publicity, a letter dated June 28, 1935, was sent from J.D. de Montenach's assistant at the League of Nations in Geneva to H.R. Cunnings in the League of Nations' London office, in an attempt to explain that C.I.D.A.L.C. was not connected to the League of Nations in any way, and that this confusion had existed for years.

However, no official public correction was ever made, and the error continued to appear in magazine stories, books, and elsewhere for decades.

On November 17, 1988, the United Nations and UNICEF *did* honor Mickey on his 60th birthday as an Emissary of Goodwill in recognition "of the joy he has brought to the children around the world." The ceremony was held in the Economic and Social Chamber.

Mickey Mouse Code Word for D-Day Invasion

Since the 1940s, one of the most frequently quoted "fun facts" about Mickey Mouse is that his name was used as the code word for the launch of the Allied Invasion of Normandy (D-Day) on June 6, 1944.

No one, however, could find any documented confirmation either in the personal files of Dwight D. Eisenhower, the U.S. military archives, or the Disney Archives. For several decades, it troubled Disney researchers as a story simply too good to be true.

Then, Disney historian Michael Barrier uncovered a press release from the United Press dated June 8, 1944, from London, that clarifies where the story originated. The press release states:

> Mickey Mouse played a part in the invasion of northern France, it was revealed today. Naval officers gathering for invasion briefing at a southern port approached the sentry at the door and furtively whispered into his ear the password of admission: "Mickey Mouse".

"Mickey Mouse" was the password for the officers to enter a meeting where they would receive orders for the invasion. It was not the name that launched the actual invasion. Recognition passwords used at U.S. military sentry points often were based on information or names considered uniquely American, such as baseball facts and cartoon characters.

Creation of Mickey Mouse

As mentioned, the story of Walt Disney being inspired by a real mouse during his days as a young artist in Kansas City to create the character of Mickey Mouse on a train trip from New York to Los Angeles has become mythology. However, modern research has debunked the specifics of the legend while maintaining that Walt may have done some rough sketches on the train and may have considered a mouse as a replacement for Oswald the Rabbit.

Here are some of the variations of the legend that Walt shared with reporters in the earliest years of Mickey Mouse's popularity.

From W.T. Maxwell *Daily Sketch* (1938):

> While riding in the upper berth of the train taking Walt from New York to Hollywood, Walt heard the continuous but slight creaking of the woodwork in his compartment that sounded like a million mice in conference. The idea made him laugh and in that split second Mickey Mouse was born.

Walt later told another interviewer that the repeating rhythm of the sound of the wheels and the sound of the extended whistle slowly blowing on the train seemed to sound like the word "mouse" over and over. Neither of these stories is true but rather examples of Walt's inventive storytelling.

From *Photoplay* magazine (June 1932):

> Legend has it that (Walt) Disney, broke and discouraged, was sitting on a park bench wondering where the next coffee and cakes were coming from. He laughed at the funny antics of a mouse scurrying about a nearby trash can. "If that critter made me laugh," reasoned Walt, "he might do the same for the world!" And he certainly has!

This account tosses in another odd, untrue story about the creation of Mickey Mouse that appears nowhere else.

From the Athens, Georgia, *Banner Herald* (December 26, 1933):

> It was Disney's brother's daughter, aged six, who was chiefly responsible for "Mickey"... Six years ago Disney had a five dollar a month studio over a garage where he sat at night and watched the antics of a pair of mice. After weeks of patient persuasion, he tamed them so that they would climb upon his drawing board. There they sat up and nibbled bits of cheese in their paws or even ate from his hand.
>
> As he watched them, he occasionally wrote letters to his niece. The letters described the activities of the mice and sometimes were illustrated with drawings of them doing funny, fantastic human things.

Walt never had a studio above a garage, and Walt's niece (the daughter of his older brother Herbert) would have been eleven years old, a significant age difference. More important, "six years ago" in 1927, Walt was living and working in Hollywood not in Kansas City. These letters were never discussed in any other article or surfaced during Walt's lifetime. They are yet another bit of hokum on the creation of Mickey Mouse.

From *Psychology* magazine (November 1933):

> [In Kansas City, Walt] made the acquaintance of Mickey. One evening as he was bending over his drawing board, two little mice scampered across his table. Amused at their capers, he began to make friends with them. And presently they were serving as his models. For hours they would sit on his drawing board, while he worked, combing their whiskers

and licking their chops in true mouse fashion. And Walt would weave them into human situations and make them tell funny human stories.

Again, this story is not true. Sometimes Walt would say it was an entire family of mice that he captured and tamed. Other times, he would say that it was just one mouse that he made a prisoner in an overturned wire waste basket and eventually trained it (by hitting the mouse on the nose with the eraser on the end of his pencil) to stay inside a large circle he drew on a sheet of paper at the top of his drawing board.

When Walt decided to go to California, he supposedly took the mouse to a vacant lot "in the best neighborhood" he could find to release it. Walt told a reporter:

> The mouse that had played on the drawing board didn't seem to want to go. He stood around looking at me. I had to stamp my foot on the pavement and yell at him to make him beat it. That's the last I ever saw of him.

None of these stories are literally true, but Walt loved embellishing how he created Mickey Mouse.

The story of Mickey's birth on a train ride from New York became so polished by repetition over the years that it overshadowed any other variation and became as much an oft-told myth as young George Washington chopping down the cherry tree and then confessing it to his father.

Even today, people still insist that the story Walt told about being inspired by a real mouse and using that inspiration on the train to create Mickey Mouse is the gospel truth.

An article in *Cosmopolitan* magazine (February 1934) stated:

> [F]iction has it that a mouse roamed Walt's workroom; that the two became friendly, and the Mickey mouse originated in this room. It is a nice story, but false. As a matter of fact, Mickey Mouse's papa is not overly fond of mice. He jumps out of their way, and doesn't go looking for them.

In response to that article, John C. Moffitt wrote in the *Providence Bulletin* newspaper (April 1934):

> A magazine writer recently dismissed the story of the [real Kansas City] mouse which inspired Mickey as a myth. But Walt Disney spent one whole morning telling it to me and he insisted it was true.

Walt's engaging and magical tale of the creation of Mickey Mouse was so powerful that it overcame any reasonable doubts with ease.

Audiences wanted to believe in the story of one brief burst of inspiration in a moment of deep desperation that resulted in the birth of the world's most beloved cartoon character as well as that it was inspired by the kindness Walt had shown to a helpless little mouse.

In fact, audiences still want to believe that story today despite any and all factual evidence to the contrary.

The Mickey Mouse Comic Strip

By the end of 1929, Mickey Mouse had already appeared in fifteen theatrical animated adventures.

Inspired by Mickey's popularity, the Disney Company introduced a daily Mickey Mouse comic strip on January 13, 1930, distributed to newspapers by King Features Syndicate. Walt explained:

> [I considered] other ways to exploit characters like the Mouse. The most obvious was a comic strip. So I started work on a comic strip hoping I could sell it to one of the syndicates. As I was producing the first one, a letter came to me from King Features wanting to know if I would be interested in doing a comic strip featuring Mickey Mouse. Naturally, I accepted the offer.

In a letter to King Features dated October 19, 1929, Walt wrote:

> Due to the fact that we have increased our production schedule from twelve to thirty-one pictures for the coming year, we have been unable to devote much time to the making up of the specimens of the MICKEY MOUSE COMIC STRIP that you requested. The comic strip is an entirely new angle for us and we have been somewhat puzzled as to the best policy to carry out in this strip. The artist that we have had working on this angle [Ub Iwerks] has made up quite a few specimens but we have not as yet been able to satisfy ourselves with the results.

A month later, on November 19, 1929, Walt wrote again to King Features:

> I mailed you yesterday the first specimens of the MICKEY MOUSE Comic Strip... the popularity of MICKEY has been increasing by leaps and bounds and the pictures are now being distributed in every country in the world. Several of the big theater circuits in this country have already re-booked the first series... to play return engagements in their theaters. We are also starting a national campaign on what is known as the MICKEY MOUSE CLUB.

Several days later, on November 21, 1929, Walt received a reply from King Features:

> I just received the six strips of "Mickey Mouse" and everyone here thinks they are great. We believe Mickey has the makings of a top-notch strip judging from these samples... we would like to have another six strips right away. One reason for this is that [newspaper publisher William Randolph Hearst] will be here next week and we want to show "Mickey Mouse" to him.

On December 18, 1929, Walt sent the second batch of six strips (one for each day of the week, except Sunday) and the third set a few days after that, and then the fourth during the week of December 30.

The actual contract was not signed until January 24, 1930, but Walt gave permission by telegram for King Features to run the first strip, which appeared on January 13. Until May 17, 1930, those early strips were written by Walt Disney himself.

Many papers headed the strip as *Mickey Mouse by Iwerks* (or Ub Iwerks), with Walt Disney's famous signature not appearing until Iwerks left the Disney Studio to start his own animation venture. Iwerks' name had appeared on many early Mickey Mouse items, including movie posters, promotional items, and the title cards for the shorts.

Ub Iwerks had drawn the first few Mickey Mouse animated cartoons virtually by himself and was the natural choice to transfer Mickey's antics to the newspaper page, fulfilling a dream of most cartoonists to have their own syndicated newspaper strip.

After three weeks and eighteen strips, Iwerks left the Disney Studio. His inker, Win Smith, took over both the penciling and inking of the gag-a-day format with the February 10, 1930, strip, until he was replaced on May 5 by Floyd Gottfredson, who would draw the strips for four-and-a-half decades and who was responsible for a series of continuity stories that have rarely been surpassed.

During those first two months of the strip, Mickey's airplane activity echoed his experiences in *Plane Crazy* (1928), and Mickey becoming a castaway fighting off wild animals and cannibals in the strip helped inspire *The Castaway* (1931).

Near the end of March 1930, rather than a series of unconnected gags, the strip began to have a loose story continuity. Clarabelle Cow was first used in the strip on April 2, 1930, and Horace Horsecollar showed up the next day.

In 1931, Walt offered (in the comic strip itself) an autographed picture of Mickey free to interested readers to try to judge the size of the readership. Over the next two weeks, eight to ten sacks of mail each day were received by the studio full of thousands of letters from readers asking for the picture. Walt happily posed for a publicity photo standing next to a pile of letters with a Charlotte Clark Mickey Mouse doll on top.

Just as in the animated cartoons, the strips featured the slapstick violence popular during that time period. Mickey got into actual fistfights as he faced bandits, pirates, crooks, mad scientists, and a host of other menaces.

Unfortunately, such pluckiness was not in keeping with Mickey's corporate image, which demanded an inoffensiveness of character to help sell his plethora of merchandise.

In the February 16, 1931, issue of *Time* magazine, the editors stated:

> Great lover, scholar, soldier, sailor, singer, toreador, tycoon, jockey, prizefighter, automobile racer, aviator, farmer. Mickey Mouse lives

in a world in which space, time, and the law of physics are nil. He can reach inside of a bull's mouth, pull out his teeth and use them as castanets. He can lead a band or play violin solos; his ingenuity is limitless; he never fails.

Sadly, that early, raucous Mickey could soon be found only in Gottfredson's newspaper comic strip.

Floyd Gottfredson was about twenty-four years old when he moved from his home in Utah with his wife and two children to Los Angeles in the hope of becoming a cartoonist for one of the seven major newspapers in the Hollywood-Los Angeles area.

Gottfredson learned cartooning through a correspondence course from The Federal Schools of Illustrating and Cartooning (now more commonly known as Art Instruction Schools, Inc.). Arriving in Los Angeles but finding no work in his field, he overheard that Walt Disney was looking for artists. He took his samples to the Disney Studio and was immediately hired as an animation in-betweener and possible backup artist for the Mickey Mouse daily strip.

At that time, Disney had already put in about six months of preparatory work on the strip which was to be officially launched about twenty-three days after Gottfredson had been hired.

The trend at that time was for all strips, comic and illustrative, to do continuities, following the example of Sidney Smith's big comic strip hit, *The Gumps*. By April, a month before Gottfredson took over, the Mickey Mouse strip was also using story continuities at the request of its syndicator, King Features.

In an interview in 1978 for an Italian magazine, Gottfredson recalled:

> Walt had continued to write the strip, including the first seven weeks of the first continuity. He had been trying to get Win Smith to do the writing as well as the drawing but, for some reason, he didn't want to. This was one of the reasons for Smith's leaving the studio.
>
> I took over the drawing with the May 5, 1930, episode [Gottfredson's 25th birthday] and I took over the writing with the May 19, 1930, release. I wrote the daily until late 1932. After that time, the continuities were written by five different writers: Webb Smith, Ted Osborne, Merrill de Maris, Dick Shaw, and Bill Walsh.

Interestingly, Gottfredson did not want to do a comic strip any more. Working as an in-betweener (the entry-level artist who provides drawings "in between" the animator and his assistant's key drawings to create a smooth flow of movement), he had become very interested in animation and wished to stay with it. Walt promised Gottfredson that he would only have to work on the strip for two weeks while Walt found another artist. Gottfredson ended up working on the strip for more than 45 years. He recalled:

Walt checked my work the first couple of months after I took over the strip but after that and all through the years, except to pass on an occasional suggestion, he very seldom concerned himself with the strip or the department. He seemed to be relieved not to have to be concerned with them. He had bigger things to worry about.

In an interview with Disney archivist Dave Smith in 1975, Gottfredson explained the creation of Morty and Ferdie, Mickey's nephews:

Walt asked me to take a couple of the mice in the audience in *Orphan's Benefit* and make nephews out of them for Mickey. Bill Walsh came in [as a writer] and we decided the two nephews who looked exactly alike and had exactly the same personality [was] being duplicated with the three nephews in the Duck strip... So, Bill and I decided that we'd just let Ferdie fade out of the picture so we could develop Morty as a little mechanical genius type... We haven't used Ferdie in the comic strip since mid-1945 at least.

Gottfredson plotted all the *Mickey Mouse* daily continuities from May 19, 1930, to June 1943. Other writers became involved with the strip as early as 1932, but Gottfredson edited all the writing until 1946, and he would have "lively bull sessions on the upcoming week's work" with the writers. Besides penciling, Gottfredson also inked the strip from May 5, 1930, until late 1932.

He said:

I always felt that Mickey should have been a little [Charlie] Chaplin mouse against the world and I tried to promote that idea when they dropped the continuity and started the ... gag-a-day strips. Mickey had become bland and wishy-washy, too much like Dagwood and Blondie, in the neighborhood format. But my idea for changing Mickey's personality was rejected.

Adding to his workload was a Mickey Mouse Sunday strip which Gottfredson penciled from January 10, 1932, until mid-1938, when Manuel Gonzales took over. Gonzales, with some occasional assistance from artists Bill Wright, Tony Strobl, and Gottfredson, continued to do the Sunday strip until his retirement in 1981.

In 1938, approximately 20,400,000 people read the daily Mickey Mouse comic strip.

Despite his artistic skill and dedication, Gottfredson never held his early work in high esteem. In a 1967 interview, he remarked:

In the 1930s, Mickey's figure construction-wise was crude, anatomically bad, bumpy, stodgy. There was no flow in composition; the design wasn't there. For me, I shudder to look at the work I did during that period. I just don't like to look back on any of my work done more than six months ago. In fact, I wouldn't ever want to see it reprinted. I think it's aged too much.

Gottfredson retired on October 1, 1975, and passed away at the age of 81 on July 22, 1986. Roman Arambula and various other artists took over the artwork for the strip through 1989.

In January 1990, the Mickey Mouse comic strip became a "semi-continuing" strip, meaning that the gag-a-day format alternated with short-story continuities.

From September 1, 1958, through March 17, 1962, there was another daily Mickey Mouse comic strip that ran concurrently with the regular strip entitled *Mickey Mouse and His Friends*. It used a gag-a-day format with no dialog balloons or captions. Disney felt that such a pantomime strip would be easier to sell overseas because there were no translation issues.

Originally, the strip was written by Milt Banta with artwork by Ken Hultgren. In 1959, Manuel Gonzales and Riley Thomson did the art. By May 1959, Roy Williams was doing the gags and Julius Svendsen the drawing.

Despite the contributions of many talented writers and artists, the daily Mickey Mouse comic strip, like all newspaper comic strips, faded in popularity as readers abandoned print media and as the reproduction of the artwork shrank to miniscule scale.

Sometime in the early 1990s, Disney's contract with King Features ended, and the strip was cancelled.

Artist and author Floyd Norman, the last writer on the Mickey Mouse comic strip, said:

> With Mickey Mouse in fewer than thirty newspapers, both companies realized that Mickey's time was nearing the end of a long and successful run. Over the years the Mickey strip had grown old and stodgy. The strip was not funny, nor was it allowed to be funny. With scrappy little Mickey reduced to an animated Ozzie Nelson it was no wonder the strip was on its last legs.
>
> I don't think anybody even noticed the strip was no longer being published. Times had changed and media had seen a revolution. Yet, I think Mickey could have survived the revolution had we only had creative leadership that would allow us to take the mouse in a bold new direction (of short adventure stories like in the early days). Personally, I think Mickey would have survived. However, this is something we'll probably never know.

Floyd Gottfredson Interview

Born May 5, 1905, cartoonist Floyd Gottfredson was inducted as a Disney Legend in 2003 for his contributions over four-and-a-half decades to the Mickey Mouse comic strip.

He started drawing the Mickey Mouse comic strip on May 5, 1930, and drew his last Sunday strip on September 19, 1976, and his last daily strip on November 15, 1976.

In 2011, Fantagraphics Publications began releasing a multi-volume prestige format book series with reprints of Gottfredson's Mickey Mouse comic strip. Edited by Mickey Mouse expert David Gerstein and publisher Gary Groth, the books contain not only the comic strips themselves but important and entertaining supplemental material. When the first volume was released in 2011, Gerstein said:

> Instead of seeing Mickey as a cheerful, but one-dimensional character — like a lot of people do — Gottfredson portrayed him as this stubbornly optimistic, determined, two-fisted young guy trying to prove himself in wild, adventurous situations. Floyd called Mickey "a mouse against the world."

> Mickey's brave, witty, imaginative and incredibly daring in Gottfredson's stories. He's a scrapper, ready to fight for what he believes in; but he's not always right about what he thinks is right, so he can create a mess for himself and have to do some great soul-searching afterwards.

Gottfredson's work influenced many artists. He once recalled:

> I've always felt that it was our job to try to capture the spirit of animation... I tried to design the characters as if they were moving in animation.

I interviewed Floyd Gottfredson in fall 1979 for an article, "The Mouse Man", that I wrote in issue #6 of the Disney-oriented fanzine, *The Duckburg Times*.

I later used some of the interview for a series of introductions that I wrote for the *UnCensored Mouse* comic book collections that reprinted early public domain Mickey Mouse comic strips. That short-lived project was published by Malibu Graphics in 1989.

KORKIS: How did you decide to apply at the Disney Studios?

GOTTFREDSON: Looking for another job, I went to Vermont Avenue in Los Angeles, California, where all the film exchanges were and one of them had a one-sheet Mickey Mouse movie poster standing in front of it.

As a projectionist in Utah, I had run all of Walt's Oswald the Lucky Rabbit animated cartoons so I was familiar with the Disney name but I had never seen or heard of Mickey Mouse before.

Out of curiosity, I went in and the fellow there and I started talking and he told me he had heard that Walt was going to New York the following week to look for artists. I lost no time in putting together my samples and rushing out to the Disney Studio which was then located on Hyperion Avenue. I figured I would get the jump on the fellows who might be applying in New York since I was already there in Los Angeles.

Korkis: Did you get to meet Walt?

Gottfredson: Walt himself looked over my samples and asked me what sort of work I was interested in doing and I told him I wanted to do comic strips. Well, at that time, Disney wasn't doing any comic strips. Walt was quite a salesman. He told me I didn't want to get involved in doing comic strips because it was a rat race.

He said that the future would be animation and he was so convincing that I said, "Fine. Do you have any openings in animation?" And he said, "Sure, we'll put you in as an in-betweener."

Then he said that he and Ub Iwerks were just beginning to put together a Mickey Mouse comic strip for King Features and that it would be good to have me around as a back-up man in case they needed some help.

Korkis: Did you start working at Disney immediately?

Gottfredson: I went to work the following day, December 19, 1929. I was 24 years old and had been married for five years. I had been earning $65 a week as a projectionist and Walt was offering $18 a week but I took it because he had really convinced me that animation was the future. I did some free-lance cartooning on the side by mail and within eight months I was making more than I made as a projectionist.

Korkis: What did you do as an in-betweener?

Gottfredson: I only worked about four months in animation as an in-betweener. I did in-between work for Johnny Cannon and later Dave Hand and Wilfred Jackson. I even did a few in-betweens for Ub Iwerks.

It was all work for the *Silly Symphonies*. Norm Ferguson and Dave Hand gave me a little piece of animation to do on *Cannibal Capers* (1930). It was a lion running out of the jungle and a cannibal beating on a drum. That was really the only animation I ever did but it worked out pretty well and I was just fascinated with animation.

Korkis: How did you finally end up with the Mickey Mouse comic strip?

Gottfredson: The Mickey Mouse comic strip debuted in January 13, 1930, with Walt doing the writing and Ub penciled them and an artist named Win Smith was doing the inking. After the first eighteen strips, Ub left and Win took over the penciling and the inking. The strip was straight gags adapted from the Mickey Mouse movie cartoons.

King Features wanted continuity, that is to say, they wanted the strip to have a story and a plot because other strips like Sidney Smith's *The Gumps* were very popular being "story strips". Walt tried to convince Win to take over the writing and Win kept stalling but I don't know why. Finally, Walt met with him and told him he was going to take over the writing and Win who had a short fuse wasn't going to be told what to do and so he quit. He came by my desk and said, "I think you've got a new job".

Korkis: So it was as simple as that?

Gottfredson: About a half hour later, Walt called me into his office and asked me whether I would like to take over doing the strip. By now I had become very interested in animation and was reluctant to change. I told Walt that he was right and that I would prefer to stay with animation. Well, Walt was quite a salesman. He told me to just take the strip for two weeks to give him some time to find another artist.

I wanted to help out so I agreed. After all, he had told me that part of my job was to be a possible back-up on the strip. At the end of a month, I wondered if he was really seriously looking for anyone. After two months, I began to worry that he might actually find someone because I was enjoying doing it and wanted to continue with it.

Nothing more was ever said about it and I continued to draw the Mickey daily strip for about forty-five and a half years until my retirement on October 1, 1975.

Korkis: When did your first strip appear?

Gottfredson: My first strip appeared May 5, 1930, and the strip had gone into continuities April 1, 1930. Walt had written a story about Mickey finding a treasure map to a gold mine in Death Valley. To help me get started, Walt continued to write about two weeks' worth of strips for me to draw and then I took over the writing on May 19 in the middle of the story and continued to write the daily until 1932 when five different writers took over writing the continuities.

Korkis: How closely did the comic strip follow the animated cartoons?

Gottfredson: We tried to follow the spirit of the Mickey animated cartoons but because we were doing adventure stories we had to go beyond them. The animated cartoons had just a loose story structure where there could be a lot of gags building to a conclusion.

That isn't how stories are done in newspaper strips. We had to develop the characters more to help sustain the story. I loved doing these little adventures but keeping them as humorous as possible. Straight gags are too thin. Not enough meat to them. I think going back to gag-a-day was a step backwards and I think this was proved by the drop in popularity of the strip.

Korkis: Weren't some of your early strips influenced by Mickey's animated adventures?

Gottfredson: Walt himself set the precedent for borrowing ideas from the cartoons. The strip was influenced by the cartoons but also the fads and movies of the day. *The Mad Doctor* influenced the strip story "Mickey Mouse in Blaggard Castle", although the mad professors in our story were modeled after a Boris Karloff movie I had just seen.

"Mickey and the Seven Ghosts" was inspired by the animated cartoon *Lonesome Ghosts*. "Mickey Mouse Runs His Own Newspaper" was inspired by the gangster movies of the time like *Scarface* and *Little Caesar*.

Korkis: Did you ever run into the same censorship issues that Walt was facing with the animated cartoons?

Gottfredson: There was one sequence in the "Blaggard Castle" story where Mickey grabs a pole and vaults over this alligator pit but as he is leaping, the pole breaks. King Features sent us a frantic telegram that they were going to cut out the entire sequence because the alligators would upset women and children reading the newspaper.

I took the photostats to Walt and he just laughed. He thought it was a good adventure and was confident that we had a way of making the resolution of the peril humorous. So he contacted the syndicate and they left it in.

We also got censored when we did the "Monarch of Medioka" story because it kind of paralleled what was actually happening in Yugoslavia at that time where the archduke was trying to overthrow the king. Over the years, there was very little censorship because our goal was to try to stay true to the spirit of Disney animation.

Korkis: Did Walt have to approve your work before it was sent to the syndicate?

Gottfredson: Walt checked my work for the first couple of months after I took over the strip, but after that and all through the years, except to pass on an occasional suggestion, he very seldom concerned himself with the strip or the department.

He seemed relieved not to have to be concerned with them. He had bigger things to worry about. We were just supposed to follow the general studio rule that any violence was to be done in a comedic manner. And we labored over the artwork to make it the highest quality we could.

Korkis: So Walt had no direct input into the direction of the strip?

Gottfredson: In the early days of the strip, I was always intrigued by details in the background like houses and picket fences and rain spouts. So one of the hardest things I had to learn was to simplify, to streamline. In the first couple of months that I worked on the strip, I would take the strips personally to Walt in his office for his approval.

Later, as I said, he became too busy to take the time to do that or maybe he just felt I was doing okay. I do know he would still look at the proof sheets closely because sometimes I would get memos but that was usually about any changes that was going to happen in animation that we needed to do in strips.

The only direct input I would get from Walt was that I was putting in too much "junk" in the strip. "Why do you put so much junk in there? Simplify." I don't know if that was to help the storytelling or because of his experience in animation where you didn't want the background too complicated.

One time when he was in Florida, he sent me a copy of the strip that had appeared in the local paper and he wrote in the margin "Too damn much junk. Clean it up." Still, that is pretty good if that is the only complaint I would get from him. Looking back on those old strips, I think the old stories were too wordy and overloaded with dialogue.

Korkis: I notice your Mickey Mouse continues to change his look over the decades. Some people even thought a different artist was doing the strip at times.

Gottfredson: Mostly, I tried to keep up with the changes the Studio made to Mickey. I tried hard to match the Mickey I was drawing for the newspaper strip with the Mickey of the films.

In January 1933, I dropped the thin white line above Mickey's eyes for simplicity's sake but other than that I just followed the new model sheets of Mickey that would filter down to me.

Periodically, Mickey would lose and then regain his tail. He lost his short pants in the Forties and of course got pupils in his eyes with *Fantasia* (1940). When I first saw the pupils in Mickey's eyes on the model sheets I liked them immediately.

Korkis: I am sure you watched the animated cartoons closely. Do you have a favorite?

Gottfredson: Fred Moore was the fellow who really streamlined the mouse and some of the other characters. To me, the finest Mickey short cartoon that was ever made was *The Nifty Nineties* (1941) with Fred Moore's design of Mickey. I've said this many times before but I think the best Mickeys ever done were by Fred Moore. I tried to imitate Fred but I don't think anyone could ever copy his style.

Korkis: Since you worked at the Studio, did any of the animators like Moore drop by to comment on your work?

Gottfredson: The animation department didn't even know we existed. We were so small and shoved in a back corner that it was out of sight, out of mind I guess.

In the Comic Strip department we were paid straight salaries and if we wanted a vacation, we had to get ahead a few weeks on the schedule. Our salaries were never as high as the animators. When the union got into it later, it finally was decided that scale for a Class I Comic Strip Artist was about the same as a minimum wage for an animator, I think.

Korkis: It was sort of what you had been telling me earlier about your feelings about the comic book artists.

Gottfredson: We just didn't consider [comic book artists] professional artists. There was a definite snobbishness by those of us who did newspaper strips towards comic book artists. I had nothing to do with the redrawing or reprinting of my comics strip stories in the Disney comic books. They had to change the panels for the format of the comic book so it resulted in some very bad drawings where panels had to be extended on the bottom or the sides or even sides being cut off in odd places to make them fit.

So they had to draw hands or feet or added in trees to fill spaces or cut characters off or changed balloons. I forget all the things that were done. It just ruined the design of the panel. I tried never to read the redrawn or reprinted strips. We considered them second-generation material and why spend time on them?

Korkis: The story continuities in the Mickey Mouse strip seem to stop in the mid-1950s.

Gottfredson: We began to phase out of continuities and go back to a gag-a-day format at that time because it was a decision of King Features to help counteract the effects of television on newspapers. They felt that with a few exceptions that comic strip stories couldn't compete with television.

At first, I missed the continuities but gradually daily gags became a relief. Continuities were very demanding. We had to do them so fast. I don't think we had the time to really develop them because we were producing them daily. In animation, they always seemed to have plenty of time.

Korkis: Were you bothered that readers never knew your name and thought that Walt was doing the strip?

Gottfredson: People ask me all the time if I was annoyed that I wasn't allowed to sign my name on the strip. Not at all. That was just the tradition of the comic strip where ghosts did the work and the artist who created the strip still signed his name.

It wasn't Walt's fault. I know he asked King Features to let me sign my name and they told him it would dilute the thing and confuse people and make it more difficult to sell. And they were right. People wanted Walt Disney. They thought he did everything. I have no complaints or regrets.

Korkis: What was your impression of Walt Disney?

Gottfredson: Walt and Roy were great people to work for. Under them, the creative freedom was unbelievable. Roy was a little warmer to us than Walt. Walt was a tough taskmaster. I don't think he even realized when he was being harsh. He was always just so focused on whatever project he was doing and was passionate that it be done right. That was all that mattered.

The rest of us were just the tools he used. If, as you said earlier, I kept the "real" Mickey alive, I was just doing the best I could as an extension of Walt and his dream. There was only one Walt Disney. There will never be another

Mickey on the Radio: Mickey Mouse Theater of the Air

One of the many forgotten aspects of early Disney history was the short-lived (only twenty episodes) radio show *Mickey Mouse Theater of the Air* produced by the Disney Studio in 1938 to showcase Mickey Mouse and his friends and to help promote the general release of *Snow White and the Seven Dwarfs* (1937).

During the Golden Age of Radio, listeners could tune in the dial on their huge radio (which was actually a piece of living room furniture) and hear adventure, comedy, drama, horror, mystery, musical variety, romance, and thrillers, as well as classical music concerts, Big Band remotes, farm reports, news and commentary, panel discussions, quiz shows, sidewalk interviews, sports broadcasts, talent shows, weather forecasts, and more.

The Golden Age of Radio lasted from the early 1920s until the invasion of television in the 1950s. In the beginning, American radio network programs were almost always presented live, since the national networks prohibited the airing of recorded programs until the late 1940s.

As a result, prime-time shows would be performed twice — once for each coast. Some programs, however, were recorded as they were broadcast, typically for syndication or so advertisers could have their own copy.

Fortunately, the estate of Felix Mills, musical director of the *Mickey Mouse Theater of the Air*, donated all of his original discs of the show to the Pacific Pioneer Broadcasters for future researchers to enjoy and study.

Mills' daughter, Betsy Mills Goodspeed, wrote:

> I remember Walt being very excited about doing the show. He was constantly amazed by how much grown-ups loved and admired his work.
>
> My father thought *Snow White and the Seven Dwarfs* was the most marvelous film that was ever produced. As far as I know, he didn't go to the Disney Studios to discuss the music for the radio show but went to [Walt] Disney's house, or Walt came to ours. Walt obviously believed that Felix was the best choice for the job, and Felix thought the radio program was a fantastic endeavor by all those who were involved. He felt highly honored to have been awarded the contract.

Walt Disney and his animated friends were no strangers to radio. Walt (often doing the voice of Mickey Mouse and sometimes accompanied by Clarence Nash voicing Donald Duck) popped up on several radio shows during the Golden Age.

In summer 1937, Lever Brothers (which made products like Rinso and Lifebuoy) were looking for a half-hour program to precede and build an audience for their *Al Jolson's Lifebuoy Program* on CBS that was being massacred in the ratings by its competition on NBC, *The Jack Benny Program*.

Looking for additional funds and publicity for the nearly completed *Snow White and the Seven Dwarfs*, Walt Disney hesitantly agreed in September to do an audition record for a weekly Disney radio show.

The show was scheduled to debut on October 5, 1937. Written by comedy writer Ken Englund, the premise was that Mickey Mouse would host the half hour and present a weekly guest star (actor Leslie Howard was chosen for the pilot), but that Donald Duck would mess things up.

Deeply involved in the final months of making *Snow White* Walt wouldn't be available to do the voice of Mickey Mouse, so actor J. Donald Wilson was selected as his substitute. One newspaper reported that it was "the first time anyone other than Walt Disney himself was allowed to speak for Mickey". Clarence Nash, of course, did the voice of Donald Duck and the musical chores were handled by Meredith "Music Man" Wilson.

Roy Disney flew to New York in September to close the deal, but it fell apart because of a dispute over money.

Some news stories, including one in the *Hollywood Reporter,* hinted that "Disney is afraid [his characters] may sour on him if they [air] every week" and that Walt "refuses radio because he doesn't think his Mickey Mouse and others would broadcast well".

Despite this setback, other sponsors, even the makers of Lucky Strike cigarettes, were trying to woo Walt into doing a weekly radio children's show. Pepsodent, thanks to a guaranteed weekly budget of between $10,000 and $12,000 weekly and some other concessions, finally got Walt's commitment to create a show to air Sunday afternoons on NBC in the same time slot used by Amos 'n' Andy during the other six days of the week.

Walt probably agreed because the show coincided with the release of *Snow White* and because he saw it (just as he later did with television) as an opportunity to publicize his latest film.

The original option was for thirteen weeks with Walt doing the voice of Mickey Mouse until a suitable replacement could be found. Despite what others report, Walt only did Mickey's voice for the first three weeks.

Starting with the fourth show, the voice of Mickey was comedian Joe Twerp, whose comedy relied on him being an excitable stutterer who confuses words. He had been considered for the role of Doc, a similar personality, in *Snow White*, but Roy Atwell was chosen to supply the voice instead.

The writers were Bill Demling, who had supplied material for big-name radio comedians like Ed Wynn and Joe E. Brown, and Eddie Holden, a radio actor who had voiced the giant in the Mickey Mouse short *The Brave Little Tailor* (1938) and who had done incidental voices in *Dumbo* and *Bambi*.

Music direction was by Gordon "Felix" Mills, one of radio's most active orchestra leaders of the era, who directed thirty-three musicians for the show. Six of those musicians also performed as Donald Duck's wacky novelty "gadget" band, the Webfoot Sextet, with instruments like cowbells, bottles, a meat grinder, an auto horn, a Bob Burns-style bazooka, and a "syrup-cruet hurdy gurdy". Amazingly, all of this cacophony sounded pretty good and very funny.

In his unpublished memoir, Felix Mills remembered:

> I called in a young drummer from the [Eddie] Cantor show when one of our drummers had the flu, and for several weeks he hung around at rehearsals. [His name was Spike Jones.] Spike asked what I was going to do with the Duck's music and I said, "I'll never use it again; do you want it?"

(Later in 1941, the musical group Spike Jones and The City Slickers appeared on the scene and became popular for playing this same type of cacophonic music.)

The show featured a twelve-voice female choir (with four members who specialized in bird whistling so they could also perform as Minnie Mouse's Woodland Bird Choir) and an eight-voice male choir. The opening theme song for the show was the still popular "Who's Afraid of the Big Bad Wolf?" and the closing theme was "Heigh Ho" from *Snow White*.

Broadcast from a theater studio on the RKO lot (RKO was releasing the Disney animated films), Joe Twerp did the voice of Mickey Mouse. Minnie Mouse was performed by Thelma Boardman who would later supply Minnie's voice in some of the Disney cartoons of the 1940s.

Pinto Colvig, the original voice of Goofy, had left the Disney Studio by the time the show started, so Goofy was voiced by Stuart Buchanan, the official "casting director" at the Disney Studio who had supplied the voice of the huntsman in *Snow White*.

Donald Duck was voiced by Clarence Nash and Clara Cluck by Florence Gill. Both of them had performed the same roles in the Disney animated cartoons.

Radio announcer John "Bud" Hiestand (who appeared in many movies in 1938 as a radio announcer) announced the show, and also voiced the Magic Mirror, which was the primary form of transportation that allowed Mickey and the gang to journey through time and space to meet everyone from Long John Silver to Mother Goose to Robin Hood.

While the Disney version of the Snow White character appeared on at least two episodes (and in one episode Walt danced with Snow White), the gang also got to visit Cinderella and Sleeping Beauty almost two decades before their films were made.

(Incidentally, on some of the later shows, Walt was too busy to attend rehearsals and performances, and so Hiestand had to impersonate him when the script called for an appearance.)

Hiestand's brother-in-law Glanville Heisch, a skilled writer of verse and song as well as the creator of the popular radio show the *Cinnamon Bear*, was also on board as a writer and director.

Other voices on the show were supplied by such popular performers as Billy Bletcher (Old King Cole and Judge Owl; Bletcher was the voice of Peg

Leg Pete in the cartoons), Hans Conreid (the Pied Piper; many years later he would voice Captain Hook), Bea Benaderet (Miriam the Mermaid in the kingdom of King Neptune), Walter Tetley, and many others, including Mel Blanc.

Mel Blanc? The voice of Bugs Bunny, Daffy Duck, and countless other cartoon characters who always told the story that the only voice he did for Disney was the voice of Gideon the Cat in *Pinocchio* and it was later cut out except for a hiccup? (Of course, Blanc also supplied the voice for the Audio-Animatronics Cousin Orville in the Carousel of Progress attraction.)

Then twenty-nine years old, Blanc was a regular on the show portraying a variety of characters as well as one of his earliest continuing characters, a man who gets so excited that he starts hiccupping so violently he can't stop. Perhaps this performance gave Walt the idea to use him in the production of *Pinocchio* which was in development at the time.

Initially, Walt Disney tried to be excited about the show. He wrote in a 1938 issue of *Radio Log* magazine:

> I'm letting Mickey and the rest of my gang go on the air, although I've been advised against it. We consider this a good omen, for we were also strongly advised against ever creating Mickey, doing our pictures in sound, branching into Technicolor, and creating a feature length picture.

Despite this optimistic statement, Walt had deep concerns that the success of his cartoon characters depended primarily on their visual antics and not their distinctive voices. He once joked that part of Donald Duck's popularity in foreign countries was that no one could understand what he said and so had to use their own imagination based on the Duck's body language and tone of voice.

Walt continued:

> Many sponsors have whispered the siren song of [radio's] riches in our ear. Several tried, but none of them had the feeling for our characters. Then we realized that what we had begun to suspect was true: if Mickey went on the air we'd have to build the program ourselves.

But Walt was distracted by the release of *Snow White* and by other issues at the Studio. He took the chance on radio because he hoped it might be a good way to advertise his films and might spark the creation of new characters or new ideas. He said:

> It's a rather logical direction in which we can expand. We expect to develop new ideas and personalities we can use in our pictures. We look upon radio as a new stimulus, a challenge — something which will give us fresh ideas and a better perspective on our work.

No new significant characters were created from the venture, but his foray into radio gave Walt insight on how later to handle his entry into television.

When Pepsodent's contract ended after thirteen weeks, the company signed a renewal to cover the remaining seven weeks of the season, but after that

The Mickey Mouse Theater of the Air quietly disappeared, as did so many other radio shows that didn't capture the imagination of their audiences.

Walt had been proven right. Even before the show premiered, he had said

> I don't think this show will work. You have to see the characters to fully appreciate them.

Contemporary critics agreed. Aaron Stein of the *New York Post* wrote:

> All the strength, the vigor and logic of the Disney films lies in the pictures. The voices, the music and the sounds are usually funny and effective, but they register only as sound effects which point up the pictures. On the air they offered only disembodied sound effects.

In the final episode, which aired on May 15, 1936, Mickey and the gang save Old MacDonald's farm. With the tune "Heigh Ho" playing in the background, the announcer said:

> And so with Mickey and the Gang headed for Vacation Land we bring to a close the last program in the present series. This program has come to you from the Disney Little Theatre on the RKO lot.

Walt, distracted by *Snow White*, had never been able to devote his storytelling skill and his famous attention to detail and innovation to the show, which remains an interesting if little-known footnote in the history of Disney and Mickey Mouse.

Here is the list of all twenty episodes of *The Mickey Mouse Theater of the Air*:

- January 2, 1938: "Robin Hood"
- January 9, 1938: "Snow White Day"
- January 16, 1938: "Donald Duck's Band"
- January 23, 1938: "The River Boat"
- January 30, 1938: "Ali Baba"
- February 6, 1938: "South of the Border"
- February 13, 1938: "Mother Goose and Old King Cole"
- February 20, 1938: "The Gypsy Band"
- February 27, 1938: "Cinderella"
- March 6, 1938: "King Neptune"
- March 13, 1938: "The Pied Piper"
- March 20, 1938: "Sleeping Beauty"
- March 27, 1938: "Ancient China" (Snow White guest appearance!)
- April 3, 1938: "Mother Goose and the Old Woman in a Shoe"
- April 10, 1938: "Long John Silver"
- April 17, 1938: "King Arthur"
- April 24, 1938: "Who Killed Cock Robin?"
- May 1, 1938: "Cowboy Show"
- May 8, 1938: "William Tell"
- May 15, 1938: "Old MacDonald"

The Birth of Mickey Mouse Merchandise Magic

Today, Mickey Mouse merchandise is distributed worldwide and includes everything from toys and clothing to furniture and food products to almost anything else that can be imagined.

In the early 1980s, it was estimated that on an average day in the United States alone, more than five million items in the shape of Mickey Mouse or with Mickey's smiling face on them were sold to eager Mouseketeers.

The flood of Mickey Mouse merchandise began a year after Mickey's birth.

In fall 1929, Walt Disney was in New York to meet with his film distributor, Pat Powers, and to handle some business matters. Walt stated:

> I made the first commercial [merchandising] deal. I was in New York and a fellow kept hanging around my hotel waving $300 at me and saying that he wanted to put the Mouse on the paper tablets children use in school. As usual, Roy and I needed money, so I took the $300.

It was so unimportant to Walt that he neither wrote down the name of this person nor the company. By 1975, no example of such a product had surfaced, so it was assumed the story was another Walt embellishment, even though in 1971 Roy O. Disney verified the date, the amount of money, and the item, but could recall nothing else about it.

Enthusiastic searching by Disney memorabilia collectors finally unearthed the tablet. The black, white, and red cover features Mickey Mouse sitting at his school desk holding a red apple in his left hand for the teacher and a history book propped open on his desk. The back cover is plain cardboard. The 5.5 x 8.75 inch tablet includes the copyright "1930 — Walter E. Disney".

Another school tablet of similar vintage from the same company and in the same format, but not bearing a copyright, has also been discovered. The cover of this tablet features a smiling Mickey facing left and hunched over as he roller skates to school. In his right hand he clutches a strap attached to two school books flying in the air behind him.

These pie-eyed Mickeys are remarkably well-drawn and "on model", especially compared with other Mickey items released during the same time period.

Disney historians now assume that the person who paid for this first piece of Disney merchandise was Pat Powers (a different Pat Powers from the one who distributed Disney's films) of Powers Paper Company in Springfield, Massachusetts. While no documentation exists, Powers continued as a licensee from 1931 to 1940, and the 1930 school tablet was very similar to later Powers Paper products.

More offers to merchandise Mickey Mouse quickly followed.

In January 1930, Carolyn "Charlotte" Clark, who had been making her livelihood selling cookies and novelties during the Great Depression, came up with an idea of how to use her talents as a seamstress to earn extra money.

She sent her fourteen-year-old nephew, Bob Clampett, who later would become a legendary Warner Bros. cartoon director and the creator of *Beany and Cecil*, to the Alex Theater in Glendale, California. Clampett sat through three consecutive showings in order to see a Mickey Mouse short several times so he could sketch the character. There were no illustrations of Mickey Mouse available at that time other than on movie posters.

From those sketches, Clark made the first stuffed Mickey Mouse doll. Clampett's father advised her to get Walt Disney's permission before she started selling them. He drove her to the Disney Studio. Both Walt and Roy loved the doll. They rented a house near their Hyperion Studio, later nicknamed the Doll House, where Clark worked on making the doll in three different sizes.

Bob Clampett earned thirty cents per doll stuffing each one with kapok and brushing off the excess. Clampett's father became the head salesman.

At first, the dolls were purchased by Walt and Roy to give to friends, business acquaintances, and special visitors to the studio. Clampett recalled:

> Walt Disney himself sometimes came over in an old car to pick up the dolls. One time, his car loaded with Mickeys wouldn't start, and I pushed while Walt steered until it caught and he took off.

In 1930, after a photo of Walt with one of the dolls appeared in *Screen Play Secrets* magazine and in several newspapers, the demand from the general public became overwhelming. Stores were swamped with calls from customers wanting a doll just like the one they saw in the photos.

By November 1930, Clark was producing 300-400 dolls per week for sale at two large Los Angeles area department stores, May Company and Bullock's, for five dollars each. The department stores only paid two dollars and fifty cents per doll, and so made an amazing profit. Clark had to employ six full-time seamstresses to meet demand.

Roy O. Disney wrote in 1931:

> The doll we are having manufactured [by Clark] is, as many buyers have stated, the truest character doll of its kind that they have ever seen. You must realize that this means far more to [Walt and me] than the mere royalties involved in the sale of the doll.

When demand continued to exceed what the overworked staff could make, the Disney brothers decided to release the Charlotte Clark doll pattern to the general public and let people make their own dolls. They were not concerned about the profit from the dolls being sold but rather with satisfying public demand for the dolls. Some families simply could not afford the price of the doll in those hard times, and Walt felt that every child who wanted a Mickey Mouse doll should have one.

The McCall Company of New York released Printed Pattern No. 91 in early 1932 with twenty seven pieces, one transfer, and one tissue sheet of directions at a cost of thirty-five cents. The pattern was printed in English, French, and Spanish, and it was sold from 1932 through 1939 in the United States and Europe. Although the pattern came with the warning that it was sold "for individual use only and not to be used for manufacturing purposes", many out-of-work seamstresses during the Great Depression earned a nice living making and selling the dolls in quantity for a monetary "donation".

In 1934, Knickerbocker Toy Company in New York started producing Mickey and Minnie dolls based on Clark's patterns. Clark designed other dolls for the company, and when Gund Manufacturing took over the production of the dolls after World War II, Clark designed their Disney dolls until 1958. She passed away on December 31, 1960, at the age of 76.

In early 1929, Disney Legend Les Clark drew several poses for Mickey Mouse. This model sheet, however, was used only for merchandising and publicity artwork. It had fifteen images of Mickey and two of Minnie penciled by Clark and inked by Win Smith, who inked the Mickey Mouse comic strip.

It was Clark who drew the famous pose of Mickey standing with legs apart, one hand on his hip and the other high in the air that was used on countless movie posters, house ads, and other products. He did two versions of the same pose, one as a classic "clear line" image, executed in graphite pencil on two-hole animation paper, and the other superimposed within a scaled-off grid. This grid would then be used by other artists to help recreate the pose in exact proportion at a larger or smaller size, a common practice at the time.

Both of these historical originals from Clark's personal estate were offered for sale at Hake's Auctions in 2009.

The first merchandising contract signed by Roy O. Disney (who was in charge of the business end of the Disney Studio) was with George Borgfeldt & Company in 1930.

The deal allowed the New York-based Borgfeldt to manufacture and sell "figures and toys of various materials, embodying your design of comic Mice known as Minnie and Mickey Mouse, appearing in copyrighted motion pictures." The first item released was a box of Mickey and Minnie Mouse children's handkerchiefs decorated with the pair doing some domestic chores.

Borgfeldt made its first Disney-themed toy in 1930: a wooden Mickey Mouse with jointed hands, arms, legs, and a tail. It came in two sizes (seven-and-a-half inches and nine-and-a-quarter inches) and had a painted composition head and a tail made of cloth-covered electrical wire. Heavy-duty elastic held the doll together, with the head being connected by a metal hook. Everything moved, including the head, hands, arms, and legs, and the doll was designed to be able to sit or stand. Each doll was hand-painted: Mickey's shorts were colored either red, yellow, or green, with matching shoes.

Mickey Mouse animator and director Burton Gillett made the original sketch for the wooden toy. In the sketch, Mickey was depicted as facing forward and from a side view.

Disney received a 2.5% royalty for products selling for fifty cents or less, and 5% for items costing more.

The Disney Brothers considered merchandise primarily as a means to publicize the characters outside the theaters and to secure intellectual property protection across various avenues other than the films themselves.

Roy O. Disney famously said in October 1929:

> We are a movie studio, not a toy store. We have no desire to go into the business of manufacturing or distributing toys and novelties, but we greatly desire to take advantage of the wonderful opportunity that exists.

Borgfeldt also produced comic character toys for the King Features newspaper syndicate. When King Features contacted Walt about producing a syndicated comic strip featuring Mickey Mouse, they also recommended that Disney use Borgfeldt as their toy manufacturer.

Unfortunately, Borgfeldt was known for making cheap novelties for five-and-dime stores, using inexpensive overseas manufacturing facilities, and had no concern for quality.

In 1931, Borgfeldt flooded stores with such branded Mickey Mouse items as a drum, a metal drummer, a sparkler, crickets, a wooden squeak toy, a wooden dancer, a walking toy on a board, express wagon, a wooden-jointed Mickey Mouse, a tumbling circus toy, a ring nose puzzle, a rubber sport ball, four velvet dolls, a wooden bobbing head figure, a shooting game, a quoits game, and two stencil sets.

By the holiday season, Borgfeldt hoped to also release a kite, a marble game, a celluloid rattle, a speed boat, a bubble pipe, an inflated rubber doll, and a magic lantern with Mickey Mouse slides. These toys were all produced under the Nifty Toy Company label.

Roy wrote to Borgfeldt on October 30, 1931:

> Walt had the opportunity of seeing the display of all Borgfeldt Mickey Mouse toys and novelties in the Biltmore Hotel. Walt was not disappointed. He was positively disgusted with the majority of the merchandise... Evidently in your opinion this is good merchandise at the price and competition demands that you keep that price down. However, we have built our business on the theory of trying to make a better product than the other fellow, and we still believe we are right.

Early in 1932, Walt Disney received an unexpected long distance call from Herman "Kay" Kamen, a successful and ambitious advertising executive in Kansas City. He expressed his disappointment in the quality of Disney merchandise and wanted to become involved.

Walt was impressed with his ideas and told him that the next time he was in Hollywood to drop by and they could continue the discussion. Within hours, Kamen was on a train to California.

When Kamen arrived, he immediately went to the Disney Studio and met with Walt and Roy, who were impressed with his enthusiasm and commitment to quality. In a 1968 interview, Roy O. Disney recalled:

> Kay walked in our office one day and said, "I don't know how much business you're doing but I'll guarantee you that much business, and give you 50% of everything I do over." We made a deal with him. He was a merchandising-minded fellow. He did a terrific job for us.

The Disney Company signed a contract with Kamen on July 1, 1932. For the next seventeen years, until he died in a plane crash in 1949, Kay Kamen handled the licensing of Disney merchandise.

He cancelled existing contracts with manufacturers who lacked prestige, raised their prices on products to compensate for the Disney royalties, produced poor quality material, and exhibited no enthusiasm for significantly improving their output.

The Disney-Kamen partnership quickly became one of the most successful collaborations in business history. Within six months, Kamen had doubled retail sales of character merchandise to $6,000,000.

By 1935, over $35,000,000 worth of Disney character merchandise had been sold. One Mickey Mouse book sold over 2.4 million copies. Kamen reported that as of October 1935, he had turned down over a thousand applications for licenses to use Disney characters. The companies he turned down generally produced such items as cigars, cigarettes, alcohol, and medicine.

By the late 1930s, revenue from merchandise exceeded revenue from film rentals.

It was this income that gave Walt Disney the funds for producing *Snow White and the Seven Dwarfs* (1937) and helped convince Bank of America that the Disney brothers were a good risk to lend money.

From his New York office, Kamen and his group of in-house artists and sales reps successfully marketed Disney's stable of characters to hundreds of manufacturers whom Kamen visited personally and frequently.

Kamen had the secretaries answer the phone with a school girl inflection saying "Mickey Mouse". When asked in 1932 by *The New Yorker* magazine why he had them do that, Kamen replied: "Mickey is better known than I am."

Kamen was responsible for two legendary merchandising landmarks.

Early in 1933, the Ingersoll-Waterbury Company of Connecticut was almost bankrupt. Kamen approved a license for them to make the first wristwatches featuring Mickey Mouse. Kamen helped get the watch featured at Macy's Department Store in New York City where 11,000 were sold in a single day. After only eight weeks of production, Ingersoll-Waterbury had to add 2,700 employees to its existing 300 to fill the demand for the watches. By June 1935, the company had sold over 2.5 million watches.

On May 7, 1934, the Lionel Corporation went into receivership with liquid assets of only $62,000 and liabilities of $296,000. Kamen believed in the company and so on July 19, 1934, he licensed them to produce a metal wind-up handcar with Mickey and Minnie Mouse at the handles pumping up and down in a see-saw manner. Supposedly, it was inspired by the ending of the Mickey Mouse short *Mickey's Choo-Choo* (1929) where they did the same thing. The handcar came with eight sections of curved metal track to form a twenty-seven inch circle. It sold for one dollar and advertisements claimed "loaded with fun and a thousand thrills, they circle the track ten or more times at a single winding".

In four months, 253,000 sets were sold. The $296,000 Lionel owed its creditors was paid in full on December 31, 1934. On January 1, 1935, Lionel had $500,000 in liquid assets. It was not just the sale of the Mickey Mouse handcar but the fact that the company was associated with Mickey Mouse that made the rest of its products and the company itself popular.

In a story picked up around the world, Federal Receivership Judge Guy L. Fake, who turned a healthy Lionel company back to its owners on January 21, 1935, gave Mickey Mouse the credit for saving the company. *The New York Times* ran this headline on January 22, 1935: "Mickey Mouse Saves Jersey Toy Concern; Carries It Back to Solvency on His Railway".

A 1934 survey of seventy manufacturers of Disney and Mickey Mouse character merchandise revealed that approximately ten thousand jobs had been created to meet public demand.

In the March 10, 1935, issue of *New York Times Magazine*, L.H. Robbins wrote:

> New applause is heard for Mickey Mouse, rising high above the general acclaim for him that already rings throughout the earth.
>
> The fresh cheering is for Mickey the Big Business Man, the world's super-salesman. He finds work for jobless folk. He lifts corporations out of bankruptcy. Wherever he scampers, here or overseas, the sun of prosperity breaks through the clouds.
>
> Shoppers carry Mickey Mouse satchels and briefcases bursting with Mickey Mouse soap, candy, playing cards, bridge favors, hairbrushes, chinaware, alarm clocks and hot water bottles wrapped in Mickey Mouse paper tied with Mickey Mouse ribbon and paid for out of Mickey Mouse purses with savings hoarded in Mickey Mouse banks.
>
> [Children] wear Mickey Mouse caps, waists, socks, shoes, slippers, garters, mittens, aprons, bibs and underthings, and beneath Mickey Mouse rain capes and umbrellas. They go to school where Mickey Mouse desk outfits turn lessons into pleasure.
>
> They play with Mickey Mouse velocipedes, footballs, baseballs, bounce balls, bats, catching gloves, boxing gloves, doll houses, doll dishes, tops, blocks, drums, puzzles, games.

Paint sets, sewing sets, drawing sets, stamping sets, jack sets, bubble sets, pull toys, push toys, animated toys, tents, camp, stools, sand pails, masks, blackboards and balloons.

Harper's Magazine (May 1934) reported that Disney's "chief income from Mickey Mouse was not from films but rather from by-products".

In 1988, on Mickey's 60th birthday, during that year alone, he appeared on over 9,000 products from ice cream treats to 18-karat-gold and diamond brooches ($5,800) in more than fifty countries.

Mickey Mouse merchandise in the 1930s pioneered a business practice that would become standard in Hollywood — that of utilizing a variety of products not only to generate additional income but to support a core franchise.

Mouse-ka-Tales

The appeal of Mickey will continue, because if he hasn't reached a saturation point by now, he never will.

— George Lucas
Film producer and director (1988)

On the following pages are several sections devoted to intriguing facts, quotes, and anecdotes about Mickey Mouse organized in different categories.

Mickey Mouse Memorabilia

- "When our girls were little, he [Walt] made a point of not having Mickey Mouse toys around the house. The only ones they acquired were gifts from people outside the family." Lillian Disney, Walt's widow, in "I Live With a Genius" (*McCall's* magazine, Feb. 1953)

- Since 2006, Janet Esteves of Celebration, Florida, has held the *Guinness World Records* honor of the largest documented Mickey Mouse memorabilia collection in the world. Her collection at the time included 2,100 items; in 2013, the collection had grown to 4,127 items, filling her 1,900-square-foot condo.

  Esteves estimates her actual collection at nearly 6,000 items, but many of them were packed away and unavailable for the final official count.

- In an interview with the *New York Times Magazine* in 1947, Kay Kamen, Disney's licensing agent, said: "Mickey Mouse is the greatest thing in the history of merchandising."

- In 1935, against Disney's strict merchandise policy of not putting Mickey on anything unpleasant for children, such as cigarettes or liquor, Walt allowed Mickey Mouse to promote Scott's Emulsion, a cod liver oil, but only in South America because of the high incidence of rickets there.

- In 1936, twenty million dollars of Mickey merchandise was sold in Europe alone.

- In 1934, General Foods puts Mickey Mouse on the Post Toasties cereal box, making him the first licensed character to appear on a cereal box.

  The boxes featured cut-outs of the Disney characters and were an inexpensive way for children in the Great Depression to have a Mickey Mouse toy after they finished eating their corn flakes.

  General Foods paid Disney an annual fee of $1.5 million (over $20 million today) to produce these boxes that cost families roughly 12 cents per box. General Foods continued the contract through 1941.

- In 1935, one-third of the population of the small town of Norwich, New York, were earning enough money from overtime for making Mickey Mouse sweatshirts to comfortably support their families. That year, over one million Mickey Mouse sweatshirts were sold.

- A British company introduced a new toffee in 1934 with Mickey Mouse on the wrapper. In the first week, they sold 36 tons. Six months later, the company was selling 150 tons per week.

♥ In 1935, it was reported internationally that the favorite toys of the famous Dionne quintuplets of Canada were their Mickey Mouse rattles.

♥ From 1935-37, the Geuder, Paeschke and Frey Company of Wisconsin produced a tin litho lunch box pail measuring 8¼" by 5" by 5" high called the Mickey Mouse Lunch Kit. It featured Mickey on the side walking in the woods carrying a picnic basket as well as a big image of Mickey on the top.

It was the first licensed cartoon character lunch pail and included an oval pie tray in the oblong container. Disney did not license another lunch box until 1954, when ADCO Liberty produced one with Mickey on one side and Donald on the other.

♥ The most successful school lunch box ever made was the Disney School Bus (with a dome lid) first produced by Aladdin in 1961 and kept in release for many years. On the lunch box, Mickey and Pluto stand beside a yellow school bus filled with Disney characters including Pinocchio, Dumbo, Mickey's nephews Morty and Ferdy, Dopey, Brer Rabbit, and good old Goofy behind the steering wheel. It sold its nine-millionth unit in 1976.

The designer, Disney Legend Al Konetzni, was an idea man and artist for the Disney Character merchandising division from 1953-1981. Konetzni was also a marketing account executive who coordinated licensing with such industry giants as General Electric (for the Mickey Mouse night light); Lever Brothers (for the Mickey Mouse toothbrush); and Bradley Time and Elgin (for Mickey Mouse watches and clocks, among others).

He was also responsible for the development and licensing of the now-collectible Mickey and Donald Pez candy dispensers. "Mickey always makes me smile," said Konetzni in 2003.

♥ Dwight Stones, a track-and-field athlete, wore a Mickey Mouse T-shirt in the 1976 Montreal Olympics where he won his second and final Bronze medal. Stones was known for wearing Mickey Mouse shirts.

♥ In its January 16, 1937, issue, *The New Yorker* reported: "Mr. Kay Kamen holds the contract with Walt Disney to use Mickey Mouse's picture on toys, sweat shirts, etc. (When you call up Mr. Kamen, the switchboard girl says, "Mickey Mouse.") He has 9 artists working for him, and he summons them to his private office by ringing the buzzer once for Artist No. 1, twice for No. 2, etc. The other day he rang for all nine at once. 45 buzzes - hell of a commotion. The artists dropped everything and hurried into Kamen's sanctum. He waited until they were all lined up at attention, then cleared his throat and said, 'Gentlemen, Mr. Disney has just sent word that henceforward Mickey's eyes are not to be highlighted'."

🐭 Disney Legend Ward Kimball remembered: "I recall when I was in the animation department the man who was the head of merchandising (Kay Kamen) often tried to convince us animators that there was a lot of money to be made by the company in selling Mickey Mouse merchandise. He'd pay us a visit in our department and show us the latest little toy or knick knack that was being produced.

"The animators were always disappointed with these items because the little toys never looked like the Mickey that we drew. We'd wait until the merchandising manager was out of ear shot and we'd toss all those toy samples he'd leave with us into the wastebasket… toys that I see going in auctions today for as much as a thousand dollars."

🐭 In its December 1994 issue, *Toy Collector* magazine reported: "Though Donald (Duck) did well in the merchandise marketplace, his success never equaled that of Mickey, who found overwhelming commercial favor. Merchandise seems to have been Mickey's specialty, and from the beginning Mickey toys, dolls, games and figurines vastly outnumber similar articles featuring Donald."

🐭 Imagineer and artist Alice Davis, wife of Disney Legend Marc Davis, said: "When Marc and I went to New Guinea in 1978, a group of us went with a guide into the rainforest to meet the natives. They'd had almost no contact with the outside world. In fact, the only white person they'd ever seen before was the guide. Yet, as we stood there, suddenly out of the forest, this little child came running toward us wearing nothing except a Mickey Mouse t-shirt. Somehow, Mickey had made it there before anyone else."

🐭 Disney Legend Ward Kimball revealed: "I own many Disney items from the early days that I happened to buy back then but not with the thought that one day they would be valuable. For instance, I bought the Lionel Mickey Mouse circus train when it was first issued (in 1935) because I'm a train buff and I just wanted to have it."

🐭 In 2000, Lego introduced five Mickey Mouse-themed sets: Mickey's Fire Engine, Minnie's Birthday Party, Mickey's Car Garage, Mickey's Mansion, and Mickey's Fishing Adventure. The majority of the parts for these sets were from the Fabuland theme (1979-1989) and the figures were sized to the same scale as the Fabuland figures. Only three mini-figures were made: Mickey Mouse (in three variations), Minnie Mouse, and Pluto. In 2013, a Mickey Mouse and Friends theme was produced with Mickey done in DUPLO bricks.

🐭 In 2012, Disney donated more than 100,000 Mickey Mouse plush toys to the Red Cross to give to children who have lost everything in natural disasters. Gail McGovern, president and CEO of the Red Cross, said: "The Mickey Mouse plush bring comfort to those impacted by disaster, which brings a sense of normalcy back into children's lives".

Roy E. Disney, Walt's nephew, remembered: "Our house was filled with Mickey Mouse toys and watches and games. As soon as my father brought home new toys, I'd see how fast I could destroy them."

Mickey Mouse Watches

The first Mickey Mouse wristwatch was featured at the 1933 Century of Progress Exposition in Chicago. At the Exposition, it outsold the World's Fair commemorative watch by a 3:1 margin, with as many as 5,000 Mickey Mouse watches selling per day, usually to adults who stood in long lines to purchase one.

On Wednesday, March 27, 1957, in Disneyland, U.S. Time officials presented Walt Disney with the 25th million Mickey Mouse watch. By 1946, U.S. Time had absorbed the Ingersoll-Waterbury Clock Company, the original manufacturers of the watch, but they continued to display the Ingersoll brand on Mickey Mouse watches until 1948.

Cartoonist Charles Schulz, creator of the *Peanuts* comic strip, wrote: "I did want a Mickey Mouse watch [in the 1930s] in the worst way, though. In those days, it cost $2.95 and I saved up my money for one. My mother took me to the local jewelry store to buy one. She asked them if they were really good watches and the guy said that they were okay but for a dollar more, I could have a really good watch. So I never did get my Mickey Mouse watch."

In 1969, it was reported that comedienne Carol Burnett once refused an offer of $500 for her classic 1930s Mickey Mouse watch, a gift from her husband, Joe Hamilton.

In 1968, comedian Bill ("Jose Jimenez") Dana gave his new Mickey Mouse wristwatch to astronaut Walter Schirra, who carried it with him on the Apollo 7 spacecraft as it orbited the Earth. According to the *Navy Times* in 1969, astronaut Eugene Cernan wore the Mickey Mouse watch given to him by the Commander of the Blue Angels during the Apollo 10 mission to the moon.

Mickey in Print

A trade advertisement for David McKay, the company that in 1931 published the first professional Mickey book, *The Adventures of Mickey Mouse*, proclaimed: "Mickey Mouse is close to a child's heart long after his frisky form has faded from the screen. A Mickey Mouse Book is a permanent companion for children who want to have their pal with them always."

The book was kept in print for nine years and McKay later published three others, all Mickey Mouse titles.

The slogan for the 1935 version of the *Mickey Mouse Magazine* was "A Fun Book for Children to Read to Grown-ups." Roy O. Disney told publisher Hal Horne that the slogan was accurate because his young son (Roy E. Disney) spent an entire evening at a polo match reading the first issue and pestering his father by reading him the jokes.

Charles Schulz recalled: "I used to subscribe to *Mickey Mouse Magazine* [in the 1930s] and even won a contest for Mickey Mouse's crazy invention. I remember that my invention had to do with a movie theater that didn't show pictures for people who didn't like Mickey Mouse. I didn't win the big prize but I did win a Mickey Mouse pen."

Walt Disney ordered six subscriptions to *Mickey Mouse Magazine* for the Orthopedic Hospital and School in Los Angeles, one of his favorite charities at the time.

In the mid-1930s, silent movie actress Mary Pickford made arrangement with publisher Hal Horne to purchase at a reduced price copies of the *Mickey Mouse Magazine* that were returned by newsstands. She distributed those issues to local hospitals.

The first issue of *Mickey Mouse Magazine* appeared in newsstands on May 15, 1935 and sold nearly 150,000 copies. It lasted until September 1940 when Kay Kamen converted it into a comic book, *Walt Disney's Comics and Stories*, which appeared in October 1940.

The first Mickey Mouse book, published in 1930 by Bibo and Lang, was called simply *Mickey Mouse Book* and at fifteen pages long was more magazine than book. It came with a game and game board as well as a marching song. The main four-page story, written by Bobette Bibo, the eleven-year-old daughter of one of the publishers, recounted how Mickey was kicked out of Mouse Fairyland and met Walt Disney. Roughly 100,000 copies were printed and sold over a six-month span at fifteen cents apiece.

Another first, the *Mickey Mouse Coloring Book*, was produced by the Saalfield Publishing Company of Ohio in 1931. It was an oversized 11"x15" book with thirty pages of drawings and short captions. Some of the drawings were partially colored to show young artists which colors they should use.

Saalfield was also responsible for the first Mickey and Minnie paper doll book.

Whitman Publishing of Racine, Wisconsin, released its first ten Big Little Books in 1932, with Mickey starring in one of them. Each book was 4"wide, 4½" high, and about 1½" thick. Text would be printed on one page, and then on the facing page there would be a black-and-white illustration. Each book cost only a dime.

Over two dozen different Mickey Mouse Big Little Books were published between 1932-1949. The first Mickey Mouse Book (#717) came in two different versions: the first had a crudely drawn Mickey and Walt Disney's signature on the cover, while the other had a more pleasing, standard Mickey without the signature. Even though the front and back covers of the book were different, both versions share the same interior and number, #717.

Several Big Little Books published by Whitman Publishing were used as premiums. *Mickey Mouse The Mail Pilot* was given away by the American Oil Company and Clark Drugstores. *Mickey Mouse Sails for Treasure Island* was a premium for Kolynos Dental Cream. Two special editions were produced for Santa at Macy's Department Store to hand out to children during the holiday season: *Mickey Mouse and Minnie at Macy's* (1934) and *Mickey Mouse and Minnie March to Macy's* (1935).

Mickey Goes to War

In 1930, the German Board of Film Censors prohibited the Mickey Mouse short *Barnyard Battle* because they felt the kepi-wearing Mickey Mouse shown in the film fighting the helmeted cats negatively portrayed the Germans and would "reawaken the latest anti-German feeling existing abroad since the War."

Perhaps the most oft-reprinted quote about Nazis hating Mickey Mouse is this: "Youth, where is thy pride? Mickey Mouse is the most miserable ideal ever revealed. Mickey Mouse is a Young Plan medicine to promote weakness.

"Healthy emotions tell every independent young man and every honorable youth that the dirty and filth-covered vermin, the greatest bacteria carrier in the animal kingdom, cannot be the ideal type of animal...Away with Jewish brutalization of the people! Down with Mickey Mouse! Wear the Swastika Cross!"

This diatribe was reprinted in the October 1931 issue of *The Living Age* magazine on page 183 in a small news blurb section entitled "Against Mickey Mouse", prefaced with: "one of their [Nazi] newspapers in Pomerania has published the following malediction attacking young people who decorate themselves with little emblems of Mickey."

The Nazis were well aware of the power of film and the popularity of Mickey Mouse, in particular, since young people wore images of Mickey including buttons and patches rather than swastikas.

In his diary entry for December 22, 1937, Hitler's propaganda minister, Joseph Goebbels, wrote: "I am giving the Fuhrer... 18 Mickey Mouse films (as a Christmas gift). He is very excited about it. He is very happy about these treasures which will hopefully bring him much fun and relaxation."

Goebbels chose to give this gift because he knew that during July 1937, in Hitler's private screening room, the Fuhrer had watched five Mickey Mouse cartoons and laughed loudly.

During World War II, Mickey Mouse appeared on thirty-seven military insignia for units like the signal corps and the chaplain's unit. Mickey was just not perceived as very threatening or war-like. Donald Duck appeared on two-hundred-and-sixteen insignia.

The very first Disney military insignia was designed in 1933 for the Naval Reserve squadron stationed in New York. It featured Mickey Mouse sitting on a diving bird that held a bomb in its claws. Disney did not do the design but merely gave permission for the use of Mickey's image.

A prominent and feared Mickey Mouse insignia first appeared around 1937, when German flying ace Adolf Galland of the Luftwaffe painted a homemade version of Mickey on all the fighters that he flew. Mickey had a cigar in his mouth and held a pistol in one hand and an axe in the other. When asked why he chose Mickey Mouse, Galland replied: "I like Mickey Mouse. I always have. And I like cigars, but I had to give them up after the war."

During World War II, the Sun Rubber Company of Ohio made a children's Mickey Mouse gas mask designed by Bernard McDermott, in the hope that the mask would seem less frightening. The company sent samples to President Franklin Roosevelt for his grandchildren. However, the rubber shortage and the lack of any real threat of gas attack resulted in the product never being mass produced in the U.S.

In 1938, based on the Ministry of Popular Culture's recommendation, the Italian Government banned foreign children's literature except for Mickey Mouse. Mickey was exempted from the decree because of his "acknowledged artistic merit". Actually, Mussolini's children were fond of Mickey Mouse, so they managed to delay the eventual ban on Mickey as long as possible.

In 1949, on the verge of the Korean War, the American Army asked a group of prominent Koreans to suggest what sign over the door of its Information Center would immediately make it clear to Koreans that Americans were inside. "After a brief consultation, the Koreans' vote went 100 percent for Mickey Mouse," reported *Collier's* magazine April 9, 1949.

🐭 Emperor Hirohito of Japan was a huge Mickey Mouse fan. He was given a Mickey Mouse watch during his special tour of Disneyland in 1975. For years, even on formal occasions, His Majesty was observed wearing the watch. In 1979, there was panic when the watch stopped ticking, and a concerned Palace Chamberlain rushed it to experts in Tokyo who specialized in American timepieces. Fortunately, the watch merely required a new battery. When Hirohito died in 1989, he was buried at his request with the Mickey Mouse watch.

🐭 At the end of December 1980, Disneyland in Anaheim, California, received a letter addressed to Mickey Mouse. Inside was a form letter requesting that Mickey send in his correct birth date information so he could be properly registered for the draft.

Mickey Mouse Music

🐭 Disney composer Paul Smith had this to say about the first Mickey Mouse cartoon he ever saw: "Mickey was playing the piano and I noticed that the sound of the keys was perfectly matched to his finger action. But, what impressed me the most, he was playing the correct keys!"

🐭 A fox trot released in 1930 with words and music by British lyricist Harry Carlton includes the lines: "There's a certain animile, making everybody smile. What's this fellow's name? Mickey! Mickey! Tricky Mickey Mouse!"

It was not an authorized Disney song, though the sheet music features a picture of Mickey and the name of the song as "Mickey Mouse".

🐭 Jimmy MacDonald, one of the official voices of Mickey Mouse, appears on screen as a drummer on the tympani in *Fantasia* (1940), causing colored lights to glow from inside the drum. He also appears as a circus band drummer in *Toby Tyler* (1960).

🐭 The song "Minnie's Yoo Hoo", written by composer Carl Stalling and Walt Disney, was Walt's only official song-writing credit. The song begins with the line: "I'm the guy they call little Mickey Mouse..."

🐭 Lyrics from the Mack Gordon and Harry Revel song "It's the Animal in Me" sung by Ethel Merman in the film *The Big Broadcast of 1936* include: "Look at Mickey Mouse. Look at Minnie Mouse. They just live on love and cheese."

🐭 Lyrics from the popular Cole Porter tune "You're the Top" (1934) include: "You're a melody from a symphony by Strauss. You're a Bendel bonnet. A Shakespeare sonnet. You're Mickey Mouse."

🐭 A music colleague approached conductor Leopold Stokowski, who appeared in *Fantasia* (1940), and said, "I'll bet you don't know why I admire you so much. It's because you're the only man I know who shook hands with Mickey Mouse [in the film]!" Stokowski wagged his finger and replied, "No! No! No! *HE* shook hands with *ME*."

🐭 The term "Mickey Mousing" refers to the close synchronization of music with cartoon action as in the earliest Mickey Mouse shorts. The music literally punctuates every physical motion on the screen, usually for comedic effect. Around the mid-1940s, the term began to be used as a pejorative in film-scoring circles and has sometimes been cited as one of the reasons the term "Mickey Mouse" itself became a derogatory term in later years.

🐭 Author Bob Thomas explained: "[Mickey Mousing music] stemmed from circus bands and can-can in which the effects corresponded closely to what was happening on the stage or in the ring."

🐭 The *Mickey Mouse Disco* album was released in 1979, peaked at #35 on Billboard's Pop Albums Chart, and was certified 2x Platinum by the Recording Industry Association of America.

🐭 The left library in the Walt Disney World Twilight Zone Tower of Terror attraction has a trumpet on a bookcase in reference to a *Twilight Zone* episode. Underneath the trumpet is the sheet music for the song "What! No Mickey Mouse?" (1932) by Irving Caesar. The lyrics for that song include: "What? No Mickey Mouse? What kind of a party is this? So where's that tricky mouse? That slicky, wacki, wicki, bolsheviki Mickey Mouse?"

🐭 The song "Hey Ra Ra Ray — Happy Birthday Mickey Mouse", written by Al Kasha and Joel Hirschhorn, was first sung by Davy Jones of the Monkees along with "a Million Kids", according to the label on the Warner Bros record released in England in 1978.

Mickey Milestones

🐭 In 1931, Madame Tussaud's wax museum in London unveiled a likeness of Mickey Mouse. It stood roughly three-feet tall and featured Mickey sitting on a stool and playing a piano. His left arm was raised high in the air while his right hand played the keys. The piano with squiggly legs was bending in the middle from the force of Mickey's playing. The pose was very reminiscent of Mickey's picture on the cover of the sheet music for "Minnie's Yoo Hoo".

🐭 In 1937, on Mickey's ninth birthday, The Boy Scouts of America bestowed upon him membership in the Cub Scouts.

🐭 Mickey Mouse was on the front of the first Disney Dollar released in 1987. A special Disney Dollar was released in 1993 to celebrate Mickey's 65th birthday: on it, a smiling Mickey adjusts his bowtie to look neat and pretty. Disney artist Matt Mew, the original designer of the Disney Dollars as well as the designer for Mickey's 60th birthday celebration, stated: "Right from the start we had no doubt in our minds that Mickey would be on the front of the one dollar bill."

Mickey Mouse was the Grand Marshal for the 116th Tournament of Roses Parade in Pasadena, California, on New Year's Day 2005. He was the first cartoon character to receive the honor and the second fictional character. (The first was Kermit the Frog in 1996, unless you also count ventriloquist dummy Charlie McCarthy who was co-Grand Marshal with Edgar Bergen in 1940.)

In announcing that Mickey would be Grand Marshal, Tournament of Roses President Dave Davis announced: "Mickey Mouse has brought entertainment, joy and laughter to families around the world for 75 years and we couldn't think of a more ideal Grand Marshal to help us *Celebrate Family* in 2005. He is a friend to families around the world."

Talk show host Larry King said: "When Mickey Mouse waves at you in a parade or on the screen, you almost *have* to smile. There is no other comparable cartoon figure anywhere. When Mickey Mouse is around, somehow things seem a little brighter."

The first Mickey Mouse balloon appeared in the 1934 Macy's Thanksgiving Parade and was a collaborative effort between Walt Disney and Macy's Tony Sarg.

It was forty-feet tall, contained 2,664 cubic feet of helium, and lasted through 1939. Mickey appeared in 1972 (wearing an open-collared yellow shirt) to celebrate the first anniversary of the Walt Disney World Resort.

Mickey returned again in 1973 to mark fifty years of Disney cartoons. In 2000, a new Bandleader Mickey balloon was introduced, and Sailor Mickey debuted in the Macy's Thanksgiving Parade of 2009 to mark the announcement of the *Disney Dream* and *Disney Fantasy* cruise ships.

Mickey Mouse was the first animated character to receive a star on the Hollywood Walk of Fame on November 13, 1978, in honor of his 50th birthday. The star is located at 6925 Hollywood Boulevard in front of Grauman's Chinese Theater.

At the 1939 New York World's Fair, A.W. Robertson, Chairman of the Board of Westinghouse, and Grover Whalen, President of the 1939 New York World's Fair, placed a Mickey Mouse wristwatch into a sealed time capsule not to be opened for five thousand years (the year 6939) and buried fifty feet deep. Also included were a kewpie doll, a pack of Camel cigarettes, a Gillette safety razor, a dollar in change, copies of *Life* magazine, and more.

- In 1934, Mickey Mouse first appeared as an entry in the Encyclopedia Britannica. Today's entry states: "Mickey Mouse, the most popular character of Walt Disney's animated cartoons and arguably the most popular cartoon star in the world."

- In May 1928, Disney filed a trademark petition for the name "Mickey Mouse". The trademark (#247,156) was granted to Disney in late September 1928, which may help explain why that month was considered Mickey Mouse's birthday for many years. The Disney Company actually owns sixteen separate trademarks for the name "Mickey Mouse" granted between 1928-2011 to cover a variety of uses.

- A U.S. commemorative stamp was released in 1968 with the smiling face of Walt Disney but not Mickey Mouse. Postal regulations at that time prohibited the placing of a Disney copyright notice on its stamps. However, other countries around the world did not have similar restrictions, so Mickey first appeared on a ninety lira stamp from the tiny republic of San Marino in 1970 with an appropriate copyright notice.

- The "Art of Disney: Friendship" stamps, issued in 2004 by the U.S. Postal Service, included Mickey Mouse. These designs were created by Dave Pacheco and Peter Emmerich. The "Art of Disney: Celebration" stamps in 2005 featured Mickey Mouse with Pluto; The "Art of Disney: Romance" stamps in 2006 featured Mickey Mouse with Minnie Mouse; The "Art of Disney: Magic" stamps in 2007 included Sorcerer Apprentice Mickey; and The "Art of Disney: Imagination" stamps in 2008 had Mickey as Steamboat Willie.

- In 1986, a gigantic 10-story hot air balloon in the shape of Mickey Mouse's head and called *Ear Force One* took to the sky to celebrate Walt Disney World's 15th birthday. Made by Cameron Balloons Ltd. of Bristol, England, and inspired by the Mickey helium balloons sold in the Disney parks, the balloon had ears 35 feet in diameter, a nose that stretched 33 feet, and eyes 16.5 feet high.

The diameter of the head was 168.3 feet. Uninflated, the balloon weighed 330 pounds without the basket. With pilots Robert Carlton and David Justice, it toured the nation (including a visit to Disneyland) in 1988 to celebrate Mickey's 60th birthday.

While this balloon was decommissioned many years ago, a new Mickey Mouse-headed balloon dubbed "The Happiest Balloon on Earth" from Cameron Balloons made its debut to celebrate Disneyland's 50th Birthday on April 2006. It sported a Golden Ears mouse cap like the souvenirs that guests could purchase and the cap was carefully removed after the celebration year for its appearances at other events.

"The Happiest Balloon on Earth" stands 98-feet tall and spans 53 feet from ear-to-ear. Mickey's pupils are 6 feet across, his nose is 5.5 feet wide, and it took over nine miles of thread to sew together this special shape. It was piloted by Scott Spencer and his wife, Laurie, for its initial four-month tour of the West Coast.

In 1988, to help celebrate Mickey's 60th birthday, the Disney Company had the Pitzenberger family of Sheffield, Iowa, plant a cornfield in the shape of Mickey's head on their farmland over the course of a day and a half. The profile of Mickey's head consisted of 6.5 million corn plants surrounded by 300 acres of oats. The distance between the tip of Mickey's nose to the end of his ear was 1.1 miles. Fifteen thousand people showed up in Sheffield (total population of 1,244) to celebrate Mickey's birthday, and for many months planes flying overhead would point out the field to passengers.

Mickey Moo, a white Holstein cow with a black Mickey Mouse head silhouette shape naturally occurring on her side, was housed in Big Thunder Ranch at Disneyland's Frontierland in 1988. The cow was born in 1982 in Maine and passed away in 1993 at the age of eleven from intestinal problems.

Minnie Moo, a similar white Holstein with a similar black silhouette, came to the Walt Disney World Resort from Edgerton, Minnesota, in 1990, living first at Grandma Duck's Farm in the Magic Kingdom and then at the Petting Farm at the Tri-Circle D Ranch in Disney's Fort Wilderness Resort and Campground. She passed away in 2001 at the age of 15.

In 1971, for the first time, *Webster's Third New International Dictionary* listed "mickey mouse" as an adjective defined as "lacking importance or serious meaning". The use of "mickey mouse" as a derogatory term is traced back to soldiers in World War II.

To promote the opening of Disney MGM Studios in 1989, Mickey Mouse toured thirty-seven cities in a forty-foot long "LiMOUSEine". The interior was supposed to be "Mickey's House" and included a soda fountain, cheese cabinet, satellite tracking system, a radio remote DJ booth (to be used by disc jockeys in the cities along the tour), four sunroofs, and many more technical enhancements.

The 9,000-pound, six-wheeled, maroon-colored limo with Mickey's famous head silhouette on the front grille toured East Coast cities for four months. The car was built by Ultra Limousine of Los Angeles at a cost close to $300,000.

For Disneyland's 35th birthday celebration, Ultra Limousine of Los Angeles created "Mickey's Mouseorail" to travel the country to promote the event. The Mouseorail body consisted of the shell and interior compartment of the Mark III Monorail Red lead car (with bubble top for the driver) fused to a stretched Chevy commercial truck chassis. Mickey's Mouseorail debuted at the Pasadena Tournament of Roses Parade on January 1, 1990, and then led the 35th anniversary parade at Disneyland on January 11, 1990, before going on a national tour with Mickey Mouse. The famous Mickey "tail lights" were included along with "ear-view" mirrors and a license plate that said "35Ears".

Mickey Miscellaneous

A survey of American children taken during the Great Depression revealed that many of them thought Mickey was a dog or a cat, even though his last name was Mouse, according to an article in a 1935 issue of *Time* magazine: "Anyway, a current survey shows that children don't think of Mickey as a mouse. A good many of them were asked whether Mickey Mouse is a dog or a cat. Almost half of the tots answered brightly, 'A cat'."

A witch doctor in the Belgian Congo reportedly used a homemade mask of "Mikimus" to provide a little extra magic. When actor Douglas Fairbanks went on a world tour, he showed Mickey Mouse movies to South Seas head-hunters to keep them friendly.

In the 1930s, Kaffirs, members of a South African tribe, refused to take cakes of soap unless they were embossed with a Mickey Mouse image, just as they had years earlier refused to take coins not marked with the image of Queen Victoria.

Reporting on experiments that animals may be instinctively capable of aesthetic appreciation, reporter Tony Osman reported in the *Sunday Times* in the early 1970s that a monkey's response to images on a television screen revealed that "an unfamiliar animal could hold his interest for a few minutes, and he would watch a Mickey Mouse cartoon for as long as the film continued."

On a trip to South America in the 1940s, Walt Disney was begged by people time and again to sketch a picture of Mickey as a souvenir. As *Collier's* magazine reported in its April 9, 1949, issue: "When he complied, the only Mickey Mouse he could draw, or perhaps would draw, was the outmoded string-bean Mickey of a decade or two ago."

At the time of singer Elvis Presley's death in 1977, according to his biographer Albert Goldman, Elvis was the second most commonly reproduced face in the world. The first was Mickey Mouse.

- Worcester, Massachusetts, proclaimed May 12, 1935, as Mickey Mouse Day. A Mickey Mouse Mall was set up in front of City Hall. School children, the Mayor, and City Council members paid homage; restaurants had Mickey Mouse on their tablecloths; clerks had Mickey Mouse on their smocks; and the *Boston Herald* began its lead editorial: "They are making history today in Worcester. They also made money."

- *McCall's* magazine had this description of Mickey's presence at the Disney Studio in its August 1932 issue: "On the walls inside the [Hyperion] studio, in private offices as well as in conference rooms, are framed drawings of Mickey Mouse in every conceivable pose. Painted on one door in red and gold is a shield bearing Mickey's Coat of Arms. The mystic words 'Ickmay Ousmay' are inscribed on this heraldic emblem and they have puzzled studio visitors a good deal. But guests who recall a jargon almost universal among American children grin and translate the gibberish into 'Mickey Mouse'. This was the language whereby dark secrets were kept from inquisitive adults."

- The 91st meeting of the American Psychological Association was held in Anaheim, California, September 1983. Because of the location, the members decided to prepare a "brief Psychohistory" of Mickey Mouse. Their conclusion: "Mickey Mouse is actually Walt Disney in smaller form, with a long tail. Plucky, spirited and optimistic and much like his creator, ready to take a chance!"

  Generally, they found the Mouse had a pretty stable ego.

- In the greenhouse of EPCOT's The Land pavilion in Florida, watermelons, pumpkins, and cucumbers are grown in the shape of Mickey Mouse's head. These edible treats are served to guests and when sliced properly retain their familiar form. The EPCOT Science team shapes the young watermelons in special plastic molds until the fruit forms the familiar three-circled Mickey head.

- Around 1957, Dr. Tom Dooley of the Medical International Cooperation Organization (MEDICO) got special permission to put the image of Mickey on the side of his hospital ship anchored off a southeast Asian coast. Mickey succeeded in luring young patients for free examinations and treatment where even the Red Cross sign painted on the ship had not.

  They had never seen Mickey before, but the kids happily boarded the ship. Disney Legend John Hench said: "Obviously, hardly any of them had ever seen a picture of Mickey. But they recognized something. It wasn't the cartoon character; it was the symbol."

- Farfur (also spelt Farfour) was a costumed character who looked exactly like Mickey Mouse and who spoke in a high-pitched voice on the Arabic children's television program, *Tomorrow's Pioneers* (2007).

The show advocated anti-Semitism and anti-American values. Disney CEO Robert Iger said, "We were appalled by the use of our character to disseminate that kind of message." Diane Disney Miller called the character "pure evil".

- To promote the Beijing Olympics in 2008, the Chinese erected several statues depicting a cartoony athlete mouse with red shorts and white gloves. When asked about its resemblance to Mickey, a spokesperson replied, "They have square holes in their ears. They are not copies." The spokesperson suggested the statues are unique because they incorporate the themes of old Chinese coins (the square holes), the year of the rat, the Olympics, and the financial district into the design. However, children passing by the statues were seen pointing and saying, "Look! It's Mickey!"

- In 1932, famed artist Thomas Hart Benton included Mickey Mouse in a set of murals painted for the library of the Whitney Museum in lower Manhattan. When the Whitney moved uptown the mural panels wound up at the New Britain Museum of American Art.

- In summer 1932, a display of Mickey and other Disney animation art at New York's Kennedy Galleries was so popular that it was extended from its initial two week run to six weeks, then transformed by the College Art Association into a show that began a national tour at the Art Institute of Chicago in December 1933.

  Disney-and-Mickey exhibitions were seen at the Toledo, Cleveland, Milwaukee, Dallas, and Los Angeles County museums, among other venues. In Evansville, Indiana, in December 1933, an exhibition entitled "The Art of Mickey Mouse" was on display in the city's Temple of Fine Arts.

- Morty and Ferdie (sometimes spelled Ferdy), Mickey's nephews, first appeared in September 18, 1932, in the *Mickey Mouse* Sunday newspaper comic strip. Their mother, Mrs. Fieldmouse, asks Mickey to babysit them. Officially, they appear together (with Shirley Reed supplying their voices) in only one animated short, *Mickey's Steam-Roller* (1934), though were frequently featured in comic books and storybooks.

  As Mickey Mouse authority David Gerstein has pointed out, as early as *Giantland* (1933) the horde of orphan mice in the Mickey Mouse cartoons were referred to as "nephews" in story conferences but never identified as such in the films or storybooks.

- Young actresses Shirley Temple and Jane Withers each had extensive collections of Mickey Mouse dolls in the mid-1930s. Temple was an official member of the 1930s Mickey Mouse Club and proudly displayed her certificate in a publicity photo. In the film *Captain January* (1936), she sang "What makes life the sweetest, bestest and completest? Not a big doll house, or a Mickey Mouse, but the right somebody to love." (Lyrics by Jack Yellen. Music by Lew Pollack). An animated Shirley can be seen in the stands cheering on Mickey's polo team in the 1936 cartoon of the same name.

- Minnie Mouse did not have many lines of dialog in the Mickey Mouse cartoons, and in fact, does not speak at all in *Mickey's Christmas Carol* (1983). In the early cartoons, Minnie's voice was provided by Marcellite Garner (who worked in Disney's Ink and Paint Department), Leone Le Doux, Thelma Boardman, Ruth Peterson, and Ruth Clifford. Russi Taylor has supplied the voice since 1986.

- On January 14, 1933, the Mid-Winter Snow Carnival in Lake Arrowhead, an event sponsored by the theater Mickey Mouse clubs, was dedicated to Mickey Mouse. Walt Disney, along with nearly 50,000 children, attended.

- A Gardner Rea cartoon in the March 20, 1931, issue of *Life* magazine showed a group of wealthy, sophisticated socialites walking out of a movie theater upset and despondent. The caption underneath read: "No Mickey Mouse!" ("What! No Mickey Mouse?" was a popular saying in the 1930s to express displeasure of a movie house not playing a Disney cartoon before the main feature.)

- On November 17, 1978, President Jimmy Carter's daughter, Amy Carter, hosted Mickey Mouse's 50th birthday party for handicapped Washington, DC, children at the White House. President Carter joined in the singing of the Mickey Mouse Club theme song. Disney animator Ward Kimball also attended, and whipped out seemingly endless drawings of Mickey Mouse for the President, Amy, other guests, and even Secret Service agents dressed as clowns

- In 1935, the Soviet government presented Walt with an antique, Russian cut-glass bowl at the First Soviet Cinema Festival. Comrade Boris Shumiatsky, the director general of the Cinematography Institute of the U.S.S.R, stated in the *New York Standard* newspaper of August 5, 1935, that Mickey was of "cosmic value". That same issue quoted Russian director Sergei Eisenstein, director of the legendary film *The Battleship Potemkin* (1925), who said that Mickey was "America's one and only contribution to world culture".

Mickey at the Movies

Mickey has a bigger screen following than nine-tenths of the stars in Hollywood.

— Louella Parsons
Hearst Newspaper Hollywood Gossip Columnist (1931)

In 1933, Mickey Mouse received 800,000 pieces of fan mail, more than any other star in Hollywood.

First Mickey Mouse Cartoon: "Plane Crazy"

While *Steamboat Willie* is officially considered the first Mickey Mouse cartoon because it was widely seen by the general public, Walt Disney and Ub Iwerks actually produced two other silent black-and-white cartoons featuring Mickey in 1928 that preceded *Steamboat Willie*: *Plane Crazy* and *Gallopin' Gaucho*.

Plane Crazy is a simple story of a rural young boy, portrayed by Mickey Mouse without gloves or shoes, who tries to emulate America's latest hero, aviator Charles Lindbergh, by building and flying his own plane.

In May 1927, "Lucky Lindy" had become a hero with his solo airplane trip in the *Spirit of St. Louis* across the Atlantic from New York to Paris, and Walt hoped to leverage the country's overwhelming interest in aviation and attract an audience for his new cartoon character.

Although Lindbergh was Mickey's hero, the aviator took a Felix the Cat doll with him on his flight for luck. Of course, to be fair, Mickey didn't exist at that time, and Felix was the most popular animated cartoon character in the world.

The first few installments of the 1930 Mickey Mouse newspaper comic strip written by Walt and illustrated by Iwerks told a version of *Plane Crazy* that included a panel of Mickey looking at a picture of Lindbergh for inspiration.

In *Plane Crazy*, Mickey is established as a resident of a barnyard with other anthropomorphic animals who help him achieve his goals. Normally, a cartoon about building and flying a plane would take place anywhere but a barnyard.

The title of the film was Walt's clever twist not only on the common expression "plain crazy" but also a commentary on the insane excitement young boys had about planes thanks to Lindbergh.

Plane Crazy was animated by Ub Iwerks, who was isolated from the rest of the Disney Studio where other animators were finishing up the commitments to produce the final Oswald the Lucky Rabbit cartoons for distributor Charles Mintz. Soon, they would abandon Walt and leave to join Mintz's new studio.

Iwerks even had drawings of Oswald that he could quickly slip over the drawings of Mickey if someone unexpectedly dropped by his desk. Walt did not want Mintz to know what he was doing, so the work on the first Mickey Mouse cartoon was done with great secrecy.

Universal Studios, not Walt, owned the Oswald copyright. It was a common business practice of the time. In an effort to save money, Mintz, who had been hired by Universal to oversee the cartoons, chose not to renew the contract with the Disney Studio but to make the Oswald cartoons on his own. Mintz hired all of Walt's animators, except for Iwerks, to produce the cartoons at his own animation studio.

Walt's only options were to become a salaried employee of Mintz or to create a new character that he did own and produce cartoons that were popular enough to sustain and grow his studio.

Along with Iwerks, Walt developed a character that bore a physical resemblance to Oswald but had some significant personality differences, the appealing Mickey Mouse.

For *Plane Crazy*, Iwerks produced over 8,000 separate drawings, an unheard of number for a single animator to draw for a short cartoon at the time. He began work during the last week of April 1928; by the second week of May, the cels were ready to be inked and painted.

When he pushed himself, Ub could produce between 600 and 700 drawings per day, a tremendous accomplishment matched only by New York animator Bill Nolan who at one time had produced over five hundred drawings per day for an animation short.

Walt put in three benches in the garage at his home on Lyric Avenue for a makeshift studio where Walt and Roy's wives (Lillian and Edna) along with Walt's sister-in-law (Hazel Sewell) inked and painted Ub's artwork onto cels.

Mike Marcus, the cameraman, shot the cel artwork at night at the Disney Studio after the animators had gone home, with Walt personally cleaning up all traces of the work so it wouldn't be discovered the next morning.

Award-winning animator and historian Michael Sporn pointed out that even the first Mickey Mouse film demonstrated innovation:

> This was the first animated film to use a camera move. The POV [point of view] shot from the plane made it appear as if the camera were trucking into the ground. In fact, when they shot this scene, they piled books under the spinning background to move the artwork closer to the camera.

Iwerks was a great technician and experimenter when it came to animation. In one dramatic sequence, Mickey's plane almost collides with an oncoming car.

According to Disney Legend Frank Thomas, one of Disney's fabled "Nine Old Men", Iwerks originally planned an even more innovative ending for the film that would have included a real model.

> [Ub] made a little tower of houses and trees and things for the plane to crash into. Combining kind of a live-action device with his cartoons.

But when the film was developed, it "didn't look too well", said Thomas. So Iwerks had to quickly substitute an ending with a black background and the words "Crash" and "Bang" with stars like "those things that were used in [the 1966 *Batman* television series] later on — the words 'Wham', 'Bam'... ", Thomas explained.

Iwerks said:

> Some people got the idea that in *Plane Crazy*, Mickey was patterned
> after Lindbergh. Well, Lindy flew the Atlantic, but he was no [actor]
> Doug Fairbanks. He was a hero to boys because of airplanes and
> what he had accomplished flying the Atlantic. But Mickey wasn't
> Lindy — he was Doug Fairbanks.

Plane Crazy was finally completed and previewed at a theater at Sunset
and Gardner in Hollywood on May 15, 1928. The title card stated: "A Walt
Disney Comic — by Ub Iwerks".

Walt had coached the theater pianist on how to accompany the action
and slipped him a little extra money as well to punch up the music.
Reportedly, the picture got quite a few laughs and applause from the
audience, which Iwerks remembers as almost a full house.

Walt sent a print of the film to New York to be viewed by distributors
but received no offers. The novelty of animation was fading in popularity
and distributors were becoming intrigued by what impact the recently
introduced use of sound on film would have on the industry.

Encouraged by the audience response to *Plane Crazy* even though they
could not find a distributor, Walt and Ub began work almost immediately
on the second Mickey Mouse cartoon, *Gallopin' Gaucho*, a loose take-off on
a popular Douglas Fairbanks silent film, *The Gaucho* (1927).

Fairbanks was at the peak of his popularity and, once again, Walt
hoped that the audience would be interested in anything having to do
with a national celebrity.

By this time, the defecting animators had left, so there was no need for
secrecy in producing the new cartoon.

At least one major movie studio, MGM, saw *Plane Crazy* but made no
offer to finance a series. Reportedly, one executive claimed that a three-
foot-tall mouse would frighten women in the audience.

Walt engaged a New York film dealer, E.J. Denison, to find a distributor.
He wrote to Denison:

> I feel that I can make good cartoons and that they can be placed
> with a good distributor if the matter is handled right., But the time
> is short and there would be no second chance this year if we get off
> on the wrong foot. It is our intention to carry on an advertising and
> exploitation campaign that should, in a very short time, along with
> good pictures and a good release, make the name of "Mickey Mouse"
> as well-known as any cartoon on the market.

Denison made a valiant effort to interest major distributors in Mickey
Mouse, but when he couldn't generate even minor interest in the property, he withdrew. Walt, despite his passionate optimism, was faced with
mounting costs on the Mickey Mouse cartoons.

By the time he finished *Steamboat Willie*, Walt had gone through all the money and more that the Disney Studio had made on the Oswald the Rabbit series. Roy O. Disney, in small handwriting, entered into his ledger book the amounts (which included production and prints) for the first three Mickey Mouse cartoons:

PLANE CRAZY: $3,528.50
GALLOPIN' GAUCHO: $4,249.73
STEAMBOAT WILLIE: $4,986.69

When *Steamboat Willie* began to attract attention and it appeared that Mickey Mouse would become the star of a series of cartoons, Walt had Kansas City theater organist Carl Stalling write musical scores for both *Plane Crazy* and *Gallopin' Gaucho* so he could release more Mickey Mouse shorts quickly to take advantage of public interest in the cartoons.

Plane Crazy was released theatrically March 17, 1929, at the Mark Strand Theater in New York after a new soundtrack had been added in December 1928. Minnie Mouse (voiced by Walt himself) also utters the only line of dialogue in the cartoon: "Who? Me?" when Mickey offers her a seat in his plane.

So Minnie spoke actual words rather than just sounds long before Mickey did.

Walt Disney filed for a copyright on *Mickey Mouse in Plane Crazy* on May 26, 1928, as an unpublished work. That copyright was never updated. On August 9, 1930, Walt Disney copyrighted the sound versions of the first two silent films (*Plane Crazy* and *Gallopin' Gaucho*).

There are a lot of physical gags in *Plane Crazy*, especially since it was originally a silent cartoon. For example, Mickey grabs the udder of the cow and it sprays him with milk. The same gag re-appears in *Steamboat Willie*. Especially during the early years, Walt was notorious for recycling successful visual gags from his previous cartoons.

In an article entitled "I Live with a Genius" in *McCall's* magazine (February 1953), Walt's wife, Lillian, wrote:

> Not long ago Walt brought home the first Mickey Mouse film he ever made, *Plane Crazy*. We were screening another picture in our projection room that night.
>
> For fun, Walt ran *Plane Crazy* first. It was crude in many ways. When Walt made it he was just 25, and he hadn't perfected the technique of animation yet. Too, it had been made originally as a silent film, and sound had been dubbed in afterward.
>
> Diane and Sharon [Walt and Lillian's daughters] were horrified and wanted to forget the whole thing. I reminded them with some heat that if it hadn't been for that old crude Mickey they wouldn't be sitting in their own projection room with their own swimming pool outside.

Lillian was probably passionate because she worked as an ink and painter on *Plane Crazy* and probably remembered even decades later how the success of Mickey Mouse was essential for the Disney Studio to survive.

However, Diane and Sharon were also right that *Plane Crazy* is a very raw cartoon that could be used by Disney Human Resources today as a training tool on sexual harassment.

The climax of the story focuses on Mickey Mouse trying to force Minnie to give him a kiss. Mickey even tries to intimidate her with dangerous aeronautical maneuvers in hopes of scaring her into kissing him so he'll stop.

When he does finally grab Minnie to force her kiss him, Minnie angrily slaps Mickey in the face and finally has to jump out of the airplane.

Steamboat Willie received a great deal of attention because of its innovative use of synchronized sound and because it was the first Mickey Mouse cartoon to receive a general theatrical release. Certainly, the Mickey Mouse in that cartoon is much more identifiable with the Mickey that audiences grew to know and love over the decades compared to the version in *Plane Crazy*, but that doesn't change the fact that *Plane Crazy*, not *Steamboat Willie*, was the first Mickey Mouse cartoon.

In 2001, the International Cartoon Museum was unsuccessful in trying to sell off the illustrated, six-page, thirty-six-panel animation story script done by Walt Disney and Ub Iwerks at the listed price. The story script had been donated to the museum by famed collector Stephen Geppi, who had obtained it through a former Disney publicist.

When the museum experienced financial trouble, it sought to alleviate the problem by selling the script. The museum had originally valued it at more than $3,000,000, the cost of insuring the script with Lloyds of London when it traveled to Italy for a special exhibition in 1993.

However, the bidding went no higher than the $700,000 range. That was not enough to save the museum, which closed in 2002.

Cartoonist Mort Walker, the founder and chairman of the museum, had originally offered the illustrated story script to the Disney Company. According to Walker, the response was that Disney already had lots of artwork from that time period and weren't interested.

The Making of "Steamboat Willie"

Steamboat Willie, the first Mickey Mouse cartoon, is perhaps the most important and well known of the early animated cartoons. It transformed a fading novelty into an art form and became the foundation of the Disney Company.

In early February 1928, Walt Disney and his wife, Lillian, journeyed to New York where Walt planned to negotiate a new contract for his popular Oswald the Rabbit cartoon series.

Walt wanted a modest $250 increase per cartoon so that he could experiment with some improvements. Instead, distributor Charles Mintz offered $450 less per cartoon than what he was currently paying the Disney brothers.

Walt discovered that Universal Studios not only owned all the rights to Oswald (a common practice in the industry for a movie studio to own the rights to its characters and films) but that Mintz had contracted with all of Walt's animators, except for Ub Iwerks, to produce future Oswald cartoons for Mintz directly.

While Walt and Lillian were in New York, his latest Oswald the Rabbit cartoon, *Rival Romeos*, premiered at the Colony Theater on February 26. It was the same theater where *Steamboat Willie* would make its premiere later that same year.

One of the gags in this latest Oswald cartoon had a goat eating Oswald's sheet music and Oswald opening the goat's mouth and cranking its tail to make the music come out like a hurdy gurdy. The very same gag shows up in *Steamboat Willie*. It was not uncommon for Walt to re-use visual jokes if they had gotten a strong audience response, especially since the audience would not likely see the original cartoon again.

When Walt returned to Hollywood during the last week of March 1928, he and Ub Iwerks, and probably Walt's brother Roy O. Disney, developed Mickey Mouse.

Disney legend maintains that shortly after the westbound train crossed the Mississippi, Walt created a mouse character named "Mortimer" and then, at Lillian's insistence, changed the name to "Mickey".

There is some truth in that story. Walt's nature was to be in a state of constant activity and, judging from later trips he took, it is indeed likely that he was furiously sketching away in an attempt to come up with a character that would save his studio. Walt would often casually sketch ideas, whether the contours of Tom Sawyer Island at Disneyland or the initial layout for Epcot in Florida, on whatever paper was available from a napkin to an odd scrap that had been discarded. Documentation does exist that Walt was planning to originally name the new character "Mortimer" until Lillian objected.

But most animation historians agree that while the idea may have been conceived during the train trip, the design (which resembled Oswald but with a mouse's ears and tail) and final decision to go with the mouse character did not occur until after Walt had arrived in Hollywood.

Walt and Roy had been able to save over $25,000 and decided to use that money to fund a new series of cartoons to save the studio.

Ub was given the job of animating by himself the first Mickey Mouse cartoon, *Plane Crazy*, which was previewed at a theater on Sunset and Gardner in Hollywood on May 15, 1928. Encouraged by the audience's favorable response, Walt and Ub began work almost immediately on the second Mickey Mouse cartoon, *Gallopin' Gaucho*.

Walt was not just trying to devise a new cartoon series to save his studio or to exact revenge against Mintz. Walt genuinely loved producing cartoons. Lillian recalled an incident shortly before they were married:

> My sister and I were visiting a friend that night, so Walt decided to go to the movies. A cartoon short by a competitor was advertised outside, but suddenly, as he sat in the darkened theater, his own picture came on. Walt was so excited he rushed down to the manager's office.

> The manager, misunderstanding, began to apologize for not showing the advertised film. Walt hurried over to my sister's house to break his exciting news, but we weren't home yet. Then he tried to find Roy, but he was out too. Finally he went home alone. Every time we pass a theater where one of his films is advertised on the marquee I can't help but think of that night.

The same joy motivated Walt to develop a new series.

On May 29, 1928, Walt threw a party for Iwerks, Les Clark, Wilfred Jackson, Roy O. Disney, and others at his house to come up with gags for *Gallopin' Gaucho* . The cartoon was completed and ready for preview just three months later, on August 28.

During the cartoon's production, Walt saw the sensation caused by Warner Bros.' *The Jazz Singer* (1927), the first movie featuring synchronized sound on film of a character talking, and realized that distributors would now have less interest in a new silent cartoon series. Walt became intrigued by the idea of applying synchronized sound to animation.

Animator Wilfred Jackson recalled:

> Walt didn't know if people would believe that the character on the screen was making the noise. Nobody had ever seen a drawing make noise, and there was no way to be sure that the people would believe it.

> It might just look like some kind of fake thing, and Walt wanted it to seem real, as if the noise was coming right from what the character

was doing. So to find out whether the whole thing would be believable... when a few scenes had been animated... they set up this test.

Walt arranged a test screening at the Hyperion Studio. The opening scene had been put on a loop of film so that it would constantly repeat. Roy Disney positioned himself outside a window so the projector noise would not be audible as he ran it.

Iwerks rigged up a microphone and customized an old crystal radio into a makeshift speaker which was placed behind a bedsheet hung on a doorway, onto which the film would be projected.

Before the screening, Walt had gone to a nearby five-and-dime store and purchased items like noisemakers, cowbells, tin cans, a frying pan, slide whistles, ocarinas, a washboard, and a plunger.

Jackson played his harmonica. Iwerks played the washboard and the slide whistles and produced various sound effects. Les Clark did percussion and sound effects. Johnny Cannon vocalized sounds for the barnyard animals. Walt supplied the voices and additional sound effects.

Jackson said:

> When Roy started the projector up, I furnished the music, with my mouth organ... and the other fellows hit things and made sound effects,. We had spittoons everywhere then, and they made a wonderful gong if you hit them with a pencil. We practiced with it several times, and we got so we were hitting it off pretty well. We took turns going out there ourselves, and looking at the thing [from the other side of the bedsheet], and when I went out there wasn't any music, but the noises and voices seemed to come from it just fine. It was really pretty exciting, and it did prove to us that the sound coming from the drawing could be a convincing thing.

Each of the men took turns going in front of the screen to watch as the loop of film ran over and over and the others did their sounds. On the other side of the bedsheet in chairs were the wives of the Disney brothers and Iwerks, as well as Jane Ames, Jackson's girlfriend who would later become his wife.

Walt later complained that when it was his turn to go out and view the film, the ladies were paying little attention to the experiment and were instead spending their time gossiping and talking about babies and exchanging recipes. Lillian recalled:

> What did they expect? We had absolutely no idea what was going on. And it any case, it sounded terrible.

The screening went on for several hours, repeating the same loop of film and readjusting the sounds over and over, so it is understandable that the spouses lost interest.

Iwerks remembered the process as a magnificent experience:

> It was wonderful. There was no precedent of any kind. I've never been so thrilled in my life. Nothing since has ever equaled it. That evening proved that an idea could be made to work.

Ever the perfectionist, Walt re-ran the film repeatedly, trying to perfect the synchronization of music and sound effects with the cartoon images being projected on the screen.

Walt, Iwerks, and Jackson came up with a rough score that would align sound with action.

Jackson, whose mother was a music teacher, understood rudimentary musical notation and the principle of a metronome to keep time. He developed the first crude bar sheet in animation.

Although this initial bar sheet did not contain conventional musical notation, it did include a measure-by-measure breakdown of the songs, delineating each musical beat. The orchestra later received a musical score using this beat and measure breakdown as a guide.

Despite its crude form, the bar sheet represented an important innovation that made it possible to time and synchronize the soundtrack precisely to the picture. Even without the proper musical notation, the sheet contained all the essential characteristics of the "dope sheets" still used today.

Jackson played harmonica and worked together with Disney to adapt two popular songs, "Steamboat Bill" and "Turkey in the Straw" (one of Jackson's favorite harmonica pieces), for the soundtrack.

Apparently, it was Walt who suggested the tune "Steamboat Bill" and the Mississippi river boat setting. From this idea, Walt hosted a "gag" meeting at his house where Jackson, Iwerks, Les Clark, and others suggested possible funny business that could be derived from the premise.

Walt journeyed to New York early in September 1928 to get the film recorded but encountered chaos as movie companies scrambled to get recording equipment and recording time.

He first approached Fox and its Movietone system, but they were uninterested because they were already overwhelmed with work. The representative at RCA not only kept padding the estimated price but was also condescending about the idea of accurately synchronizing sound to a cartoon.

When Walt asked for a demonstration of RCA's work, the studio showed him a copy of *Dinner Time*, an *Aesop's Film Fables* cartoon produced by Paul Terry, for which they had recently synchronized the sound and which premiered in theaters on September 1, 1928, a full six weeks before *Steamboat Willie*. In a letter to his brother Roy, Walt shared his opinion of the film:

> My gosh... terrible... a lot of racket and nothing else. I was terribly disappointed. I had expected to see something halfway decent. But honestly... it was nothing but one of the rottenest fables I ever saw and I should know because I have seen almost all of them. It merely had an orchestra playing and adding some noise... The talking part does not mean a thing. It doesn't even match... We sure have nothing to worry about from these quarters.

RCA and Movietone had secured a monopoly on the sound-on-film system, but Patrick A. Powers had bribed company engineers into providing him with the technical information. With slight modifications, he created an outlaw recording system called Cinephone which was remarkably similar.

Powers was a notorious character in the film business. At one time, he had partnered with Carl Laemmle at Universal Pictures. When Laemmle discovered that Powers was cheating him financially, he immediately confronted Powers, who protested his innocence.

With dramatic flair, Powers took the doctored financial record books and threw them out his upper-floor office window, where they were retrieved and spirited away by a waiting accomplice below.

Powers needed a high-profile project to help publicize and legitimatize his bootleg sound system, which is one of the reasons Walt's cartoon intrigued him. Powers' warm Irish charisma and his claims of acquaintance with important people in the business persuaded Walt that this was the man who would give his cartoon special attention.

Powers arranged for the services of Carl Edouarde, who most recently had led the pit orchestra at the Strand Theatre on Broadway. Despite Walt's detailed instructions, however, Edouarde seemed disinterested in the flash Walt had put in the film print to mimic the beat of the metronome and allow synchronization of the sounds and the music.

An orchestra, which Walt later said had thirty players plus three trap drummers and effects men, was assembled for the recording session. The players were receiving seven dollars each per hour, the effects men ten, and Edouarde twenty.

As the morning wore on, the expenses quickly mounted, especially since Edouarde insisted on several rehearsals.

Projecting the film on the studio wall distracted the musicians; often, the film finished with sheets of music yet to be played. Further, the bass player's low notes kept blowing out a bulb in the recording mechanism whenever he sawed his bass, so they kept moving him farther and farther away until he finally ended up outside the room.

One of the first musicians to show up was tired and unshaven from an all-night recording session. Upon opening his music case, he removed a bottle of whisky and took a swig.

In those days, no stopping, editing, or layering took place. Everything had to be recorded at the same time and in one continuous take. Once, a take was ruined by a loud cough near a microphone that blew out another bulb. The culprit? Walt himself, who accidentally coughed after doing a line for the parrot.

That morning session was a disaster. To finance another session, Roy had to sell Walt's favorite car, a Moon Roadster. Walt wrote encouragingly to Roy:

> I think this is Old Man Opportunity rapping at our door. Let's not let the jingle of a few pennies drown out his knock.

For the next recording session, which began at ten o'clock on a Sunday morning, the orchestra was reduced in size and two of the sound effects men let go, with Walt performing some of their functions.

Iwerks had made another print of the cartoon without the flashes but with a bouncing line that indicated where beats should strike. The film was projected directly onto Edouarde's sheet music. Following this new cue, the effects and music matched the action perfectly.

Carl Stalling, a theater organist from Kansas City and a former acquaintance of Walt's, arrived in New York October 26, 1928, and moved in to Walt's two-room suite at the Knickerbocker Hotel.

Walt had felt very lonely in New York, and was glad of Stalling's company of someone he knew, and more important, the company of someone with whom he could discuss his ideas.

Stalling would later have an outstanding career as the musical director for Warner Brothers' cartoons.

Once *Steamboat Willie* was finished, weeks passed with no sales.

Powers arranged special showings of the film all over town. While the bookers enjoyed it, no one bought it. Finally, at one showing, Harry Reichenbach pulled Walt aside. Reichenbach had been one of the most successful press agents in New York and was now handling films for Universal Pictures through its Manhattan outlet, the Colony Theater.

He was a flamboyant personality who, as a young gallery assistant, had gained notoriety when he displayed a print of "September Morn", a painting of a woman standing outdoors after a bath that was scandalously nude by the standards of 1913, even though all the objectionable areas were discretely covered. Reichenbach displayed the print in the window of the Manhattan gallery where he worked, and hired some young boys to crowd around and gawk. Then, he protested to Anthony Comstock who, as head of the New York Society for the Suppression of Vice, launched a protest against the moral outrage of the lady's nudity.

The ensuing publicity caused prints of the painting to sell like hot cakes, and it soon became available on postcards and calendars, the prototype for a century's pinup calendars.

Reichenbach was quite the creative publicist. Samuel Goldwyn hired him to save *The Return Of Tarzan* (1913), a film that Goldwyn feared would die at the box office. Reichenbach took special delight in his strategy for publicizing this potential box-office bomb because he could employ tricks he had learned working in the circus.

A week before the first screening of the film, the Hotel Belleclaire in New York City received a guest named Zann who had with him an enormous box that he claimed held a piano. The hotel obligingly hoisted it into his room through an outside window.

On the following day, Zann asked room service to deliver fifteen pounds of raw meat. The hotel manager delivered it himself out of curiosity, and was surprised to find Zann had an adult lion in his room. The police and a boatload of reporters quickly descended, ensuring headlines. The advertisements promised the public that Mr. T. Zann ("Tarzan") would personally attend the opening of the movie.

Reichenbach loved the challenge of marketing the synchronized sound cartoon, a gimmick he knew would attract appreciative audiences if he let them know about it. He advised Disney that he needed a good track record to entice distributors to take *Steamboat Willie*: "Those guys don't know what's good until the public tells them," he reportedly told Walt.

Walt was concerned that a short New York engagement might discourage a potential distributor if a New York premiere had already occurred. In 1966, he stated:

> Nobody wanted Mickey. Then a great exhibitor took a chance. [Harry] Reichenbach had a great talent for showmanship and exploitation. Harry sold the public on Mickey Mouse in just two weeks. Our red ink took on a blacker hue.

Reichenbach convinced Disney to forget about a distributorship until the public and the critics had a chance to see the new short. Part of Mickey's phenomenal success was due to Harry Reichenbach's shrewd publicity.

Steamboat Willie was booked in the Colony Theater for a two-week run beginning November 18, 1928.

Walt told an interviewer in 1966:

> We didn't yet have a release for Mickey but Harry [Reichenbach] wanted to book him in the Colony regardless. At the time, we were in desperate need of five hundred dollars. To put it briefly, everything owned by Roy and me was mortgaged to the hilt.
>
> So I asked Harry for five hundred dollars for exhibiting the first Mickey Mouse one week. I knew that the price was pretty steep. So did Harry. But fortunately for us, he said, "Let's compromise. I'll give you 250 dollars a week — and run the cartoon for two weeks."

The payment provided much needed immediate income that enabled the Disney brothers to pay salaries and other expenses. In some interviews, Walt claimed that Reichenbach paid five hundred dollars a week for a total of a thousand dollars, but that was unlikely.

Steamboat Willie debuted on a Sunday afternoon, November 18, 1928, at Manhattan's Colony Theatre on 53rd Street and Broadway.

The show included music by Ben Bernie and His Famous Orchestra, live stage acts, and a Pathé newsreel with sound. Also on the bill was *Gang War*, a crime drama starring Jack Pickford, the younger brother of silent-screen star Mary Pickford, who would soon become one of Mickey's biggest fans.

Gang War was primarily silent with some talking sequences. The film was directed by Bert Glennon, who directed fewer than a dozen mediocre pictures between 1928-32 and who was best-known as a cinematographer for other directors like John Ford and Cecil B. DeMille.

Glennon was later the cinematographer for the black-and-white portions of the behind-the-scenes segments in Disney's *Reluctant Dragon* (1941) and for the full-color *Davy Crockett and the River Pirates* (1956).

The music for *Gang War* was composed by Alfred Sherman, the father of Disney songwriters Richard and Robert Sherman.

Carl Stalling recalled:

> We [Walt and Stalling] sat on almost the last row and heard laughs and snickers all around us. Walt would continue to attend every performance for the entire two weeks.

In an ad in *The New York Times*, the Colony Theatre erroneously touted *Steamboat Willie* as the "FIRST and ONLY synchronized-sound animated cartoon comedy." Paul Terry's *Dinner Time* had been shown in theaters nearly six weeks earlier on September 1, 1928, but made no impact on audiences or reviewers.

Although technically not the first cartoon with synchronized sound, *Steamboat Willie* integrated music, voice, and effects into an entertaining and believable product, featuring a likeable main character and a clear story, not just a series of unrelated gags. It was a huge hit — so much so that many critics ignored the accompanying main feature and the stage show altogether.

Variety declared it "a high order of cartoon ingenuity" and "a peach of a synchronization job all the way."

In his review the next day, *Times* critic Mordaunt Hall thought the feature film (*Gang War*) was fine but not memorable. He was, however, very excited about the Mouse:

> On the same program is the first sound cartoon, produced by Walter Disney, creator of Oswald the Rabbit. This current film is called *Steamboat Willie*, and it introduces a new cartoon character, henceforth to be known as Micky Mouse [sic]. It is an ingenious piece of work with a good deal of fun. It growls, whines, squeaks and makes various other sounds that add to its mirthful quality.

The New York Times was one of Mickey Mouse's biggest supporters in those early years. Between 1934 and 1937, Mickey was featured in three articles in the *Times'* Sunday magazine, one of them illustrated by Al Hirschfeld, their top cartoonist.

Weekly Film Review said *Steamboat Willie* "kept the audience laughing and chuckling from the moment the lead titles came on the screen, and it left them applauding."

Exhibitor's Herald said, "It is impossible to describe this riot of mirth, but it knocked me out of my seat."

After its contracted two-week run, *Steamboat Willie* moved to the two-year-old Roxy Theatre.

By the way, after the cartoon's debut at the Roxy, the Colony Theatre was eventually renamed the Broadway Theatre, and *Fantasia* (1940) premiered there twelve years later.

Walt was soon flooded with offers including one from Universal Studios, who were highly complimentary and made a generous offer to Walt but only if he surrendered the copyright and control of Mickey Mouse to Universal.

Walt seemed to have little choice, as every other distributor wanted control of the product as well, which was something he would not let happen again after his experience with Oswald.

Powers, who at the time needed Disney about as much as Disney needed him due to Powers' desire to publicize his new sound system, was the only one who agreed to allow Walt independence as well as retaining the ownership of Mickey Mouse and the cartoons.

Taking 10% of the gross (plus a 10-year exclusive contract with Disney to use the Cinephone sound system for $26,000), Powers agreed to handle all expenses involved in the selling of the product via the "states rights" system. Under that system, Powers' salesmen would market Disney's cartoons to theaters in different territories. Most of the best theaters, however, were controlled by large movie production companies and were locked into exclusive block booking agreements.

Distribution of a cartoon was a crucial factor in its success and provided much-needed revenue for its producers, but while the states rights system allowed the cartoon to be seen, it also enabled Powers to perform financial shenanigans in determining fees and expenses before the Disney brothers would see any money.

To capitalize on Mickey's success, sound tracks by Carl Stalling were added to the first two silent Mickey Mouse cartoons, and final preparations were made on a fourth cartoon, *The Barn Dance*.

When Disney archivist Dave Smith began the Disney Archives in 1970, one of his first tasks was to catalog what was in Walt Disney's office, which had remained untouched since Walt's death on December 15, 1966. Smith was surprised to find in a bottom drawer of Walt's desk the original six-page illustrated story outline for *Steamboat Willie*. In a 1997 interview, Smith said:

> Things were stolen from the company before the Archives was established. Included were some scenes from *Steamboat Willie* and the story sketches for several sequences of *Snow White*. We have the [story script] for *Steamboat Willie* and most of the other films. I found the *Steamboat Willie* script in Walt's office which surprised me since everyone told me he wasn't interested in the company's past, only the next project.

In the Spring 1994 issues of *Sketches* magazine, Smith wrote:

> Back in 1928, when Walt Disney was beginning work on *Steamboat Willie*, a script was his method of planning. Sticking a sheet of carbon paper in his typewriter, between two sheets of paper, Walt typed out the descriptions of each scene of the action on the left hand side of the page.

> Then he handed his work over to Ub Iwerks, his chief animator, who illustrated the description with small drawings. The fact that he [Walt] saved the *Steamboat Willie* script proved to me that he did at least treasure this special moment in history, which had started him on the road to success.

In 1988, to celebrate the 60th birthday of its most famous cartoon character, the Disney Company donated to the Smithsonian National Museum of American History six original drawings from *Steamboat Willie* selected personally by Walt's nephew Roy E. Disney.

Hidden Secrets of "Steamboat Willie"

Steamboat Willie was inducted into the National Film Registry in 1998 as a "culturally, historically, or aesthetically significant film" deserving of preservation at the Library of Congress.

Unlike some of the other films that have been inducted over the years, *Steamboat Willie* is still easily able to be viewed and studied today, but most people still miss some of its wonderful details.

Walt Disney wrote the script descriptions with a manual typewriter so the final document includes misspellings and typed-over letters. There are differences between Walt's original script and the final animation. For instance, the script says the cow will lick Mickey with its tongue. It does not. The script says Mickey will use the cow's horns for music. He does not.

Some of the references in the script are very obscure today. In the script, Walt refers to a "Yoo Hoo" which is not the same as the later, well-known "Minnie's Yoo Hoo" but rather a different song made popular by Al Jolson in 1921.

In this section are some explanations of these script references and revelations of the differences between the original script and the final film.

Why Is It Called "Steamboat Willie"?

Most articles refer to the cartoon as a parody of comedian Buster Keaton's last independent silent comedy, *Steamboat Bill Jr.*, which had been released in May 1928.

Both films *do* feature a steamboat, and Keaton's character *is* named Willie, but the Disney cartoon makes no direct references to Keaton's film, unlike *Gallopin' Gaucho*, which parodies the action and style of the Douglas Fairbanks' silent film, *The Gaucho* (1927). While Walt may have hoped that audiences would associate his cartoon with the popular Keaton film, no direct parody was intended. It was just Walt's way of drawing attention to the cartoon.

The opening music for *Steamboat Willie* is a popular song called "Steamboat Bill," which also inspired the title, and again, the hope of audience familiarity. While Walt and many others assumed the song was in public domain and could be used freely, it was, in fact, still under copyright at the time.

In addition, audiences were aware of two things: the well-known Broadway musical *Showboat*, which premiered in 1927, and the tragic Mississippi River flood of 1927, which led to vast improvements in flood control. As a result, Mississippi steamboats loomed large in the general public's imagination.

Audiences had never heard of Mickey Mouse, so titling the cartoon *Steamboat Mickey* would have brought zero box-office recognition. More important, Walt insisted that when an audience went to see a Mickey Mouse cartoon they were not seeing the adventures of Mickey Mouse. Mickey was merely an actor performing a role just as Clark Gable or Cary Grant would do.

This conceit was one of the things that positioned Mickey Mouse in the marketplace differently than other cartoon characters of the time. Mickey was not Steamboat Willie; he was portraying the role of a character named Steamboat Willie. In his next film, he might be portraying a different character, even if that character shared many of Mickey's own attributes and behaviors.

Did Ub Iwerks Animate the Entire Film Himself?

Iwerks animated virtually the entire film himself in what was known as "straight ahead" animation, a technique in which he did the first drawing, then the second drawing, then the third, and so on. It would be a while before production concepts such as key drawings, assistants and in-betweeners became the norm.

By this time, Walt had stopped doing any drawing at all. His primary contribution was story and character development.

However, Iwerks did have a little assistance on *Steamboat Willie* from apprentice animators Wilfred Jackson and Les Clark.

Wilfred Jackson was so eager to become an animator that he turned up at the Disney Studio one day and offered to pay Walt tuition until he had gained experience. Walt gave him a job washing the ink and paint off cels so they could be reused to save money.

Jackson started work only a week before the Oswald the Rabbit animators left. Those animators were laughing and talking throughout the week, but on Saturday they took all their personal belongings home. They didn't return on Monday... or any day after that.

Jackson quickly moved into the role of apprentice animator. His first assignment was the cycle of Minnie Mouse running along the riverbank in *Steamboat Willie*. He later became the director of several early Mickey Mouse shorts and won Oscars for his direction of *Tortoise and the Hare* (1934), *The Country Cousin* (1936), and *The Old Mill* (1937).

Les Clark, the first of Disney's "Nine Old Men", began his tenure at the Disney Studio in 1927, where he was assigned to the *Alice Comedies* and the Oswald the Rabbit series, despite his lack of formal animation training.

In *Steamboat Willie*, Clark animated the scene where Mickey shoves a pitchfork of hay down the cow's throat.

When Iwerks left the Disney Studio in 1930, Clark became the resident Mickey and Minnie expert, expanding and defining their personalities. He also animated major portions of *The Band Concert* (1935) and the "Sorcerer's Apprentice" segment of *Fantasia* (1940).

What Is the Story Behind the Music?

The Disney Studio could not afford a composer or pay royalties, so it relied on music in the public domain.

Composers Carl Stalling, Frank Churchill, Oliver Wallace, and others would eventually supply memorable original music for Disney cartoons, but at the time Walt had to rely on what limited resources were available.

In the opening of *Steamboat Willie*, Mickey is whistling the chorus of a popular parlor song called "Steamboat Bill," written by the Leighton Brothers (who also composed "Frankie and Johnny") and Ren Shields (who wrote "In the Good Ol' Summertime") in 1911.

The Leighton Brothers used the song in their minstrel act, encouraging the audience to sing along with each repetition of the chorus:

> Steamboat Bill, steaming down the Mississippi.
> Steamboat Bill, a mighty man was he.
> Steamboat Bill, steaming down the Mississippi.
> Out to break the record of the Robert E. Lee.

The song recounts the story of Steamboat Bill, commander of the steamboat *Whippoorwill*, who was attempting to break the record of the *Robert E. Lee*, which in 1870 had set a record time covering the stretch of the Mississippi between New Orleans and St. Louis.

In the song, the *Whippoorwill* is pushed beyond its limits, causing its boiler to explode. The explosion sends Bill and a gambler high into the air, where Bill bets another thousand dollars that he'll go higher than the gambler.

Walt, his staff, and most of the general public were under the impression that the song was in public domain. It was not. With the success and notoriety of *Steamboat Willie*, this fact soon came to light.

The research by Disney historian Michael Barrier shows that Columbia Pictures (who were distributing Mickey Mouse shorts beginning in 1930) paid a license settlement fee of $150 on April 25, 1931, for the permission to use the song in *Steamboat Willie*.

The other prominent song in *Steamboat Willie* is "Turkey in the Straw," one of Wilfred Jackson's favorite tunes to play on his harmonica, and which fortunately was in the public domain.

The lyrics of the tune that are unheard in the film and that come out of the goat's mouth after eating the sheet music are:

Went out to milk, and I didn't know how,
I milked the goat instead of the cow.
A monkey sittin' on a pile of straw,
A-winkin' at his mother-in-law.

What Is a Parrot Doing on a Steamboat?

Before various bans on importation were enacted in the 1930s, parrots often represented prestige and exotic taste. Even President Teddy Roosevelt kept one at the White House.

New Orleans, as a major shipping port, saw its share of imported animals. Occasionally, crates of parrots broke open and the birds found new homes in the area, which may be how they became associated with the pirates who also frequented the port.

A parrot was probably also chosen for the same reason that a bird was selected for Disneyland's first Audio-Animatronics attraction, The Enchanted Tiki Room. Rather than dealing with the problem of matching lip movements, a bird's beak merely opens and closes, making it easier to animate dialog.

Also, a parrot doesn't merely echo speech but mimics selectively, which can seem like a taunt, thus making it a comic foil.

The parrot does not appear in Walt's original script for the cartoon. Walt did, however, provide the voice for the bird, and most texts refer to its final words as "Man Overboard!" The parrot mocks Mickey twice during the cartoon with "Hope you don't feel hurt, big boy!" when Mickey falls into a bucket and later when he is made to peel potatoes as punishment.

The line "hope you don't feel hurt" comes from the Blues song "Worn Down Daddy." In 1927 Ida Cox had a hit with that song, which is about a floozy insulting her lover for having lost his potency: "You ain't young no more… your loving is weak… you're just an old has-been… like a worn-out joke." After each of these insults comes the sarcastic tag line: "I hope you don't feel hurt."

In the cartoon, especially if the parrot is a female calling Mickey "big boy," the "I hope you don't feel hurt" is shorthand for the insults, which is why Mickey reacts not just with anger but goes so far as to throw a potato at the bird.

Walt must have liked the parrot because it reappears briefly in three early Mickey Mouse cartoons: *The Barn Dance* (1929), *When The Cat's Away* (1929) and *The Gorilla Mystery* (1930).

Did Something Disappear?

In the rush to complete the cartoon, items would often disappear.

For example, Mickey starts out wearing a pilot's hat. A pilot does, in fact, steer the boat. On smaller vessels, such as the one in the cartoon, the captain and the pilot may be the same person, or they may be different persons who share similar responsibilities.

When Captain Pete appears wearing the exact same hat, he grabs Mickey and twirls him around. As Mickey twirls toward the camera, his hat disappears, never to be seen again.

The rope for blowing the whistle and the cord for ringing the bell are evident behind Mickey in the beginning of the cartoon. After Pete chews a big plug of tobacco, both ropes disappear.

The cow on the dock wears a tag labeled "F.O.B.", "Free on Board," which meant that the cow was being shipped for a rate that included cost of delivery to, and loading onto and off of, a steamboat. When the cow stretches its neck to "moo," the tag briefly disappears.

When Mickey swings the cat by the tail and it hits the lid, the lid stays in position, disappears, reappears, and then eventually disappears for good.

The goat's goatee disappears twice when it eats the sheet music on deck, although you can only see this by examining the sequence frame by frame. Also, the goat has teeth until Mickey Mouse opens its mouth. This is a common conceit in animation where a character only needs teeth to show a brief expression like laughter or anger and then the teeth disappear for the rest of the film. Several Donald Duck cartoons have the Duck with a brief exposure of teeth.

A rowboat appears in the background in medium shots but disappears in long shots.

However, the most famous piece of disappearing animation was an entire segment missing from the cartoon for decades.

Mickey pulls on the tails of little pigs suckling their mother. Then, in a scene that was removed in the 1950s, Mickey picks up the mother, kicks off the piglets still hanging on, and plays the mother pig like an accordion by pushing on her teats.

When the cartoon was to be shown to a television audience, this bit of barnyard humor was deemed inappropriate and removed, though it's been restored on the recent releases.

Actually, that scene was directly connected to another scene planned but never animated. After loading the cow onto the boat at Podunk Landing, Mickey was to load the sow, which was behind a crate when Mickey approached to hook on the loading belt. The sow was then lifted into the air, her (previously unseen) piglets hanging on to her teats for dear life.

Where Is Podunk Landing?

Podunk Landing is where Mickey's side-wheeler stops to pick up livestock, and where Minnie, arriving late, misses the boat — before being lifted on board by Mickey with the aid of a winch.

Originally an Indian name meaning "lowland" (communities called

Podunk tend toward swampiness), the dictionary defines "Podunk" as a small, unimportant, isolated town.

Some people, however, claim that the name comes from the sound of a mill wheel going "po-dunk". Others believe that Podunk is a fictional place, though there are several Podunks in the Northeast and the Midwest. Podunk is also the hometown of the country mouse in the Disney cartoon, *The Country Cousin* (1936), directed by Wilfred Jackson.

Notice that when Mickey arrives at the Podunk Landing pier, it is filled with animals and boxes. Walt's original story script also included a rooster and the mother pig with her nursing children, all of which later appear on board.

After Mickey loads the cow, there is a quick cut to Minnie running toward the landing, then a quick cut back to see that Mickey has apparently in that brief moment loaded all the animals and freight aboard the steamboat.

Haven't I Seen Some Of These Gags Before?

In the days before television and videotape, an audience might see a cartoon only once, so it was not uncommon to borrow the funniest gags from previous cartoons and recycle them.

Apparently, Walt had a great memory for gags; when actor Dean Jones argued with Walt that a gag in one of his live-action films was too corny, Walt said: "It got a laugh in 1923 and it will get a laugh today." Later, at the preview of the film, Jones admitted that Walt was right, as the audience howled at the gag.

When Pete pulls Mickey's stomach and it stretches, Walt's comment on the original story script is "same as Oswald and the Bear in *Tall Timber*," an Oswald the Rabbit cartoon from July 9, 1928.

When the goat eats the sheet music and Mickey has to crank its tail for the music to play, it is a repeat of a gag from the Oswald cartoon *Rival Romeos*, released on March 5, 1928.

At the end of *Steamboat Willie*, when Mickey is peeling potatoes and making big potatoes into smaller ones, it is a repeat of a gag of a mouse doing the same thing in *Alice The Whaler*, released on July 25, 1927.

Is Pete Doing a Product Placement?

Captain Pete is chewing Star Plug Tobacco; Walt specifically refers to it as such in his script.

Star Plug Tobacco was produced by a Missouri company, Liggett & Myers Tobacco Company, and was described in a 1888 court case that "by reason of the distinguishing mark of the star upon the plugs, it has become known to the trade and the public as 'Star Plug Tobacco'."

Plug tobacco was highly popular at the time. Every tobacco chewer prided himself on his aim, whether lobbing it over a piece of furniture without accident or making it ping-pong when it hit the cuspidor.

According to reports, Star Plug was good on the getaway with minimum drool or drip but splattered when it hit. The brand was also popular at the Disney Studio because many years later Goofy uses it as fish bait in *On Ice* (1935). The big red star was its trademark.

Incidentally, Pete is the longest continually appearing Disney character. He made his first appearance in *Alice Solves The Puzzle* (1925), and eventually appeared in four *Alice Comedies* and seven Oswald films prior to his career menacing Mickey Mouse.

Before 1930, he was sometimes called Putrid Pete or Bootleg Pete, and audiences thought he was some type of bear. Walt's original story script identifies him as a "cat Captain", and of course, a cat is the natural enemy of a mouse, even though Walt never considered Mickey and Minnie were mice. (Walt's script for *Steamboat Willie* identifies Minnie as "the girl.")

Pete is not really a villain in *Steamboat Willie*. He may be a bully, but as the steamboat captain, he wants his only crewmember, Mickey, to do the job he is supposed to be doing rather than goofing off.

Why Is Mickey Punished by Peeling Potatoes?

Walt's experience in France at the end of World War I introduced him to the military punishment of peeling potatoes, a mindless job that had to be done to feed the troops but which also built discipline. (Look how well it's worked for Beetle Bailey!) In fact, in Walt's original script he was going to have Mickey whistle the popular WW I song "Pack Up Your Troubles" as he peeled.

Potatoes were standard fare on boats since they would keep longer and helped prevent scurvy. The *Titantic* carried forty tons of them. But even when potatoes became the second-largest food crop in America, they were still used primarily as animal fodder, and that might be their purpose on this steamboat.

How Much Did "Steamboat Willie" Cost?

According to Roy O. Disney's personal ledger books, the film cost $4,986.69, which included not only the production costs but the prints.

When Does Steamboat Willie Become Public Domain?

In 2003, *Steamboat Willie* was to finally enter public domain. The copyright had been repeatedly extended by acts of Congress several times before, oddly at roughly the same times as when the film was about to become public domain.

In 2003, due to aggressive lobbying by the Disney Company, the Copyright Term Extension Act was passed. It extended the copyright of *Steamboat Willie* once again, this time until 2023. The Act is often referred to in a derogatory manner as the Mickey Mouse Protection Act.

Of course, Mickey Mouse is also a trademarked character and trademarks can be kept alive indefinitely as long as they are in use commercially and aggressively defended. So while a particular cartoon like *Steamboat Willie* may one day become public domain, the Mickey Mouse character cannot be used by others as long as Disney's trademark is in force.

Walt filed his application to trademark Mickey Mouse with the U.S. Patent Office on May 21, 1928, and the trademark was granted on September 18 of that same year.

The First Mickey Mouse Club

When *Steamboat Willie* premiered in November 1928, a star was born. Movie theaters noticed a huge increase in attendance whenever a new Mickey Mouse short was shown and often publicized the shorts on their marquees, sometimes in larger letters than the main feature.

Less than a year later, in September 1929, Harry W. Woodin, manager of the Fox Dome Theater in Ocean Park, California, approached Walt Disney with the idea of a theater-sponsored club for boys and girls that would focus on Mickey Mouse. He felt that such a club would encourage attendance at his theater.

Roy O. Disney believed that, as with character merchandise, the club would help promote the cartoons with little or no investment from the Disney Studio.

That original Mickey Mouse Club chapter was so instantly successful within its first months of existence that Roy asked Woodin to quit his job and work for the Disney Studio organizing similar clubs throughout the country. By January 1930, Woodin was on board as the General Manager of the theater Mickey Mouse Clubs.

Because Woodin had to travel almost constantly to help organize new clubs and maintain the ones in existence, Roy assigned his own personal secretary, Lucille Allen Benedict, as Woodin's assistant.

Woodin defined the two primary functions of the club as, first, "to provide an easily arranged and inexpensive method of getting and holding the patronage of youngsters" at theaters, especially important since the Great Depression had just started and was tightening the purse strings for discretionary extras like attending the movies, and two, "through inspirational, patriotic, and character building activities related to the Club, to aid children in learning good citizenship."

Woodin created a manual for theaters, developed a semi-monthly newsletter called the *Official Bulletin of the Mickey Mouse Club* (sent to theaters on the 1st and 15th of each month beginning April 15, 1930, and ending by early 1933), and arranged for Mickey Mouse Clubs to be able to purchase at minimal cost from the Disney Studio such items as membership cards, membership applications, buttons, promotional artwork, and even a short film of Mickey singing the song "Minnie's Yoo Hoo."

To help offset these costs — a one-year Mickey Mouse Club license and the bimonthly bulletin was $25, but extras like posters, cards, buttons, balloons, masks, books, etc., ran the total cost up to around $100 — the sponsoring theater partnered with local merchants.

The Disney Studio provided these extra items at cost to help support the project and to control the quality of the material. For example, two-color membership cards were $3.50 for 500 or $4.50 for 1,000. Theaters could buy the "Minnie's Yoo Hoo" sing-a-long short for $16.50. Membership buttons ran $15 per 1,000, and membership applications $1.25 per 1,000.

Participating merchants supplied many perks of their own. Local bakeries donated a free birthday cake each Saturday for Mickey Mouse Club children who had celebrated a birthday during the previous week. Local florists sent a small bouquet of flowers to sick club members. Department stores provided inexpensive toys as prizes for contests at the weekly meetings.

All of these businesses had their names flashed on the movie screen, posted in the theater lobby, and printed in the newspaper and on posters. The famous orange-and-black window card identified each merchant as an "Official Mickey Mouse Store", which of course encouraged youngsters and their parents to shop there.

Sponsoring the club allowed merchants to gain a loyal customer base during difficult economic times. Eventually, almost all the businesses in a club town, including bank, shoe store, jeweler, stationery shop, and others hopped on board as the clubs grew.

Local Parent-Teacher Associations and schools were also supporters with kids who got high marks in school given special membership cards with special privileges. Charitable, patriotic, civic, and church organizations backed the club because it offered wholesome juvenile activities and helped children to learn good citizenship.

Membership in the Mickey Mouse Club was free, but children had to pay — usually a dime — to get into the theater each Saturday for the weekly two-hour matinee meeting.

Each meeting followed a strict ritual like an adult fraternal order. There were elected officers, including a Chief Mickey Mouse, a Chief Minnie Mouse, two Sergeants-at-Arms, a Song Leader, a Color Bearer, and others.

The Chief Mickey Mouse would lead the members in the Club Creed, printed on the back of every membership card:

> I will be a squareshooter in my home, in school, on the playgrounds, wherever I may be.
>
> I will be truthful and honorable and strive always to make myself a better and more useful little citizen.
>
> I will respect my elders and help the aged, the helpless and children smaller than myself.
>
> In short, I will be a good American!

Then all the Club members would respond with the Mickey Mouse Club Pledge: "Mickey Mice do not swear, smoke, cheat, or lie." This was usually followed by members singing a verse of the song *America* as an American flag was brought on stage. (It is assumed that the British clubs omitted the American references.)

The Mickey Mouse Club Creed was similar to oaths in other clubs, especially those related to popular cowboy movie stars.

After the creed and pledge, members might voice the Mickey Mouse Club yell, sing the official song, watch and critique the latest Mickey Mouse cartoon short, view a chapter of an exciting movie serial, enter contests, and enjoy appearances by guest celebrities or performers.

Younger "Mickey Mice" were also instructed on how to brush their teeth, wash behind their ears, and make their own beds.

In 1931, Roy O. Disney told an entertainment newspaper that there were 375 licensed Mickey Mouse Clubs in existence, and he believed there were an equal number of unlicensed ones.

At its peak in 1932, the Mickey Mouse Club had more than one million members in the United States — or as the *Motion Picture Herald* put it in its October 1, 1932, issue: "Memberships approximate that of the Boy Scouts of America and the Girl Scouts combined." At that time, there were more than 800 clubs in America with as many as 1,000 members in each club.

The Mickey Mouse Clubs were popular in Canada and the United Kingdom as well. The first British club was founded in 1933 at Darlington's Arcade Cinema. Within four years, there were more than 400 British Mickey Mouse Clubs. In December 1937, *The New York Times Magazine* reported that there was even a Mickey Mouse Club in Singapore and implied that Mickey was taking over the world.

By mid-1933, however, the Disney Studio began to withdraw its support, finding that the club concept had become too unwieldy, especially since there had been some controversies and backlash, including a growing resentment toward Disney films from other theaters who didn't have a club. Support didn't cease immediately, but by 1935 no new clubs were being licensed by the Studio. Disney hoped the clubs would just fade away.

Despite lack of support, some clubs continued for years. The most famous example involved Sonny Shepherd, who managed the Biltmore Theater in Miami, Florida. The first meeting of his club was attended by 300 children; within three months, membership shot up to 1,500. Shepherd was able to keep his club successful right up to the mid-1950s, when *The Mickey Mouse Club* television show premiered.

Regional conventions of Mickey Mouse Club members were held periodically, with the first one taking place in June 1931 at the Fox Theater in Milwaukee, Wisconsin, and drawing more than 4,000 children from 30 Wisconsin cities. Milwaukee, in 1931, had ten Mickey Mouse Clubs sponsored by nine merchants and with a total membership of more than 20,000 children.

The June 20, 1931, issue of the trade magazine *Motion Picture Daily* reported on the proceedings.

At 9:30 a.m., on a Saturday, the convention opened at the Fox Theater with a performance of the 40-minute long *Fanchon and Marco's Mickey Mouse Idea* stage show.

Fanchon Simon and her brother Marco Wolf (who removed an extra "f" from his last name so it would be bigger on a marquee) had produced a series of live stage shows in Los Angeles and now toured the country to perform them in major movie theaters before the feature film. Their stage shows were called "Ideas," as in the *Beach Idea*, the *Contrasts Idea*, the *Saxophobia Idea*, and the *Syncopation Idea*. The shows were fairly lavish, elaborate production, with singers, dancers, and specialty acts like acrobats and jugglers. In 1929, *Variety* declared the Fanchon and Macro shows as "the standard by which stage shows are judged."

The *Mickey Mouse Idea* had premiered in Los Angeles just a few months earlier on March 12, 1931. A costumed Mickey (portrayed by vaudeville entertainer Toots Novelle) performed in several sketches, including one as the conductor of the Silly Symphony Ballet with outrageous costumed animals, skeletons, and flowers. The show also featured the California Sunshine Girls (who became the Fanchonettes), forty-eight beautiful young women on stage at one time, performing incredible dances and stunts in perfect unison.

The show toured only for one year, but Fanchon and Marco produced several other Mickey Mouse stage shows. In place of the Midget Village at the California Pacific Exposition in San Diego in 1936, vaudeville impresarios Fanchon and Marco managed a *Mickey Mouse Circus*, in which midgets used full-size elephants as playmates and dinner guests.

Around 11:30 a.m., a parade kicked off from the Milwaukee Auditorium and passed through the business district with floats representing the businesses and organizations that sponsored the club, and seven children's bands, including the Boy Scout Drum and Bugle Corps, the Girl Kiltie Band of Milwaukee, the West Allis High School Band, and the Hales Corner Band. The participants did not let the rain dampen their enthusiasm.

More than 300 ushers and personnel from fourteen Fox theaters lined the streets to help control the event. Milwaukee merchants decorated their windows and counters with displays of Mickey Mouse, highlighting objects for sale in their stores. Convention expenses were paid by local merchants.

At 1 p.m., an informal banquet for delegates selected from each club in Wisconsin was held at the Hotel Schroder. Immediately after the banquet, the boy delegates unanimously elected Art Zirler Jr., age 11, as their Chief Mickey Mouse. Members of the Minnie Mouse division elected Eunice Schneeberger, age 13, as their Chief Minnie Mouse. The delegates selected Appleton, Wisconsin, as the site for the next state convention.

Attending both the theater performance and the banquet were local dignitaries like Dr. J.P. Koehler (city health commissioner), Mrs. W.D. Isham (president of the Milwaukee Parent and Teachers Association), Mrs. Dorothy Enderis (superintendent of the Milwaukee public schools), Sam McKilhop (director of the Milwaukee Public Library), and Disney representatives W.H. Peters and Eddie Vaugh, who helped organize Mickey Mouse Clubs.

For publicity, the event organizers had arranged for a special Mickey Mouse insert in the Friday edition of the *Wisconsin News* and the Saturday morning editions of the *Milwaukee Sentinel*, and featured a coloring contest with a $100 total cash prize: $50 for 1st place, $25 for 2nd, and $5 each for 3rd-6th places. In addition, 3,000 free tickets to a Mickey Mouse matinee screening in the winning contestants' neighborhood theaters were awarded.

While the Mickey Mouse Club had many desirable aspects, there were also unforeseen disadvantages.

For example, in a letter written December 4, 1935, to a theater manager in St. Louis requesting information about the club, Lucille Allen Benedict wrote:

> We found that granting exclusive rights to any theater to call its junior matinee a Mickey Mouse Club in the long run caused us more trouble than it did good in the way of publicity. After all, all of the theaters are our potential customers, because if they don't buy one year, they may the next.

> We ran into all kinds of difficulties and controversies over the Clubs and finally decided to do away with any connection with them. A great many theaters are still running such clubs, but they are doing so entirely on their own, and without help or references from us.

> The success of each Club has always depended upon the resourcefulness of the theater manager, at any rate, and no matter how many suggestions we gave them from this end, the manager had to put it over in the long run.

> We also found that in the cases where the Club wasn't especially successful, the Managers felt 'Mickey Mouse' was responsible and developed a resentment against the product in general.

Even after the dissolution of the clubs, RKO (distributor of the Mickey Mouse cartoons) still gave promotional material like masks and balloons to movie theaters to help them entice young people to come in and see Mickey Mouse.

UnMade Mickey Mouse Cartoons

The reason for so many unmade Mickey Mouse shorts was not just that a story idea didn't seem to gel but that Mickey was the victim of his own early success.

In its February 16, 1931, issue, *Time* magazine ran an essay about what it described as Walt's "regulated rodent":

> Already censors have dealt sternly with Mickey Mouse. He and his associates do not drink, smoke or caper suggestively. Once, a Mickey Mouse cartoon was barred in Ohio because the cow read Elinor Glyn's *Three Weeks*. German censors ruled out another picture because "The wearing of German military helmets by an army of cats which oppose an army of mice is offensive to national dignity."

Time had earlier covered the German ban on the Mickey short *The Barnyard Battle* (1929) in its July 21, 1930, issue.

Elinor Glyn's scandalous book *Three Weeks*, while not sexually explicit, did recount a romantic fantasy of a short-lived but intense extra-marital affair between an incognito European queen who seduces a younger British aristocrat. It created tremendous controversy when it was first published in 1907.

It was still an international bestseller over two decades later when an enthralled and naked Clarabelle Cow decided to read the book in her bed in the Mickey Mouse cartoon short *The Shindig* (1930) before she goes to the big barn dance. Clarabelle then puts on a polka dot skirt to cover her huge udder because a group of film censors in Ohio had complained about visible udders, leading to a story in the *New York Herald* on January 3, 1931, entitled "They Shudder at the Udder".

When interviewed in a 1949 issue of *Collier's* magazine, Walt stated:

> Mickey's decline was due to his heroic nature. He grew into such a legend that we couldn't gag around with him. He acquired as many taboos as a Western hero — no smoking, no drinking, no violence.

In a 1978 interview, Disney Legend Jack Hannah, who worked as a Disney storyman in the late 1930s and early 1940s, told me:

> [Donald Duck's] temper made him an easier character to work with than Mickey Mouse. I remember many stories were started with Mickey but as soon as they started to rough the Mouse up, somebody would come up and say, "Well, that's more of a Donald Duck story" so they'd turn around and make it a Donald Duck story.

Mickey was a little more the hero type so it was a little bit harder to find material for him. Walt had a special love for Mickey and I don't think he wanted to see Mickey roughed up.

One classic example of a Mickey story being transformed into a Donald story is *Yukon Mickey*, an unproduced short from the 1930s that was partially storyboarded with Mickey Mouse and then completely re-boarded with Donald Duck. Neither version had enough humor to satisfy Walt.

In a story meeting on February 21, 1938, Walt talked about transforming the Mouse story into a Duck story:

> This picture might be suited better for the Duck as you would be able to use more personality with the Duck in spots where he would be laughing than you would with Mickey. The expression and the voice of the Duck would help it. It is a natural for the Duck to get in a situation like this — and the audience likes to see the Duck get it.

Jimmy MacDonald, who voiced Mickey for almost four decades, said:

> Walt was very serious about the character. I remember when Walt was in a story meeting one time and they were showing him the storyboards and reading the dialogue. He was smiling and everybody thought, "Oh, this is great". If Walt was smiling, then it was going over well. But when he was through, he said, "No, we're not going to make it". And they couldn't understand why. Then he said, "I don't want Mickey put into those situations."

It became increasingly difficult to find stories for Mickey since he was now a "reactive" character instead of one that would instigate the action, which is one of the reasons he found himself teamed up more often with Donald, Goofy, or Pluto, each of whom could participate in violent action and the consequences of that action.

In the April-June 1948 edition of the Dell magazine *Who's Who in Hollywood*, Walt wrote:

> Mickey soon reached the stage where we had to be very careful about what we permitted him to do. Mickey could never be a rat.

> Mickey had become a hero in the eyes of his audiences, especially the youngsters. Mickey could do no wrong. I could never attribute any meanness or callow traits to him. We kept him lovable although ludicrous in the blundering heroics. And that's the way he remained, despite any outside influences.

Mickey Mouse storylines underwent rigorous review from Walt himself, who would repeatedly say in story conferences, "Mickey wouldn't do that."

Sometimes a Mickey story idea was just a simple sentence or two, like this one taken from a page of a dozen other quick ideas from the mid-1930s:

> Mickey is a poor farmer... Pete is a wealthy neighbor... Mickey finally triumphs over him in some way.

Sometimes there would be a short, written story outline or a selection of quickly done gag sketches to show the potential of an idea. Further development might reveal the story to be too flimsy, too labored, or just not appropriate for Mickey. For instance, Mickey could only attack Pete if it was in defense of saving Minnie.

Here are just a few Mickey cartoons proposed in the 1930s that didn't get beyond the storyboard stage:

- *Navy Mickey*: Mickey joins the Navy (just like Roy O. Disney did during World War I) and has run-ins with an admiral who is a bulldog.

- *Hillbilly Mickey*: In the mountains, moonshiner Pete mistakes newcomer Mickey as a "revooner" sent to close down his still. Mickey would meet Minnie as a cute hillbilly girl at a dance.

- *Jungle Mickey*: Mickey as a newsreel photographer in darkest Africa.

- *Pilgrim Mickey*: This would have been the only Thanksgiving short ever made by the Disney Studio. There were several variations on the story, including Mickey recounting a tall tale to his nephews of how he went hunting for a turkey and ran into Indian trouble.

- *Tanglefoot*: Taking place at a racetrack, Mickey is the owner of a horse with hay fever named Tanglefoot who appeared in Floyd Gottfredson's *Mickey Mouse* comic strip. According to Disney historian J.B. Kaufman, "Transcripts of the story meetings confirm that Walt Disney was intrigued with the project." At one story meeting, Walt warned: "Strive for the personality of the horse rather than relying on props for gags."

- *Pluto's Robot Twin*: Mickey builds a robot dog to show Pluto how a good dog should behave. Unfortunately, the robot goes out of control and Pluto must rescue Mickey before the berserk automaton kills Mickey with its sharp teeth.

- *Mickey's Toothache*: Because of an aching tooth, Mickey takes ether at the dentist and falls asleep. He dreams that Dentist Pete takes him to court (where a gigantic wisdom tooth is the judge) and charges Mickey with dental neglect. Mickey confronts creatures that are half-animal and half-dental instruments in a nightmarish world. Disney artists spent six months coming up with elaborate pencil drawings.

- *Prehistoric Mickey*: The story of the first Mickey Mouse.

- *Mickey's Follies*: Mickey, like the Great Flo Ziegfeld, is the host for a musical revue featuring all the standard Disney characters as well as some of the popular ones from the *Silly Symphony* series.

- *Mickey's Hotel*: There were at least two versions of this story. One had Goofy and Donald as bumbling bellboys. Another had Mickey running his hotel with robots which, like all robots in animated cartoons, go out of control.

Many other story concepts are in the Disney vaults, including *The Time Machine*, where Mickey is sent back to the city of Atlantis; *Mickey's Sea Monster*, based on Walt's own suggestion of putting Mickey in a short version of Jules Verne's *20,000 Leagues Under the Sea*; and *Morgan's Ghost* (sometimes known as *Three Buccaneers*) starring Mickey, Donald, and Goofy, and later reworked into Donald Duck's first original comic-book story, *Donald Duck Finds Pirate Gold*.

Some ideas did, however, progress almost to the production stage. For example, two unreleased Mickey Mouse shorts from 1951 were over 90% completed, and many animation fans have urged Disney to either release these pencil tests or complete the animation.

One of them, *The Talking Dog*, focused more on Pluto than on Mickey, like many other Mickey shorts of the time.

Restoration specialist Scott MacQueen uncovered the scratch track (the preliminary rough voice and sound effects track) for *The Talking Dog* and some of its completed animation for use in his traveling 1997 presentation, *Unseen Disney*. MacQueen spent twelve years at the Disney Company, beginning in 1991, where he oversaw the restoration and preservation of literally hundreds of classic cartoons as well as animated and live-action features.

The Mickey animation in *The Talking Dog* was done by Disney Legend Fred Moore, known for his ability to bring the Mouse to life in a way that eluded so many others. The Pluto animation was done by Disney Legend Norm Ferguson, renowned for his earlier work on Pluto, like the scene of Pluto battling flypaper. Milt Schaffer was the director.

In the film, Pluto has been a bad dog messing up the house and a stern Mickey Mouse exiles him outside. As Pluto walks sadly along the side of the road, he is scooped up by a crooked con man (Black Pete) in a moving van lettered on its side with "Miracle Medicine Show."

Pete's concoction is "the medicine that takes warts off frogs, turns hiccups into teacups and guaranteed to cure the Texas tickle!" The tricky medicine man decides to entice customers to buy his wares by convincing them that Pluto can speak. Using his ventriloquism skills, he asks Pluto how he feels, and the poor pup seems to answer "Just like a piano... GRAND!"

Of course, to perform this "miracle", Pluto must first drink the horrible medicine, which makes him sick. Pluto soon gets tired of his sideshow career and longs to return home.

When Mickey can't find his beloved pet, he goes on a search that ends in a struggle with the medicine man on top of the careening truck as Pluto steers with his teeth. As they approach a covered bridge, Mickey and Pete leap from the top of the truck to the bridge and continue battling across it until they jump back on the truck as it exits the bridge on the other side. The driverless van soon smashes into a huge tree and Mickey recovers Pluto.

Mickey asks Pluto if he is okay, and Pluto responds, "Grand!"

Disney producer Harry Tytle claimed that the short in its rough form got a low rating when it was screened for the other animators:

I had thought *Talking Dog* was a weak story. Too much dialog and we didn't have the animators capable of doing a good job. At the time we first viewed the rough animation, I told Walt it was so bad that I called everyone concerned into a meeting. Three hundred feet of changes, new animation, went into the picture. The basic change was to make it a Pluto story but the animation by Ferguson was bad.

The Plight of the Bumblebee is the other nearly completed Mickey Mouse cartoon from 1951.

Once again, the primary Mickey Mouse animation was done by Fred Moore, with other scenes animated by Cliff Nordberg and Hal King. John Sibley may have been involved as well.

Director Jack Kinney offered his explanation why the short was abandoned before going to ink and paint:

The best Mickey ever was never finished. It was called *The Plight of the Bumble Bee*, and it was all finished in animation. It had an awkward length, but Fred and Sib agreed that it could not be cut, so it was shelved.

Most animation scholars, however, agree that length was not the major factor in the cancellation of the film.

Also, *The Plight of the Bumble Bee* is not the best "Mickey ever", but it is a nice cartoon and a little out of the ordinary for Mickey. For one thing, he is dressed in a suit and a hat (think of Mickey dressed as Don Draper from the television series *Mad Men*) and calls to mind the "look" of Goofy as an office worker from cartoons of the same time period. It was a more suburban look that was common in that era's daily newspaper strips.

The film has straight voice-over narration. I asked voice expert Keith Scott whether he recognized the announcer's voice or any of the other voices in the film:

I think the narrator could be Wendell Niles, Ken Niles' brother. The singer sounds a bit like the frog singer Bill Roberts in places, and the female sounds like Aileen Carlisle, but I am sure since the film was nearly completed that the Disney Archives could find the payment records from that time period to accurately identify the voices.

Walt always said that Mickey's voice, because of its limited range, could not sustain long stretches of dialog, so maybe that is the reason for the narration (just like in the typical suburban Goofy cartoons of the period, which were also directed by Kinney).

In the film, Mickey stumbles into a local bar, where he finds a bee named Hector singing "bebop" (a bee who is jazz bopping), but notices that the bee occasionally hits a beautiful operatic note. Mickey decides the bee is destined for bigger things, and becomes his manager by signing Hector to a contract. However, Mickey soon discovers that the reason Hector is singing in a bar is that he has a weakness for the nectar of flowers.

In fact, whenever he has a drink of nectar, he becomes a sloppy drunk. So, Mickey tries to keep Hector away from temptation. Unfortunately, for Hector's operatic debut, the stage set is decorated with flowers and Hector overindulges, sending the female opera diva on stage into a fit and a faint. Chaos ensues. After the performance, a defeated Mickey runs across a musical grasshopper outside and decides to try again.

The premise is similar to that of other animated cartoons, like *Dixieland Droopy* (MGM 1954), *One Froggy Evening* (Warners 1955), and *Finnegan's Flea* (Paramount 1958).

In 1981, Daan Jippes, who was working in the Consumer Productions division of the Disney Studio in Burbank, was browsing though some index cards in the Disney Archives when he found some information about Production 2428 (*The Plight of the Bumblebee*), including the location of three dusty boxes filled with stacks of animation, layouts, photographed storyboards, and x-sheets (exposure sheets). He also found the recorded soundtrack (with the final voices) on a transcription disc.

In an interview with Christopher Finch and Linda Rosenkrantz, Disney Legend Floyd Gottfredson, who did the *Mickey Mouse* comic strip for decades, stated

> This big model sheet up here was all made from drawings that [Fred Moore] made for... a featurette, called *The Plight of the Bumblebee*. Mickey had a bee that could buzz operatic numbers; he was a great virtuoso that way. But the bee had a weakness, he was a nectarholic: he'd get drunk on nectar, so Mickey had trouble controlling him this way. Fred got that picture about 90% animated, I understand, and Walt dumped it because he got scared of the alcoholic connotations.

The "alcoholic connotations" were probably not the reason the film was dropped because during this time period drunkenness was not considered a disease but rather a weakness and often was used as a springboard for comedic moments in films. In fact, at this same time, Walt was suggesting a cartoon based on drinking for the Goofy *How To* series. It was Roy O. Disney who stepped in and blocked that particular cartoon, according to producer Harry Tytle.

The Fred Moore model sheet was later used as the cover for a 1972 animator recruitment booklet from the Disney Studio entitled *What Do You Know About Disney?*

Under the supervision of animator and director Bunny Mattinson, and using all the elements that had been found, a picture reel of *The Plight of the Bumble Bee* was filmed and shown to Disney executives; unfortunately, Jeffrey Katzenberg (then Chairman of Walt Disney Studios) chose not to complete it.

After the screening, someone walked away with the picture reel — but fortunately, Mattinson had had the foresight to burn a one-quarter inch copy for himself. When Jippes was working on the television series *Mickey*

MouseWorks in 1999, there was talk about finally finishing the short and using it on the series — but nothing came of it.

Perhaps the real reason for these two shorts being abandoned was Walt deciding that he couldn't generate a good enough story for the Mouse. He told an interviewer in 1951:

> I'm tired of Mickey now. For him, it's definitely trap time. The Mouse and I have been together for about 22 years. That's long enough for any association.

Those harsh words did not reflect Walt's true feelings, just his frustration at being unable to find a good vehicle for Mickey. Over the decades, many possible stories for Mickey Mouse were proposed, sometimes even developed, but none made it to final production. Instead, they are filed away in the stacks awaiting some enthusiastic visionary to rescue them.

Sorcerer Mickey

Walt Disney was looking for a piece of music for his *Silly Symphony* cartoon series. In those cartoons, the action was drawn to suit the music. When he ran across Paul Dukas' "The Sorcerer's Apprentice", a scherzo for orchestra composed by Dukas in 1897, and based on Goethe's 1797 ballad poem, he was especially pleased because it already told a story — that of a lazy magician's apprentice who foolishly experiments with his mentor's magic to bring to life a broom that would do the apprentice's chores. The situation for the apprentice quickly gets out of control, leading to an exciting climax. The tale has been around in one form or another since the second century.

In May 1937, Walt began looking into purchasing the use of the Dukas score and final arrangements were made by July. Leopold Stokowski, conductor of the Philadelphia Orchestra for twenty-five years, remembered:

> I first met Walt Disney in a [Los Angeles] restaurant. I was alone having dinner at a table near him, and he called across to me, "Why don't we sit together?" Then he began to tell me how he was interested in Dukas' "The Sorcerer's Apprentice" as a possible short and did I like the music. I said I liked it very much and would be happy to cooperate with him.

On October 26, 1937, Walt wrote:

> I am all steamed up over the idea of Stokowski working with us on "The Sorcerer's Apprentice". I am greatly enthused over the idea and believe that the union of Stokowski and his music, together with the best of our medium, would be the means of a great success and should lead to a new style of motion picture presentation... In fact, I think so much of the idea that I have already gone ahead and now have the story in work with this crew, on the chance that we will be able to get together with Stokowski and possibly have the music recorded within a short time...

Walt assigned Perce Pearce as animation director for the project and had Carl Fallberg begin work on the story. By November 9, 1937, Fallberg had finished a rough draft.

As the story developed, it was strongly suggested to Walt that Dopey from *Snow White and the Seven Dwarfs* perform the role of the apprentice, especially with audiences wanting to see more of that character. Walt never seriously considered the suggestion because at the time he wanted the characters in the feature films to be separate from the shorts, and felt that too much exposure of those characters would dilute the impact of their films.

Some elements from Dopey's costume in *Snow White* remain in the final version of *Fantasia*, including the over-sized sleeves that would slip over his hands, the long robe with the distinctive neckline, and the soft brown shoes.

What Walt wanted was a good story to showcase Mickey Mouse, whose theatrical appearances had diminished because of the restrictions on the character now that he had become a role model. On November 15, 1937, all Disney Studio staff were alerted that a short was going to be made, given a paragraph synopsis of the story, and told that it would star Mickey Mouse.

Director Pearce emphasized to the staff that:

> The picture will be made without dialogue and without sound effects, depending solely on pantomime and the descriptive music... Our picture is designed to intrigue the audience, thrill them, entertain them, but not in the belly laugh manner.

Pearce's memo was also a plea for visual ideas, story suggestions, and gags, which he wanted by November 27. Even Carl Barks, who would later gain fame as the artist for the comic-book adventures of Donald Duck and his relatives, submitted gags, including one where Mickey causes two waterspouts to spring upward and do a gyrating dance.

Pearce and Fallberg were later pulled off the film to work on the animated feature *Bambi*. James Algar was assigned as the new director.

With the opening of *Snow White* just five weeks away, Walt was still holding meetings about "The Sorcerer's Apprentice". He said:

> The thought is this: Mickey is an apprentice wanting the power of the Sorcerer to do his work. Then when that happens and he has that power, then he dreams of his great power. But when he awakens and finds what the broom has done and he hasn't the power to stop the broom, we find Mickey having to resort to an axe and try to stop the broom's work.

The story continuity at the time stated that once Mickey was dreaming it was "a picture of a typical little man and what he would like to do once given complete control of the earth and its elements. In his dream Mickey is having a spectacular lot of fun without being malicious".

At a story meeting on November 13, the stenographer recorded:

> Walt expressed himself about this dream several times by saying that Mickey could be here, there — anywhere. It is like a dream actually is. There doesn't need to be any flowing continuity.

Walt saw Mickey as an orchestra conductor in his dream, directing the ocean and the stars. When it came to layout, he suggested:

> Have a lot of up-shots, looking up at the guy, you know, like you'd shoot up at an orchestra conductor as he is conducting.

Walt was briefly shocked when, on November 29, he received a letter from Stokowski suggesting that rather than use Mickey Mouse in the film, he should create a new character representing "everyman." Stokowski wrote:

> What would you think of creating an entirely new personality for this film instead of Mickey? You may have strong reasons for wishing Mickey to be the hero....I feel that if you create a new personality which represents every one of us, it might be a valuable factor in the years to come.

Walt completely ignored the letter, knowing that audiences already identified with Mickey as their "everyman" character.

The recording session with Stokowski and a full orchestra began at midnight on January 9, 1938, at the Selznick Studio in Hollywood, and ran into the early morning of the next day. The live-action shooting of Stokowski had to be delayed until January 24 because, according to Bill Garity, who was in charge of handling the recording, "Stokowski's tails had not arrived".

Jim Algar began handing out the first scenes to animate on January 21, with Preston Blair given the scene of Mickey waking from the dream in an armchair surrounded by water. Edward Love and George Rowley worked on the never-ending brooms.

Les Clark, who had become the Disney Studio's "Mickey expert" after the departure of Ub Iwerks, did much of the animation of Mickey himself, along with Riley Thomson — in particular, he did the sections from the first appearance of Mickey with buckets in his hand until the end of the nightmare. Cy Young animated Mickey being carried off by the waves.

Special effects were handled by Cornett Wood, Joshua Meador, Daniel McManus, and Ugo d'Orsi.

Fred Moore was called upon to help with the design of Mickey. Besides being an acknowledged expert on Mickey Mouse, Moore had also animated Dopey in *Snow White*. It was Moore who gave Mickey pupils for the first time in a theatrical cartoon.

Animator Marvin Woodward did the final scenes of Mickey, and these directions to him indicate Moore's importance to the project:

> Work for a cute, short, chunky Mickey in this scene. Do not let him get too tall. He should not be over three heads high. When the first key poses have been drawn, please refer them to Fred Moore for possible suggestions. Fred Moore is assisting all animators on this picture in an attempt to make the Mickeys conform to a cute style.

Bill Tytla animated the Sorcerer and slyly gave the character Walt's habit of raising one eyebrow to indicate disapproval, which Walt himself called "that dirty Disney look". The Disney Studio dubbed the character "Yensid" — Disney spelled backwards.

Nigel de Brulier, a well-known silent film star, was brought in to portray the live-action reference of the Sorcerer. Carl Fallberg went to Hollywood costume rental houses like Western Costume to find an appropriate robe and pointed hat. The hat he finally got needed to have white stars and crescent moons pasted on it.

A rough preview of the short was shown on April 12, with a handful of scenes still unfinished. Even Roy O. Disney wrote in a letter on June 10 that "the picture is practically completed. It looks grand".

However, Roy was not pleased with the final cost, which had run over $125,000, nearly four times that of a regular *Silly Symphony* short. Roy felt the only way to recover the production costs was to exploit the film as a "special" to the public, though that would entail additional expense as well.

This idea sparked in Walt the concept of putting the film together with several other musical numbers and marketing it as an animated concert. Stokowski came to the Disney Studio in September 1938 with composer and music critic Deems Taylor to discuss this proposed film, then known as *The Concert Feature*.

On September 3, Walt broached the idea of making the film an immersive experience with broom shadows marching down the sides of the theater toward the screen and the sound of water rushing from behind the audience, then through the audience, and finally crashing on the screen (made possible with the placement of coordinated sound speakers).

The music for *Fantasia* was recorded by the Philadelphia Orchestra in April 1939. Interestingly, "The Sorcerer's Apprentice" was the only piece of music *not* recorded by the Orchestra. The film uses the recording from the Selznick Studio session.

Filming was done at the Disney Studio in 1940 for the live-action introduction and conclusion, including Mickey bounding up the steps in silhouette to shake hands with Stokowski.

Fantasia premiered on November 13, 1940, at New York's Broadway Theater, the same theater where *Steamboat Willie* had premiered on November 18, 1928, nearly twelve years earlier to the day. Several New York film critics singled out Mickey's segment as the best part of the film. Walt told the newspapers:

> Perhaps Bach and Beethoven are strange bedfellows for Mickey Mouse, but it's all been a lot of fun.

Oddly, only two major pieces of Sorcerer Mickey merchandise were available during the film's initial release: a Hagen-Renaker ceramic figure and a Grossett & Dunlap storybook. It was not until the early 1980s that a flood of Sorcerer Mickey merchandise started to appear in response to public demand.

Disney Legend Woolie Reitherman stated:

> [Mickey in] "The Sorcerer's Apprentice" was a very charming thing but to me it started the trend of Mickey where he became a different kind of character from that little flip guy that was always fighting off Peg Leg Pete and all these impossible things, with Minnie and all that stuff. There was a charm, a naïve quality [to those shorts].

That image of Mickey Mouse in his Sorcerer Apprentice costume was so powerful that it evolved into another separate persona for Mickey, one in which he was elevated to full magician status.

To further that persona, Mickey Mouse appeared in his Sorcerer Mickey outfit every Wednesday on the "Anything Can Happen Day" of the original *Mickey Mouse Club* television show in 1955, entering on a bucking flying carpet. Sorcerer Mickey was animated in this segment by Hal King with Walt Disney providing the voice. The sequence, filmed in color, shows Mickey's robe colored purple not red.

In the last twenty-five years, Sorcerer Mickey has become a very prominent icon.

Sorcerer Mickey made a few appearances on the *House of Mouse* television series, including the episode "Mickey and Minnie's Big Vacation" where he has to save the nightclub from a flood caused by Donald Duck, and in "Mickey's House of Villains", where he must transform into Sorcerer Mickey to save the nightclub after it has been taken over by such villains as Captain Hook, Jafar, and Cruella De Vil.

Sorcerer Mickey appears in video games like *Kingdom Hearts 3D: Dream Drop Distance* and *Epic Mickey 2: The Power of Two* as well as in Disney Infinity.

Sorcerer Mickey was the mascot icon for Walt Disney Home Video and its home video releases beginning in 1987. Sorcerer Mickey was also the icon for Walt Disney Imagineering starting in the late 1990s and continuing through today. In *Walt Disney Imagineering* (Hyperion 1996), Imagineers Kevin Rafferty and Bruce Gordon write:

> Mickey Mouse, as the Sorcerer's Apprentice, conjures up a fitting logo for Walt Disney Imagineering. In a scene from *Fantasia*, the Sorcerer's Apprentice somehow manages to make magical things happen without expecting them to. We owe Mickey a great deal of gratitude. If it were not for him, there would probably not be an Imagineering.

In addition, Sorcerer Mickey is the mascot for the *Disney Dream* cruise ship, which launched in 2011. A full figure of Mickey with his brooms decorates the stern of the ship.

A forty-five foot tall inflatable Sorcerer Mickey balloon was one of the parade floats for Disneyland's Party Gras Parade from January 1990 to November 1990 as part of the theme park's 35th anniversary celebration. Sorcerer Mickey was also the logo for the 25th anniversary celebration of Walt Disney World in 1996.

Sorcerer Mickey is the unofficial mascot of Disney's Hollywood Studios (formerly Disney-MGM Studios), which made sense because *Fantasia* came out in 1940 and the park represents Hollywood of the 1930s and 1940s. A statue of Sorcerer Mickey is in the Mickey's of Hollywood merchandise store in that park.

A fifty-five-foot-tall inflatable Mickey rose behind the Chinese Theater for the *Sorcery in the Sky* fireworks show from summer 1990 until its cancellation with the debut of *Fantasmic!* in 1998 (though the show did return infrequently until 2004). Appearing directly behind the Chinese Theater during the last minute of the eight-and-one-half-minute show, Sorcerer Mickey had a shower of sparks shoot from the first finger of his outstretched right hand.

Sorcerer Mickey is the star of the night-time spectacular *Fantasmic!* Despite promotional material and photographs, Sorcerer Mickey never fights any villains during the show but appears triumphant in the final minutes.

The iconic hat, complete with its six stars and two crescent moons, that Mickey wore in "The Sorcerer's Apprenctice" segment of *Fantasia* was unveiled at the end of Hollywood Boulevard in Disney's Hollywood Studios on October 1, 2001, as part of the "100 Years of Magic" Celebration. The entire structure is 122 feet tall, with the hat itself 100 feet tall and 27 tons. To wear this hat, Mickey would have to be 350 feet tall. The hat size is 605 and 7/8.

As part of the "Millennium" Celebration in 2000, a twenty-five story Sorcerer Mickey's arm and hand, holding a gigantic magic wand with "starfetti", was installed next to Spaceship Earth at Epcot. By October 1, 2007, it had been removed.

Sorcerer Mickey (joined by Yen Sid) is the star of *Mickey and the Magical Map*, the new musical stage show at Disneyland.

Today, Mickey greets guests at the Disney theme parks attired as Sorcerer Mickey. Even Walt Disney himself would not have been able to foresee how popular the character has become and the plethora of merchandise that is eagerly purchased by Sorcerer Mickey's many fans.

The Making of "Runaway Brain"

Runaway Brain, an Academy Award-nominated, seven-minute short animated primarily by Walt Disney Feature Animation Paris, was released on August 11, 1995, along with the live-action feature *A Kid in King Arthur's Court*. It was re-released on July 16, 1997, with Disney's live-action *George of the Jungle*, then shown twice on The Disney Channel before its release in The Walt Disney Treasures DVD collection: *Mickey Mouse in Living Color, Vol. 2*.

The short marked the first appearance of Mickey Mouse on the big screen since the 1990 featurette *The Prince and the Pauper*.

The idea for creating a new Mickey Mouse short was to have it ready for Mickey's 65th birthday in 1992, but that deadline came and went. Fortunately, desire for a new Mickey Mouse animated short remained, and with the launch of the Disney animation studio in France, an opportunity to create one arose, since the other animation resources at Disney were committed to feature productions. Creating a new Mickey short presented a great opportunity to inaugurate the new studio with an important Disney project.

Several story ideas were under consideration when animator Andreas Deja remembered that:

> Someone at a meeting, and almost out of boredom, drew Mickey Mouse as a monster. Someone else saw it and said, "That's hysterical!" All of a sudden, the idea came up to do a satire of Frankenstein.

The film has many layers.

While it does satirize the film version of *Frankenstein*, the mad doctor is named Dr. Frankenollie, a tribute to two of Disney's legendary animators, Frank Thomas and Ollie Johnston.

The design of the character is reminiscent of Professor Ecks, a mad scientist monkey Mickey tangled with in one of his classic 1933 comic-strip adventures drawn by Floyd Gottfredson. Dr. Frankenollie's laboratory is located at 1313 Lobotomy Lane; Disneyland's street address is 1313 Harbor Boulevard.

In the film, Mickey is at home intently focused on playing a video game. Minnie arrives to find that Mickey has forgotten their anniversary. Mickey comes up with a last-minute idea to take her to a miniature golf course, but Minnie misinterprets what she is supposed to be looking at in the newspaper and thinks Mickey is taking her to Hawaii.

After Minnie leaves, Mickey uses the same newspaper to find a "help wanted" ad where he can earn the entire cost of the Hawaiian trip for one day of "mindless work."

When Mickey knocks on the door of Dr. Frankenollie's house for the job in a composition reminiscent of a classic scene from the horror film

The Exorcist, he gets sucked downward through a trap door into the mad scientist's laboratory, where the mad doctor plans to switch Mickey's brain with that of his monster, Julius. The name Julius is a reference to one of Walt Disney's first animated characters, a black cat in the *Alice Comedies*, though Julius looks more like a monstrous Frankenstein version of Mickey's nemesis, Pete.

The brain transfer is a success, with Mickey's mind ending up in Julius' giant body, and Julius finding himself in control of Mickey's body which now has wild eyes, sharp teeth, and ragged, torn ears. Unfortunately, Dr. Frankenollie crumbles to dust after the experiment and cannot reverse the effects.

The dimwitted Julius opens Mickey's wallet and finds a photo of Mickey and Minnie. The rest of the contents of the wallet are a black-and-white picture from *Steamboat Willie*, a library card from Guillard County Library (#2495 21095), a Social Security card (#746-55-2769), a stamp, a ticket stub, and a coin.

Julius falls instantly in love with Minnie's picture and escapes the laboratory to search for her. He finds Minnie shopping for a tiny bathing suit to wear on the Hawaiian trip. The real Mickey (in Julius' body) shows up to save Minnie, who mistakes him for a monster. A chase ensues during which Mickey is finally able to convince Minnie of his true identity. A climatic battle between Mickey and Julius ensues on top of a building.

During the course of their battle, Julius and Mickey fall onto electric wires, which cause their minds to transfer back to their correct bodies. Mickey is able to defeat Julius using the same technique he used defeating the giant in *Brave Little Tailor*.

This short plot summary does not do justice to the quickly paced film, which is littered with sight gags that a frame-by-frame examination is almost needed to reveal them all.

Zazu from *The Lion King* appears briefly as part of the debris being sucked down the trap door with Mickey Mouse and then is spit from Julius' mouth when Julius roars at Mickey on top of the building.

Mickey's home has a model of the starship *Enterprise* from *Star Trek* and a picture on the wall that shows a piece of cheese and the motto: "Just Say No" referencing the familiar slogan about drug addiction.

A month before the short opened, director Chris Bailey said:

> My goal was to capture the appeal Mickey had in the black and white short days but place it in a color body. People would ask "Which Mickey model are you going to use?" and they were shocked when we said, "We're going to make up our own."

Bailey claimed that Mickey's body was inspired by the short film *The Little Whirlwind* (1941) but the personality was from the black-and-white era of *Two Gun Mickey* (1934). "We watched a lot of the early shorts," Bailey remembered.

Supervising animator Andreas Deja was selected to be Mickey's supervising animator. He had previously animated Mickey in *Who Framed Roger Rabbit* and *The Prince and the Pauper*. Deja remarked:

> There's such a degree of subtlety in the work, the length of the nose, how the eyes relate. One big graphic feature is Mickey's ears. They are always round, no matter what! Whichever way he turns, they glide on his head, up and down. It's so weird a thing, and nobody questions it! It should look very strange, but it doesn't. He has lots of crazy things like that, and they make the character. It's a kick to do this character that you've grown up with. You get the opportunity to pass it on and he gets a little encore in life. We all wanted to do something a little different with the character though, a little edgier.

Deja's favorite Mickey Mouse moments in animation include *Brave Little Tailor* (1938), *Society Dog Show* (1939), *Mr. Mouse Takes a Trip* (1940), and of course, the "Sorcerer's Apprentice" segment of *Fantasia*. He used those scenes as inspiration for his work on Mickey. Deja said:

> It's a kick to do this character that you've grown up with. You get the opportunity to pass it on and he gets a little encore in life. We all wanted to do something a little different with the character, though, a little edgier.

The first animation Deja did on the short was the opening scene of Mickey playing a segment of the video game in which Dopey battles the Wicked Witch from *Snow White* who is throwing poisoned apples and has apparently already dispatched the six other dwarves since their tombstones are at the bottom of the screen. Deja recalled:

> At first I wasn't sure if we should push it with the video game sequence, but once I saw the designs and got into it, I thought it fit the character. He would do that now.

Runaway Brain was written by Tim Hauser who had worked on *Beauty and the Beast* and *House of Mouse*, and gotten his start as an animator working such project as *Sport Goofy in Soccermania*.

The music was by John Debney, son of Disney Studio producer Louis Debney (*Zorro*, *The Mickey Mouse Club*) and one of the most sought-after composers in Hollywood. Among his other Disney credits, he composed the music for the Phantom Manor ride at Disneyland Paris.

The film had its beginning and its end produced in California, but most of its middle section was at Walt Disney Feature Animation Paris, France.

When the film was released Deja told the press:

> We had to go through lots of explanation, chalk-talk and explanation about how the character's put together and how he's drawn. They have a lot of talented people there.

Although *Runaway Brain* received an Oscar nomination and was enjoyed by most of the people who saw it, many Disney Studio executives quietly commented that it was too much like a wacky Warner Bros. "Looney Tunes" with its raucous action and swift pacing. That is one of the reasons why Disney didn't widely publicize the release of the film because of lack of internal company support.

Disney Merchandise was even more horrified. They couldn't create items with Mickey in his huge monster body because it didn't look like Mickey; it looked like a huge Frankenstein Pete. And if they created merchandise of Mickey's body when Julius's brain was in it, then they had this horrific-looking Mickey with sharp teeth and torn ears.

Director Bailey defended his artistic design choice:

> We had the opportunity to play with a corporate symbol and not have it be him. We could scruff him up a little, give him shark teeth and have fun without tarnishing the image.

Animator Deja added:

> We knew we wouldn't be jeopardizing his personality because it really wasn't Mickey.

> The goal with *Runaway Brain* was to make a modern short that people wouldn't confuse with a cartoon dug from the vault. That's why I made him younger and a bit more aggressive, which was actually consistent with his early black-and-white film persona from films like *Building a Building* (1933).

In an interview many years later, Bailey recalled:

> There was a management change near the end of production and the new powers were less comfortable with a monster's brain running around in the corporate symbol's body.

> Several shots were cut, drool removed and ending changed. America's moms that didn't see the cartoon, but saw merchandise in the Disney stores thought Disney changed Mickey's design just to appeal to the skateboard crowd. In that respect, they [the Disney Studio] probably see the cartoon as a misfire.

Interestingly, Bailey's work on this short got him a job as supervising director on Kevin Smith's short-lived animated series, *Clerks*. Bailey recalled:

> Kevin Smith didn't know my name but liked the Mickey Mouse cartoon I directed titled *Runaway Brain* and wondered if I was available. I suppose he figured that anyone who could get a cartoon made at Disney where Mickey Mouse ran around like a mad monster would be a good fit for him.

Runaway Brain remains a problematic Mickey Mouse short even though merchandise, such as a comic book adaptation by Gemstone comics (*Mickey Mouse And Friends* #269), continues to be produced.

In 2009, Walt Disney Classics Collection made sculpted figures of Doctor Frankenollie and Monster Mickey. Patrick Romandy-Simmons, sculptor of the Monster Mickey figure, said:

Mickey's always happy-go-lucky and chipper and pleasant. Finally, he's Mickey as we've never seen him before, so wild and out of control and quirky. When I get really excited about a piece, I really throw myself into it. I did find myself doing the crazy Mickey voice... grunting and growling... to really feel the character.

Mickey Mouse at the Oscars

At the 50th Academy Awards Ceremony held in April 1978, *Star Wars* was a big winner with six wins out of ten nominations. Two of its characters, the droids C3PO and R2D2, were on hand to present a special technical award related to the film.

As the orchestra played "The Mickey Mouse Club March", a costumed Mickey Mouse character in a tuxedo walked on stage, greeting the droids as they left the stage. The audience roared its applause. After announcing (thanks to a live voice-over by Jimmy MacDonald who was backstage) that he was there to award the Oscar for best animated short, Mickey was joined on stage by singer/songwriter Paul Williams as co-presenter along with actress Jodie Foster.

Williams complimented Mickey on *Steamboat Willie* and joked that maybe he would get Mickey two more fingers for his 50th birthday being celebrated that year. Williams said of Mickey:

> He is forever young and he has kept us young.

Mickey then announced all the nominees. The winner was *The Sand Castle*.

Ten years later, as part of his continuing 60th birthday celebration, Mickey Mouse appeared at the Academy Award ceremonies to present the Oscar for Best Animated Short: *The Man Who Planted Trees*.

An animated Donald Duck, Daisy Duck, and Minnie Mouse sat in the audience in the front row as comedian and host Chevy Chase introduced a compilation of film clips of "one of the most beloved cartoon stars of all time", Mickey Mouse, ending with a clip from the "Sorcerer Apprentice" sequence of *Fantasia*.

At the end of the clip, an animated Sorcerer Mickey stepped off the screen and onto the stage where he was joined by an animated Donald Duck, who thought he was going to be the co-presenter. Mickey had to gently tell his friend that the Academy had chosen a human for that role. Donald is then yanked off the stage by a hook and with a little Sorcerer Mickey magic finds himself bound up back in his front-row seat.

Disney historian Charles Solomon described the scene in the April 13, 1988, edition of the *Los Angeles Times*:

> [Mickey] conjured up a giant package that burst to reveal Tom Selleck. The cartoon mouse exchanged banter with the live actor, walked across the stage and announced one of the nominees. The envelope flew out of his hand, turned circles in the air and landed on the lectern within Selleck's reach.

Although the Disney animation staff and telecast director Marty

Pasetta began planning this surprise bit of technical legerdemain in early January, directing animators Mark Henn and Rob Minkoff and free-lance artist Nancy Beman had to create two minutes of animation in just three weeks--less than half the time the work would ordinarily take. The artists used still photographs of the stage and lectern as guides when they devised the cartoon action.

It's difficult enough to coordinate the movements of actors and cartoon characters in feature films, when all the footage has been shot in advance. The awards show was a live broadcast: The action on nine separate reels of animation had to be matched to Selleck's movements in real time. The two images were combined electronically by technicians in the control room. [The audience in the Shrine Auditorium saw Selleck talking to an empty space on the stage and to Mickey on the monitors.]

Selleck was familiar to audiences for his role in the popular television series *Magnum P.I.*, but the previous year he had starred in the successful Disney film *Three Men and a Baby*.

For the 1989 Oscar ceremonies, comedian Robin Williams appeared with a Mickey Mouse headpiece and white mouse gloves to present a special award for technical achievement to animator Richard Williams

In 2003, Mickey made one more appearance at the Oscar ceremonies to celebrate his 75th birthday, presenting in the shorts category with actress Jennifer Garner. The animated shorts winner that year was *The ChubbChubbs!*.

At the time, Walt Disney Imagineering was developing a "digital puppetry" process that it would introduce at Epcot in 2004 in the Turtle Talk with Crush attraction. A hidden puppeteer performs and voices a digitally animated 3D character.

For this Oscar presentation, a CGI Mickey was created using the same technology. Backstage, a performer utilized an electronic rig to manipulate the image of Mickey that audiences saw on their television screen in "real time".

Host Steve Martin introduced actress Garner and said that "she is sharing the stage with one of the most beloved black actors in the history of cinema, Mickey Mouse".

Mickey entered from the opposite side of the stage in a black tuxedo and white tie. He searched through his suit for the list of nominees and found his parking stub and an envelope with a ring.

"Very funny, Frodo," said Mickey, making reference to the film *Lord of the Rings: The Two Towers* that was nominated for several Oscars that year.

Mickey also made a joke about being unable to read a name, asking actor Jack Nicholson sitting in the front row for help. It was in reference to the film *About Schmidt*, where Nicholson's character was unable to correctly pronounce the name of a young Tanzanian boy. Nicholson was nominated that year for Best Actor for that role.

Garner suggested that Mickey read the nominees from the teleprompter so, like many real actors on award shows who are asked to read from a teleprompter, Mickey put on a pair of glasses with black frames.

After the winner was announced, the camera cut back to Mickey who stood there smiling and applauding.

Mickey Mouse has been in nine animated shorts nominated for an Academy Award:

- *Mickey's Orphans* (1932)
- *Building a Building* (1933)
- *Brave Little Tailor* (1938)
- *The Pointer* (1939)
- *Lend a Paw* (1941)
- *Squatter's Rights* (1946)
- *Mickey and the Seal* (1948)
- *Mickey's Christmas Carol* (1983)
- *Runaway Brain* (1995)

Lend a Paw won an Oscar. Also, Walt Disney was awarded a special Oscar in 1932 for the creation of Mickey Mouse.

Behind the Stories of Mickey Mouse Cartoon Shorts

Mickey's Follies (1929)

Animator and director Ben Sharpsteen, in an interview with Disney historian Don Peri for *Working With Walt* (University Press of Mississippi, 2008), explained how Walt liked to talk about the story of a cartoon before making it:

> Walt described each act and the audience response. As each act follows, the applause gets more enthusiastic and finally when the big act comes, everybody goes crazy with applause and the cats are whooping it up and jumping so much that they all break through the roof of the privy [outhouse]. The sides of the privy fall apart, exposing a hole in the ground where naturally the cats have disappeared…I noticed that his wife [Lillian] was standing to one side and that she was not too enthusiastic. When Walt pulled the final punch about the cats all going out of sight, she said, "Humph, I don't think I want to see that picture". Even though her remark was very much to the point, it did not affect Walt the least bit, because we went right ahead and made the picture.

Traffic Troubles (1931)

Disney Legend Ben Sharpsteen, who directed many of the earliest Disney cartoons, including *Traffic Troubles*, explained what inspired the creation of this cartoon:

> In the early days, when we were making animated shorts, Walt was driving through town and was stopped by a cop, who gave him a ticket. He returned to the studio and told us about it. He reenacted his conversation with the cop in a way that revealed he did not think it was very funny. Each time he told the story, however, it became funnier, and his attitude changed. Parts of the story were added and others eliminated. One of Walt's strengths was not just creating a story but editing it, refining it. And before we knew it, we were starting a Mickey Mouse picture called *Traffic Troubles* that turned out pretty good.

The Castaway (1931)

In an interview, animator Wilfred Jackson told author David Johnson how he assembled his first short:

Walt was behind on schedule and needed something to catch up with and he had a lot of footage that had been cut out of other cartoons and it was saved in the morgue. All the animation was done and my first job was to make some kind of a story where we could use all this discarded stuff. The only way I could see to tie all this stuff together was to have Mickey be cast away on an island after his ship was wrecked and to be sort of a Robinson Crusoe character and had all kinds of materials that had come from the ship, including a piano, and all the things that were needed for all the different scenes and it would be on an island where there are jungle creatures to use gags about and jungle animals in the various out take footage.

And Walt had hired a musician when he put me to work on the thing. He said: "I got a new musician I just hired and I want you to work with him on your picture. I want to see if he's any good and if we can use him". So I said "fine". That musician happened to be Frank Churchill.

Walt did not care for the finished product. In their book *Disney Animation: The Illusion of Life*, Ollie Johnston and Frank Thomas recalled:

Wilfred Jackson never forgot the sidewalk post mortem after his first picture, *The Castaway*. "Walt had his hat way down and his coat up around his ears", he recalled. "I walked by and I heard Roy saying, 'Walt I don't know if we should release this, it doesn't look like a Disney picture'". They released it of course, but Jackson learned his lesson; he never made another film that could be called un-Disney.

The Mad Doctor (1933)

In 1988, Oscar-winning film director Steven Spielberg paid $63,800 for the first black-and-white Mickey Mouse cel overlay ever offered for sale. It was from this cartoon. In the cel, Mickey is at the top of the stairs with his back toward the audience and skeletons are starting to pop out from the tops of the stairs.

What newspaper reports of Spielberg's purchase failed to mention was that the overlay actually was not from *The Mad Doctor*. Though the background was original, Mickey and the skeletons were on a cel created in 1934, in black and white and using the same animation technique, as an illustration for page 59 of the David McKay book, *Mickey Mouse's Movie Stories: Book 2*. Because of all the publicity and the high price, other Mickey black-and-white cels came out of hiding. The next year a black-and-white cel from *Orphan's Benefit* (1934) sold for $450,000.

The British Board of Film Censors were more ruthless and aggressive than their American counterparts in banning horror films from being shown in the United Kingdom. *Snow White and the Seven Dwarfs* (1937) was given an 'A' certificate ("under sixteen must be accompanied by a parent or guardian") for its horrific elements.

The Mad Doctor, however, was deemed completely unacceptable, not because of its scenes with Mickey almost being cut in half or the proposed operation on Pluto's brain, but because of the presence of skeletons, classified as representing the "living dead", one of the forbidden items on the British censor list. In 1933, several British organizations were actively lobbying for children to be forbidden completely from attending any film with an "H" certificate, which indicated horrific content.

Mickey's Kangaroo (1935)

In 1934, an Australian admirer of Walt Disney, winemaker Leo Buring, shipped Walt a crate with the gift of two wallabies, a male and a female. By the time they arrived in California, they had given birth to a child. The Disney staff, inspired by the names of the Marx Brothers, named the male Leapo, the female Hoppo, and the baby Poucho. The wallabies were kept in a pen outside the Story Department. In *Mickey's Kangaroo*, Mickey received a crate from Leo Buring containing a boxing kangaroo and its baby.

Brave Little Tailor (1938)

Walt was determined to make *Brave Little Tailor* a great showcase for Mickey Mouse. He told his animators:

> We haven't had a good Mickey story for so long that it seems we should make an effort to put this over.

Disney Legend Jack Kinney did most of the story work and the cartoon ended up being the most expensive short ever produced up to that time. The Studio investigated why costs were so high and found out that some of it was due to Walt's insistence on the subtle handling of material.

Walt contributed significantly to the story and how it was to be told. Disney Legend Frank Thomas recalled:

> Walt was reaching the highest standard of Mickey stories. Only Walt could do it. He was the best Mickey storyteller and played up Mickey's derring-do. Yet there was so much heart and warmth.

Fred Moore drew up a new model sheet of Mickey to allow him to be more expressive and appealing. Thomas explained:

> It was one of the best Mickeys we ever had. Freddy's new design brought more fullness to the cheeks, and more flexibility around the middle. The body is more pear-shaped. It's balanced, but not symmetrical.

Brave Little Tailor was aggressively marketed with a coloring book, an installment in *Good Housekeeping* magazine, and a re-telling in the Sunday *Mickey Mouse* comic strip (August 28–November 27, 1938).

The Pointer (1939)

In their book *Disney Animation: The Illusion of Life*, Ollie Johnston and Frank Thomas relate this story of filming Walt as he recorded Mickey Mouse's lines in *The Pointer*:

> Walt had been so funny in the story meetings when he acted out Mickey's confusion [about meeting a bear] that we asked if we could shoot a film of him as he recorded the lines. Mickey's voice was always done by Walt, and he felt the lines and the situations so completely that he could not keep from acting out the gestures and even the body attitude as he said the dialog. No one but Walt would have thought of that dialog, or stretched out the situation to so much footage, or expected the animator to sustain the predicament with nothing but personality.
>
> Walt was skeptical... but our enthusiasm won him over. On that day, he wore his baggiest clothes and his favorite old felt hat [that made him] feel comfortable and relaxed. The camera was set up so far away from Walt that our image on the film was very tiny and [animator Frank Thomas] nearly went blind trying to chart the timing and to sketch the action but it paid off in a memorable little sequence [where] Walt instinctively reached out with his hand to denote the height of a little kid [for Mickey Mouse].
>
> It was the only time we ever knew just how big Walt considered Mickey to be. In spite of the help it gave us, he never let us put a camera on him again. Years later, when we wanted to look at the film once more, it had disappeared. No one knows what happened to it.

Mickey and the Seal (1948)

Disney producer Harry Tytle recalled:

> Walt had seen *Mickey and the Seal* storyboards and in his own way raved about it, saying: "That is like the old-time shorts; who did it?" etc. He wanted to know all the details. The story was originally made by Nick George and Bill Berg with the Duck [Donald Duck] in the same situation. After $900 worth of story, Jack Hannah, the Duck director, shelved it because he felt it was not a funny situation. I had disagreed with him, and it occurred to me this was one of the few stories in which the Duck could be supplanted by Mickey and I authorized the expenditure of additional story work to make the change. Nick Nichols [who directed the Mickey shorts] saw the storyboards and was very receptive to them and bought the story. Eric Guerney and Milt Schaffer [the second story team] did very little actual work in shaping [the story] and it is this story that Walt saw.

Orphans' Benefit (1941)

In the summer of 1939, with Mickey's twelfth birthday coming up, Walt wanted to produce a two-reel short film that theaters could use for the celebration. It was entitled *Mickey's Revival Party*.

The story was that the Disney characters would arrive at a theater to watch scenes from some of their classic cartoons. They would even interact with themselves on the "screen within a screen" as well as have humorous moments in the audience.

Unfortunately, these "classic cartoons" were mostly in black-and-white, and the characters had changed in appearance often drastically over the years. Since the animation would have to be redone in color and redrawn to make the characters "on model", Walt decided to just reproduce several of the old shorts completely. A soundtrack existed. The layout and staging existed. And the project would serve as good training for new, inexperienced animators who'd have a definite guideline to follow.

The black-and-white *Orphan's Benefit* was the first to be redone. The title was made more grammatically correct (as *Orphans' Benefit*). Donald's final line of "Aw nuts!" was changed to his then common catchphrase, "Aw, phooey!" Some gags did not translate well from the original, such as Donald Duck proclaiming "Am I mortified?" as a parody of performer Jimmy Durante.

The next film scheduled for reproduction would have been *Mickey's Man Friday* (1935), followed by four early *Silly Symphony* shorts and then *On Ice* (1935) to revise the look of Donald Duck. Only cartoons earlier than 1935 were seriously under consideration because the later shorts might still be in release somewhere.

During this time, Walt even had the color in *The Band Concert* (1935) retouched.

As the remake of *Mickey's Man Friday* was in production, the program was cancelled. Walt saw that re-making the black-and-white cartoons in color was not as inexpensive as he had hoped, and he was also anxious to explore new cartoons rather than re-visiting the past.

Mickey Mouse in Vietnam: Not a Disney Cartoon

Mickey Mouse in Vietnam was, of course, not created by the Disney Studio. It was the work of Lee Savage and Milton Glaser, who co-produced and co-wrote the film in 1968 for exhibition in the Angry Arts Festival, an event designed to give creative artists a forum for protesting the Vietnam War.

The silent, black-and-white cartoon finds the early 1929 version of Mickey Mouse happily walking along. He passes a billboard that reads, "Join the Army and See the World." Mickey studies the billboard, walks off-screen, and then returns wearing a helmet and carrying a military rifle.

Mickey sails off on a tugboat with the words "To Vietnam" printed on its side. The voyage is unusually quick, with Mickey crossing a calm Pacific from the USA (which is helpfully identified by a large sign posted on its shoreline) to Vietnam (which has its own large sign on its shore, along with large explosions popping over its land mass). Mickey arrives and marches into Vietnam, following an arrow-shaped sign that reads "Warzone".

Mickey is barely seconds into an overgrown jungle when he suddenly drops his rifle, goes stiff, and falls over backwards. The camera finds him flat on the ground, with a bullet hole in his forehead. Mickey's smiling face turns glum as blood trickles out of the bullet hole.

Savage, the director and animator of the short, and Glaser offered private screenings during the early 1970s. The film occasionally popped up in film festivals but was not widely known among Disney fans and was never released theatrically.

Glaser said:

> Mickey Mouse is a symbol of innocence, and of America, and of success, and of idealism. And to have him killed, as a solider is such a contradiction of your expectations. And when you're dealing with communication, when you contradict expectations, you get a result.

Despite rumors to the contrary, The Disney Company made no attempt to destroy copies of the film, but neither did it give the film any public recognition. Glaser remembers there was some talk about Disney suing them, but he was told it didn't happen because Disney didn't want to attract attention to the film and felt it wouldn't be able to recover sufficient financial penalties to justify the time and expense.

Mickey Mouse's image has occasionally popped up in other independent films such as *Uncle Walt*, an animated film made in 1964 by Bob Swarthe, who started working on the film while he was in high school and then as part of the UCLA Animation Workshop. Swarthe went on to greater success as a professional animator, even being nominated for an Academy Award for his work on *Star Trek — The Motion Picture*.

As the film begins, images of Walt Disney at various ages are followed by a pan across a cemetery showing the graves of hundreds of Perris (in 1957 Disney produced a live-action fantasy called *Perri* about the life of squirrels), then there are scenes with a very old-style Mickey and Minnie Mouse as well as racial caricatures and outhouse gags, a *Fantasia* sequence including the female centaurettes working a red light district with Goofy as a pimp, a scene of frightened little rabbit children looking at scenes from Disney cartoons like the transformation of the queen into the old hag in *Snow White*, and a scene of the Seven Dwarfs gathering to worship Mickey Mouse in a "Mouse-ka-mausoleum" reminiscent of a similar scene in *Snow White*.

Mickey's Surprise Party: The First Mickey Mouse Commercial

The 1939–1940 New York World's Fair, located on the current site of Flushing Meadows-Corona Park and also the location of the later 1964–1965 New York World's Fair, was one of the largest world's fairs of all time. More than 44 million people attended its exhibits.

Another fair, the Golden Gate International Exposition, was held in San Francisco during 1939-1940 as well. Sponsored by eleven western states and twenty-eight foreign countries, this "World's Fair of the West" was built on Treasure Island, a man-made island in San Francisco Bay.

At both of these fairs, the National Biscuit Company (Nabisco) sponsored a special Technicolor Mickey Mouse short cartoon, *Mickey's Surprise Party*. In "N.B.C. Theaters at New York and San Francisco World's Fair", published in *The N.B.C. National Biscuit Company Magazine* (January-February 1939), the company stated:

> In New York, we have a circular space in Food Building North, and … are erecting an air-conditioned motion picture theater seating approximately 266 persons.

> On Treasure Island, in San Francisco Bay our Company has erected a modern motion picture theatre in the Food and Beverages building. The theatre is rectangular in shape with rounded corners, and seats about 130 persons. There will be no charge to either theatre.

> At both Fairs, the N. B. C. screen program will be the same (except that in San Francisco a few of the products featured are different from those in the New York Version).

Mickey's Surprise Party, which Disney delivered to Nabisco on February 18, 1939, might be considered one of the very first "infomercials".

It's clear that money was spent on this cartoon because the color is much richer than in some of the other Mickey cartoons made during the same period. And when Mickey first appears on Minnie's front porch, there are shadows (even from Mickey's nose) that don't appear in other Mickey cartoons due to the labor and expense of putting them there.

In the film, Minnie Mouse and her dog, Fifi, are in the kitchen with Minnie stirring a bowl because they are going to "surprise Mickey with some cookies like his mother used to make".

When Minnie leaves the room, Fifi barks to shoo away an annoying fly from the batter. Fifi gives chase but accidentally knocks an entire box of popcorn into the batter. Minnie returns unaware of the accident and puts the cookies in the oven.

Mickey shows up with flowers for Minnie and Pluto shows up with a dog bone for Fifi. Mickey is curious what surprise Minnie has planned as she sits coyly at the piano.

Suddenly, there is the smell of smoke of burning cookies.

Mickey scoops up a bug sprayer and fills it with water from the gold fish bowl, leaving just enough for the poor fish. Using the sprayer and hiding behind an overturned table, Mickey battles valiantly against the exploding, burnt cookies.

Pluto also joins in the fray but accidentally swallows one of the cookies that continues to pop inside of him for a while.

Distraught, Minnie collapses into tears on the living room couch while Fifi howls. Her surprise for Mickey is ruined.

Minnie cries: "I wanted to make them the way your mother did." Mickey tries to comfort her with his flippant response: "Aw, my mother used to burn the whole batch all the time!"

Mickey suddenly gets an idea and he and Pluto zoom out of the house. They return shortly with a variety of Nabisco cookies: Lorna Doones, Fig Newtons, Social Tea Biscuits, Ritz Crackers, Oreos, and Animal Crackers. Pluto has even brought Milk Bone Dog Biscuits for Fifi.

"Mother used to buy them all the time and here's my favorite!" says a happy Mickey as he offers Minnie a Fig Newton. Minnie smothers Mickey with kisses and the film fades out on the Nabisco logo.

A censored version of the cartoon appears on *The Spirit of Mickey* video, with all references to the Nabisco brand name removed, including the names on the cookie boxes.

An uncensored version is available as an Easter Egg on the *Disney Treasures: Mickey Mouse in Living Color (Volume One)*. On the second disc, press the up arrow on the remote when "play all" is highlighted. Mickey's head appears in the "o" of Mouse. Press enter to see the cartoon with a short introduction by Leonard Maltin.

Mickey's Surprise Party is an interesting cartoon because a good deal is revealed about Mickey's mother, who is not mentioned in any other Mickey Mouse cartoon, and it is revealed that Mickey Mouse loves Fig Newtons!

While *The Pointer* (1939) is officially credited as the first film in which pupils appear in Mickey's eyes, *Mickey's Surprise Party* (released several months earlier) also featured Mickey with pupils.

Hollywood Party:
Mickey Goes Hollywood

Hollywood Party (1934) was planned as a lavish, star-studded MGM musical revue, but the production dragged on seemingly forever and used the talents of five directors, none of whom were credited, and seven writers, each of whom tried to make sense of the material.

The originally announced "all-star" cast slowly dwindled to inexpensive contract players like Jimmy Durante and Jack Pearl (radio's Baron Munchhausen) and a parade of cameos from non-MGM personalities.

The final film told an odd story about The Great Schnarzan (Durante), a jungle-movie star like Tarzan, who throws a huge Hollywood party in a convoluted plot to purchase some healthy lions to bring much-needed zip to his films. The party, however, is just an excuse to showcase short comedy bits by everyone from Laurel and Hardy to the Three Stooges to Mickey Mouse.

In his article "Before Snow White" for the June 1993 issue of *Film History*, Disney historian J.B. Kaufman covered in accurate detail how the Disney Studio developed animated features and special animated projects before the release of *Snow White*. Kaufman identifies several never-produced attempts at incorporating Mickey Mouse into an MGM film, including a "Mickey Mouse travelogue" for a Baron Munchausen film with Jack Pearl.

In September 1933, a contract was drawn for the Disney Studio to produce a segment in black-and-white for *Hollywood Party* in which Mickey Mouse would crash the party and interact with the main star of the film, comedian Jimmy Durante. While the sequence was only supposed to be 75 feet of footage, it ended up nearly twice that length at roughly 132 feet.

One of the challenges was that the MGM writers didn't understand how to write for Mickey, who was primarily a visual character who spoke in short phrases. When Mickey disrupts the party, for instance, the writers had him saying "Now that the tumult has subsided…," a phrase that was very un-Mickey.

Several actions were suggested for Mickey, including having him enter the party by skipping among the glasses of drinks that have been left on the bar and reaching into a martini glass for an olive to munch.

Finally, writer Ned Marin devised a script where women scream that a mouse is loose on the floor at the party and Jimmy Durante picks up the rodent by its tail to discover that it is Mickey Mouse. Mickey stretches out his snout and does an imitation of Durante including some additional good-natured banter with the star, marking the first time that Mickey interacts with a live performer on screen.

Then at Durante's urging, Mickey sits at a cartoon piano and begins to play the music for "Hot Choc-late Soldiers" that fades into a short Technicolor cartoon of the same name also produced for the film by the Disney Studio. (The rest of the film, including the Mickey Mouse segment is in black and white.)

Mickey's animation is uncredited, though J.B. Kaufman discovered:

> The Disney exposure sheets suggest that the Mouse animation was largely in the hands of Fred Moore.

Most of the production work for Mickey's scene was done in October, with final footage delivered to MGM on November 8, 1933.

Hollywood Party was released in June 1934. To indicate how important Mickey Mouse was at the time, he received his own separate title card in the credits just like the big name live-action stars. One film reviewer claimed that the Disney animation was the only bright spot in the entire film.

In the trailer for the movie is a sequence where Mickey hits Durante's nose from the film while the narrator portrays it as the two battling for the honors to host the party.

Because of the contract, the Disney sequences from the film were removed when the film was released to television in 1957. That's the way the film was shown for more than three decades, until the Disney scenes were restored for the 1992 video edition.

More Mouse-ka-Tales:
Mickey Movie Memories

Additional facts, quotes, and anecdotes about Mickey at the Movies.

- Author and illustrator Maurice Sendak wrote: "Oh, I adored Mickey Mouse when I was a child. He was the emblem of happiness and funniness. You went to the movies then, you saw two movies and a short. When Mickey Mouse came on the screen and there was his big head, my sister said she had to hold onto me. I went berserk."

- In an issue dated October 3, 1936, the *Literary Digest* reported: "Today, four hundred employees are required to turn out a Mickey Mouse cartoon and a Silly Symphony each month. Of these, 300 are artists, thirty-five in the story department, most of the others are musicians, sound crew or cameramen."

- In an issue dated February 28, 1931, The *Seattle Motion Picture Record* reported on Charlie Chaplin's request for Mickey Mouse: "Word has come that Charlie Chaplin has requested that his latest production, *City Lights*, be accompanied wherever possible with a Mickey Mouse cartoon. This unusual request bears upon Chaplin's high regard for the cartoon character and surety in that his own presentation will meet with a greater acclaim after an audience has been amused by Mickey's antics."

- By 1931, Van Beuren Studios produced three *Aesop's Film Fables* cartoons with Mickey and Minnie Mouse imitations named Milton and Rita Mouse. The Disney Studio sued and won on copyright infringement. In 1931, Warner Brothers produced three cartoons featuring an imitation of Mickey called Foxy who looked like Mickey except for fox ears and tail and even "borrowed" the plots from *Gallopin' Gaucho* and *Trolley Troubles*. The Foxy character was created and directed by former Disney animator Rudy Ising, who had also worked on the Oswald the Rabbit cartoons.

- In the Paramount Pictures movie *The Princess Comes Across* (1936), actress Carole Lombard played a Swedish noble woman. When reporters asked Lombard to name who her favorite film star was, she replied, "Meeky Mouse", always getting a huge laugh from theater audiences.

🐭 Excerpts from Mickey Mouse cartoons appeared in movies from other studios. A short clip from Mickey Mouse's *Ye Olden Days* (1933) is seen at the beginning of the Fox film *My Lips Betray* (1933). The Republic Pictures Corporation film *Michael O'Halloran* (1937) features an excerpt from *Puppy Love* (1933). In Paramount's *Sullivan's Travels* (1941) there's an excerpt from *Playful Pluto* (1934).

🐭 In the RKO film *Bringing Up Baby* (1938), when Cary Grant and Katharine Hepburn are mistaken for bank robbers and ordered to name their accomplices, Grant replies: "Mickey-the-Mouse and Donald-the-Duck".

🐭 On November 18, 1932, at the Fifth Annual Motion Picture Arts and Sciences' banquet held at the Ambassador Hotel in Hollywood, Walt Disney received a special Oscar for the creation of Mickey Mouse. It was only the second time a special Oscar had been awarded. (The first went to Charlie Chaplin.) One of the congratulatory telegrams that Walt cherished was one from Ub Iwerks who had left the Disney Studio in 1930 and who was responsible for the design of Mickey Mouse.

🐭 England's King George V refused to go to the movies unless a Mickey Mouse cartoon was shown, and his wife Queen Mary once came late to tea rather than miss the end of a charity showing of the cartoon short *Mickey's Nightmare (1932)*.

🐭 *The Band Concert* (1935) received awards from the 3rd International Cinematographic Arts Exhibition in Venice and from the Brussels International Festival.

🐭 Disney Legend Ward Kimball once told animator and director Richard Williams: "You can have NO IDEA of the impact that having these drawings suddenly speak and make noises had on audiences at that time. People went crazy over it."

🐭 In 1935, Romanian authorities banned Mickey Mouse films after they feared that children would be "scared to see a ten-foot mouse in the movie theatre."

🐭 Disney Legend Frank Thomas wrote: "Years back someone told me how popular one of the Mickey cartoons I'd worked on was around the world, even in countries that were having troubles. In Ireland, for instance, folks who were fighting would sit side by side at the movies and laugh. I couldn't get over the fact that for one brief moment, they all agreed on something... that Mickey was fun. That stayed with me."

🐭 Between 1941 and 1965, the Disney Studio released 109 Donald shorts, 49 Goofys, and only 14 Mickeys. In most of the Mickey Mouse shorts, Mickey played straight man to Pluto.

🐭 In a letter to Walt Disney sent circa 1931, silent screen actress Mary Pickford wrote: "Dear Mr. Disney. Will you ask Mickey why he doesn't make more pictures? It is not fair to his public to keep them waiting so long between appearances."

🐭 In an issue dated July 21, 1931, *Time* magazine reported that when asked to name her favorite movie hero, Mary Pickford would demurely reply: "Mickey Mouse".

🐭 In coverage of Mickey's eighth birthday in 1936, the *Literary Digest* reported in its October 3, 1936, issue that 468 million tickets had been sold for Mickey's cartoons in 1935.

🐭 On September 13, 1929, at the Fox Dome Theater in Ocean Park, California (managed by Harry Woodin, the originator of the Mickey Mouse Clubs in the 1930s), it was announced that for the noon matinee: "In Person. Mickey Mouse's Daddy, the man who originated the world's most popular sound cartoon character: Walt Disney assisted by Carl Stalling at the piano and U.B. Iwerk [sic], cartoonist. They'll show you how they do it, and introduce 'The Mickey Mouse Theme Song'. Mothers and Fathers are urged to attend this program."

🐭 During the early 1930s, Walt tried to release a new Mickey Mouse cartoon every month. Each short took roughly ten weeks to produce and could require as many as 125 people to finish it. At a cost of about $20,000 each, the short would run approximately seven minutes.

🐭 In 1975, Ward Kimball said, "You've got to realize that by 1930 Mickey Mouse had been in existence just two years and by 1932, you can safely say that Mickey was a worldwide character, just like Chaplin. Four years after he was invented, Mickey was a household word whether the house was in China, Moscow or Beverly Hills. We would get one Mickey out every two weeks, but the shows in theaters then changed twice a week, and we just couldn't make enough of them to satisfy the demand."

🐭 Until 1932, theater lobby posters of Mickey Mouse were the same general use artwork pose of Mickey Mouse with specific film titles printed on a blank strip that ran across the poster. In 1932, artwork representing the actual cartoon short was used. The standard poster for 1929 read: "He Talks! He Sings! He Dances! The Laugh Riot in Sound & Synchrony! A WALT DISNEY comic Drawn by 'UB' IWERKS."

🐭 In *Photoplay*, November 1930, Howard Greer wrote: "In London, a Ruth Chatterton picture was playing at one of the biggest theaters. Her name was in lights but above in letters five times as big was A *Mickey Mouse Comedy*. In Berlin, one theater advertised for its feature *Five Mickey Mouse Pictures*. There were hundreds standing in line waiting to get in. In out of the way towns in the south of France,

I found Mickey Mouse comedies. Tucked away off the highways in Spain were Mickey Mouse comedies. They speak of him as 'Mickey' as they once called Charles Chaplin 'Charlot'."

- In its October 3, 1936, issue, the *Literary Digest* reported: "Close study of a Mickey Mouse film will reveal that he wears gloves with but three fingers and a thumb. The missing digit saves Disney several thousand dollars a year in artists' time."

- When United Artists took over distribution of the Disney shorts in 1932, it hired a theater in Stockholm, Sweden, to run an entire program of nothing but *Mickey Mouse* and *Silly Symphony* cartoons to demonstrate the popularity and value of a Disney cartoon. The show was so popular that it ran for seventeen weeks.

- Actor Dick Van Dyke said: "Mickey was the first animated cartoon I ever saw. Mickey was my first introduction to humor and comedy. Mickey's character was always visually funny to me. He was the good guy."

- Actress Marion Davies, the companion of newspaper magnate William Randolph Hearst, threw a Mickey Mouse party at Hearst Castle in San Simeon, California, where all the celebrity guests came dressed as Disney characters as well as other cartoon stars of the day. Marion Davies told interviewers that she wanted to "make a motion picture with Mickey".

- Actor Bela Lugosi, famed for his portrayal of Dracula, was a fan of Walt Disney and of Mickey Mouse in particular. He had a photo taken with a Charlotte Clark Mickey Mouse doll on Mickey's 5th birthday in 1933 at a Hollywood restaurant. In 1935, he had to fill out a press biography for Cameo Pictures Corporation (where he was starring in the film *Murder by Television*) and one of the questions was his favorite film star. At first, he wrote "none" and then crossed it out and wrote "Mickey Mouse".

- Former First Lady Eleanor Roosevelt, wife of U.S. President Franklin D. Roosevelt, said: "My husband always loved Mickey Mouse and he always had to have [a Mickey Mouse animated short playing] in the White House." In addition, Mrs. Roosevelt even sent Walt Disney a possible story idea for a Mickey Mouse cartoon. Her letter and Walt's response are in the Disney Archives. That cartoon was never made.

- An original 1935 hand-painted animation production cel with background from Mickey Mouse's *The Band Concert* sold for a record $420,000 in a private sale in 1999. The cel set-up shows Mickey and company at the beginning of the cartoon, greeting their audience. It was later re-sold for an undisclosed amount.

❣ In December 2012, a 1928 vintage color Mickey Mouse movie poster was sold by Heritage Auctions to an anonymous buyer in Dallas, Texas, for $101,575. It was the typical generic poster that did not advertise a specific cartoon.

❣ In 1934, Hollywood Film Enterprises (HFE) exclusively licensed the use of Mickey Mouse cartoons primarily for the Keystone hand-crank 16mm home movie projector. HFE was a film laboratory that went into the home-movie business of releasing a variety of product including edited Westerns, comedies, and more to keep their equipment running between their regular outside orders. Each Mickey Mouse cartoon was issued silent without a soundtrack and ran about one to three minutes because HFE/CineArt would take a theatrical short and cut it down to make several different films.

In the process, they would create new titles for each of these edited cartoons, leading some current collectors to believe they had discovered a "lost" Mickey Mouse cartoon. *Football Manglers* and *Forward Pass* were two edited cartoons taken from *Touchdown Mickey*, *Mickey's Brigade Turns Out* was an excerpt from *The Firefighters*, and *Donald Duck's Trained Seals* was a segment from *Mickey's Circus*.

 Other edited titles included *Mickey's Little Eva*, *Ice Cold Mickey*, *Running Wild*, *Mickey's Best Girl*, *Mickey's Close Shave*, *Mickey's Bad Dream*, *Mickey Plays Santa Claus*, *Movie Star Mickey*, *Donald Duck The Mechanic*, *Gold Rush Mickey*, *Mickey and the Giant*, *Mickey and the Lilliputians*, *All American Mickey*, *Mickey Gives a Party*, *Mickey Saves The Air Mail*, *Mickey's Trick Horse*, *Mickey and Simon Legree*, *Mickey's Exciting Picnic*, *Robinson Crusoe Mickey*, and *Flying High*.

HFE also offered 8mm versions beginning in the 1940s.

Most of these were black-and-white and silent, although in the 1950s about a dozen previous black-and-white titles were offered in 16mm sound; and by the 1960s a number were available in 8mm Eastman Color. The HFE license was terminated when Disney decided to go into the home movie business for themselves.

In 1974, the Disney Company introduced Walt Disney Home Movies. However, this new division wouldn't release any of the classic black-and-white shorts, thinking that modern audiences didn't want to watch black-and-white cartoons, even going so far as to put a disclaimer card in the commemorative edition: *Mickey Mouse: The First 50 Years* that included *Steamboat Willie*.

In 2001, *American Bandstand* producer Dick Clark stated: "I grew up with Walt Disney. My father had a 16 millimeter movie projector, and the only thing I wanted to watch were Mickey Mouse cartoons."

Songwriter Richard M. Sherman wrote: "My memories go back to when my dad would run black-and-white short films of Mickey Mouse on the wall of our New York apartment. The images filled the room. Mickey was my best friend. One day, part of the film burned in the projector and it broke my heart. Dad spliced the film but there was always a skip. I still watched it over and over."

In 1981, the Disney Company negotiated with CBS to have an hour-long Saturday morning Mickey Mouse television series similar to *The Bugs Bunny/Road Runner Show* then running on CBS. The classic Disney cartoons were to be censored to meet the current Saturday morning guidelines regarding violence and other matters.

For the proposed Saturday morning series, Disney had some of the old black-and-white Mickey Mouse cartoons colorized so they could be used in the show. These colorized cartoons were later used when The Disney Channel debuted in 1983. The show never aired. Beginning September 26, 1981, CBS ran the Disney weekly anthology series (then titled simply *Walt Disney*) on Saturday evenings until September 24, 1983.

When Disney Legend Ward Kimball called musician Carl Stalling (then in his mid-seventies) about the song "Minnie's Yoo Hoo" to use on the Disney television episode *The Mickey Mouse Anniversary Show* (1968), Stalling replied, "What do you want with that old thing? It was written for Mickey's tenth picture. I just made it up. Nothing special about it." Kimball later used the tune as the closing theme song for the syndicated Disney television series, *The Mouse Factory* (1972).

Mickey Mouse Annotated Filmography (1928–2013)

I'd liken [Mickey] to the stars of the Golden Age, who could play any role from tragedy to comedy. Like Cary Grant or Fred Astaire or Laurence Olivier. Mickey represents class.

—Animator Mark Henn

First animated Mickey Mouse in *Mickey's Christmas Carol* (1983)

Theatrical Films

In addition to the official theatrical Mickey Mouse films, this filmography also includes the films where Mickey Mouse made just a cameo appearance, was in a film produced by another company, or appears in some film that was out-of-the-ordinary from the regular theatrical releases. These films are indicated after the film's title by the designation: *SPECIAL*

1928

Plane Crazy *SOUND VERSION*

March 17, 1929 | Director: Walt Disney

To emulate his hero, Charles Lindbergh, Mickey builds an airplane in his barnyard and flies it with Minnie Mouse as an uncooperative passenger.

Notes: Although *Plane Crazy* was the first Mickey Mouse cartoon, completed in May 1928, it was not released until after *The Barn Dance* (1929). Mickey wears no shoes or gloves. When sound was added, Minnie Mouse says one line of dialog (voiced by Walt Disney): "Who? Me?" when Mickey offers her a plane ride. So, Minnie spoke actual words long before Mickey.

Gallopin' Gaucho *SOUND VERSION*

December 30, 1928 | Director: Walt Disney

Bandit Pete kidnaps Minnie who is a barmaid and dancer at Cantina Argentina. Mickey rides to the rescue on a rhea, a bird resembling an ostrich, for a climatic sword fight.

Notes: The cartoon featured parodies of scenes from the Douglas Fairbanks silent film *The Gaucho* (November 1927), such as sitting in an upper window and lighting a cigarette. Mickey smokes and drinks in this short. It was the second Mickey Mouse cartoon made, and completed in August 1928.

Steamboat Willie

November 18, 1928 | Director: Walt Disney

Mickey is a pilot on a steamboat captained by Pete. He loads aboard cargo as well as Minnie as a passenger, and the two mice perform music using the animals on board as instruments. A disgusted Pete assigns Mickey to peel potatoes for neglecting his chores.

Notes: This short is considered the first Mickey Mouse cartoon because it was the first to receive a wide theatrical distribution.

1929

Cartoons released in 1929-1930 have conflicting general release dates because the cartoons were distributed through the regional "states-rights" system. For the most part, the dates listed here match the official dates given in Disney's internal All Pictures Book (1996 edition), used by the Disney Company to determine the official release dates. Some release dates could not be completely verified and so are left blank.

The Barn Dance

March 15, 1929 | Director: Walt Disney

Minnie goes to the dance with Pete in his car, but when it breaks down, she goes with Mickey in his horse cart. At the dance, Mickey proves to be a clumsy dancer, and so Minnie chooses Pete as her dance partner.

Notes: The cartoon featured multi-cel background of dancing couples, something uncommon for cartoons at the time. Walt continued to supply the squawks for Minnie as well as for Mickey.

The Opry House

March 20, 1929 | Director: Walt Disney

Mickey is the owner and star of a small vaudeville (misspelled "vaudville" on the outside banner) theater in a Midwest town where he performs as a snake charmer, a belly dancer, and a hapless piano player.

Notes: Mickey wears his white gloves for the first time when he sits down to play the piano about four minutes into the film. They are not in evidence at the beginning of the cartoon. Minnie appears only on a poster outside the theater as part of the Yankee Doodle Girls performing troupe which may explain the use of the tune *Yankee Doodle*. The short has no dialog, only music.

When the Cat's Away

May 3, 1929 | Director: Walt Disney

Mickey Mouse organizes his mice friends to break into a cat's house and have a party.

Notes: Mickey and Minnie were drawn roughly the size of real mice for the first and only time. Originally, the ending was for the parrot to phone the police and report the break-in; when the police arrive, however, the mice have already scattered, and so the police officers mistake the parrot for the intruder. The songs are all public domain.

The Barnyard Battle

Release Date Unknown | Director: Walt Disney

Pete's cat army threatens Mickey's farmhouse, so Mickey joins the mouse army to defeat the invaders.

Notes: Since the cat's helmets resemble those worn by Germans in World War I, Germany banned the cartoon from being shown in the country. The July 21, 1930, issue of *Time* magazine covered this incident.

The Plow Boy

June 28, 1929 | Director: Walt Disney

Mickey is a farmer plowing his field when Minnie drops by to have him milk her cow. She later spurns his romantic advances and a bee-stung horse ruins the field and the plow.

Notes: Many researchers consider this cartoon the first official appearance of Clarabelle Cow and Horace Horsecollar, though they are portayed as animals, not friends, and do not speak words.

The Karnival Kid

July 31, 1929 | Director: Walt Disney

Mickey is selling hot dogs at a carnival where Minnie is a dancer. Later that evening, Mickey tries to serenade Minnie outside the window of her trailer with a guitar accompanied by two screeching cats. The concert ends when the annoyed Cat Barker in a nearby trailer trying to sleep throws things at the cats and Mickey.

Notes: Mickey voices his first word: "Hot Dog!" (not "Dogs" plural as some claim). He tips his ears to Minnie like a hat, a gag that inspired storyman Roy Williams to create the famous Mouse Ears caps in the mid-1950s. Oswald the Rabbit first tipped his ears in July 1928, almost a year earlier, in *Sleigh Bells*, and the gag was borrowed for this cartoon. It was rumored that musician Carl Stalling supplied Mickey's voice. *The Karnival Kid* marks the first animated appearance of "pie-eyed" Mickey. Originally, the second half of the cartoon was printed on blue film stock to indicate night-time.

Mickey's Follies

August 28, 1929 | Director: Wilfred Jackson

Mickey and his barnyard pals put on a homemade show with song and dance numbers similar in style to the famous Ziegfeld Follies.

Notes: Mickey sings his theme song "Minnie's Yoo Hoo" for the first time. It's rumored that Carl Stalling provided the singing voice for Mickey in this cartoon.

Mickey's Choo-Choo

Release Date Unknown | Director: Walt Disney

Mickey operates a small-town railroad with an anthropomorphic train engine. He takes Minnie on a ride during which the train goes out of control as it travels up and down the hilly landscape.

Notes: This was the first cartoon with Mickey's familiar falsetto voice definitely done by Walt Disney speaking words rather than just sounds. Supposedly, Mickey and Minnie pumping a handcar at the end of the film inspired the creation of the famous Lionel wind-up toy from 1934 that helped save the company. *Mickey's Choo-Choo* features the first animation by legendary Norm Ferguson in the early scenes of the train engine. Recent scholarship suggests that it was Ub Iwerks, not Walt Disney, who directed the cartoon.

The Jazz Fool

October 15, 1929 | Director: Walt Disney

Mickey and Horace have a traveling road show packed into a wagon. Mickey performs on a calliope, a xylophone, and a piano.

Jungle Rhythm

November 15, 1929 | Director: Walt Disney

Mickey rides an elephant into the African jungle where his gun falls apart and he uses music to soothe the savage beasts.

Notes: The instrumental "Minnie's Yoo Hoo" was played over the title credits for the first time. The Disney Channel once banned this cartoon under the assumption it has cannibal caricatures. It does not.

The Haunted House

December 2, 1929 | Director: Walt Disney

During a storm, Mickey hides in a house filled with dancing skeletons that force him to play an organ.

Notes: Recent scholarship suggests that Jack King may have directed this short as his name appears as director on the draft script. King later directed several Donald Duck shorts. Some of the animation of the skeletons was reused from *The Skeleton Dance* (1929) released several months earlier the same year. One example of the most noticeable reused animation was four skeletons dancing in a circle while holding hands.

Wild Waves

Release Date Unknown | Director: Burt Gillett

At the beach, Minnie is swept out to sea, and lifeguard Mickey must rescue her. When he brings her back to shore, he cheers her up by singing and dancing along with walruses, pelicans, seals, and other sea creatures.

Notes: Carl Stalling told Disney historian Michael Barrier that he did the singing for Mickey Mouse and the walrus in this cartoon. *Wild Waves* was Stalling's last cartoon score for Disney before he left the studio. Marcellite Garner voices Minnie, and it sounds like Walt does Mickey's dialogue after Minnie's rescue.

1930

Minnie's Yoo Hoo *SPECIAL*
Release Date Unknown

This five-minute film features Mickey and the Mickey Mouseville Jazz Band on a stage performing "Minnie's Yoo Hoo" from *Mickey's Follies*. Mickey encourages the audience to sing with the lyrics that appear on the screen. Then he encourages them to sing along the mostly forgotten second verse as well and applauds the audience at the end.

Notes: This film was meant to be shown at theaters hosting a Mickey Mouse Club. Some of Mickey's animation is reused from *Mickey's Follies*. Walt Disney sings the first chorus as Mickey. An unknown baritone sings the second chorus. "Minnie's Yoo Hoo" is credited jointly to Carl Stalling and Walt Disney.

Another short film produced for the Mickey Mouse Club featured animation of Mickey and Minnie interacting with live-action vaudeville performer "Noodles" Fagan. No prints have ever surfaced.

Just Mickey / Fiddlin' Around
March 21, 1930 | Director: Walt Disney

Mickey comes on stage and plays several musical selections on his violin to an unseen audience. The cartoon features only Mickey.

Notes: The original name of this short was *Fiddlin' Around* (sometimes spelled *Fiddling Around*). It was copyrighted under that name, which also appeared on the movie poster. *Fiddlin' Around* was the first Mickey Mouse cartoon with little or no input from artist Ub Iwerks who by then had left the studio. It was also the first cartoon released by Columbia so a new title card is used at the beginning of the cartoon.

The Barnyard Concert
April 10, 1930 | Director: Walt Disney

Mickey conducts an unruly orchestra composed of barnyard animals in a concert featuring the "Poet and Peasant Overture" (Dichter und Bauer).

The Cactus Kid

May 15, 1930 | Director: Walt Disney

Minnie is performing in a Mexican cantina when she is kidnapped by Pete. She is rescued by Mickey as Pete tumbles down a cliff.

Notes: This was the last Mickey Mouse cartoon officially crediting Walt Disney as director. It has the first appearance of Pete with a peg leg in a Mickey Mouse cartoon. Marcellite Garner remembers it as the first time she did Minnie's voice, although she is heard doing that voice in earlier cartoons as well. Mickey's warning to Pete of "When you say that… smile" is a parody of Gary Cooper's line in the Western *The Virginian* (1929), and got a good laugh from the audience. Beginning in the 1980s, censors have repeatedly censored the film, including removing a beer glass and by cutting out scenes of gunplay.

The Fire Fighters

June 25, 1930 | Director: Burt Gillett

Minnie Mouse is trapped in a burning building and it is fireman Mickey to the rescue, despite several misadventures along the way.

The Shindig

July 29, 1930 | Director: Burt Gillett

Mickey and Minnie go to a barn dance and have fun partying with their barnyard friends.

Notes: Clarabelle Cow puts on a skirt to cover up her udder following the new motion-picture ruling about not exposing that anatomy. She also reads the banned book *Three Weeks* by Eleanor Glyn which resulted in angry letters from the Ohio censorship board. Mickey snaps Minnie's underwear, but this apparently upset no one but Minnie.

The Chain Gang

September 5, 1930 | Director: Burt Gillett

Mickey is on a chain gang breaking rocks. During a riot, he escapes prison but finds himself back behind bars at the end of the film after a wild horse ride.

Notes: Disney has always claimed that the bloodhounds, animated by Norm Ferguson, were the prototypes for Pluto.

The Gorilla Mystery

October 10, 1930 | Director: Burt Gillett

An escaped gorilla breaks into Minnie's house and ties her up. Mickey overhears this on the phone and rushes over to rescue her.

The Picnic

October 23, 1930 | Director: Burt Gillett

Mickey and Minnie take her dog, Rover, along for a nice picnic in the woods but it is ruined when forest animals and insects steal their food, Rover chases rabbits, and a rainstorm dampens the day.

Notes: Rover is the prototype for Pluto.

Pioneer Days

December 5, 1930 | Director: Burt Gillett

Mickey and Minnie are on a wagon train heading West when she is captured by Indians. Mickey tries to rescue her and is captured as well, but Minnie drops hot coals down the Indian's pants and he runs away. Finally, the two imitate a large army unit and scare off the Indians.

Notes: The 1940 reissue print ends with the hot coals (and was the version most commonly seen for decades). The original version has an extra minute of Mickey and Minnie carrying a log with branches that look like rifles. The Indians can only see the top so think an army is marching toward them. Restoration expert Scott MacQueen not only discovered the original ending but that there were alternate cuts with variant backgrounds for other scenes in the cartoon, though without documentation to explain the reasons for those changes.

1931

The Birthday Party

January 7, 1931 | Director: Burt Gillett

At his surprise birthday party, Mickey Mouse receives a piano as a gift and all of his animal friends join in the celebration with raucous dancing.

Notes: Later remade as *Mickey's Birthday Party* (1942), the short was often re-released in the fall to theaters hosting a birthday party for Mickey.

Traffic Troubles

March 17, 1931 | Director: Burt Gillett

Mickey is a reckless taxi driver. His second fare is Minnie on her way to a music lesson, but problems arise when Pete's elixir is poured into the gas tank and the car goes out of control.

Notes: The cartoon was inspired by a real-life incident of Walt getting a traffic ticket.

The Castaway

April 6, 1931 | Director: Wilfred Jackson

Mickey is washed ashore on a tropical island where he has adventures with a piano and with wild animals including a gorilla, a lion, and a crocodile.

Notes: Wilfred Jackson put together *The Castaway*, his first Mickey Mouse cartoon, with segments discarded from previous cartoons because Walt was running behind schedule. There is an alternate version with a few more seconds of the piano washing up on the beach. There is also reused animation from previous shorts like *Wild Waves* (1929). The cartoon featured composer Frank Churchill's first score for Disney, with some original incidental music by Bert Lewis. Walt did Mickey's characteristic nervous giggle for the first time.

The Moose Hunt

May 8 1931 | Director: Burt Gillett

Mickey thinks he has accidentally shot Pluto while the two are in the woods hunting for moose. Pluto is okay, but a real moose appears and causes problems.

Notes: In this cartoon, for the first time, Pluto was portrayed as Mickey's pet dog and for the first time called Pluto. It was the only time that Pluto officially speaks (he says "Kiss Me"). The scene of Mickey shooting at Pluto has been cut from recent releases.

The Delivery Boy

June 13, 1931 | Director: Burt Gillett

Mickey is delivering musical instruments in a wagon but takes time out to flirt with Minnie, who is doing her laundry in a pasture. A hornet's nest mishap scatters the instruments and there is a barnyard hoedown.

Around the World in 80 Minutes *SPECIAL*

June 30, 1931

Mickey does an approximate thirty-second cameo dancing to Siamese music. The cameo (which is original animation) was added to the film at the request of its director and star, Douglas Fairbanks. The film was released through United Artists.

Mickey Steps Out

July 7, 1931 | Director: Burt Gillett

Mickey goes to Minnie's house for a date but leaves Pluto behind. Pluto follows anyway and causes havoc chasing a cat.

Notes: Pluto also talked in this cartoon, saying "Mammy!" at the end when all the characters' faces are covered with soot. Since this was a blackface gag, it has been cut from recent releases. Mickey shaves in the cartoon.

Blue Rhythm

August 18, 1931 | Director: Burt Gillett

Mickey and Minnie perform to ragtime jazz music on a big theater stage with an animal orchestra that gets so intense in its performance on the final number that it breaks through the stage.

Notes: Mickey imitates bandleader Ted Lewis and plays a clarinet.

Fishin' Around

September 25, 1931 | Director: Burt Gillett

Mickey and Pluto go fishing in a "No Fishing" lake and find that the fish are too smart for them.

Notes: Walt did the voice of a fish. It is suspected that Lee Millar (Verna Felton's husband) did Pluto's barks.

The Barnyard Broadcast

October 10, 1931 | Director: Burt Gillett

Mickey is running a radio station in his barn but a howling cat and her kittens ruin the show.

The Beach Party

November 5, 1931 | Director: Burt Gillett

Mickey, Minnie, Horace, Clarabelle, and Pluto spend a day at the beach that is disrupted by an octopus.

Notes: Marcellite Garner probably voiced Clarabelle's squeal of joy. Lee Millar may have done the sounds for Horace.

Mickey Cuts Up

November 30, 1931 | Director: Burt Gillett

Mickey playfully helps Minnie with her yard work, but when Pluto pulls a lawnmower while chasing a cat he tears up the yard.

Notes: Mickey trims a potted bush into a topiary with a face.

Mickey's Orphans

December 9, 1931 | Director: Burt Gillett

A basket of orphan kittens are left on Mickey's doorstep at Christmas and they proceed to destroy the house.

Notes: Nominated for an Academy Award, *Mickey's Orphans* lost to another Disney short, *Flowers and Trees*. It was the first Disney cartoon with a Christmas theme.

1932

The Duck Hunt

January 28, 1932 | Director: Burt Gillett

Mickey and Pluto go duck hunting but the ducks end up getting the final laugh.

The Grocery Boy

February 11, 1932 | Director: Wilfred Jackson

Mickey goes shopping for Minnie and later they make dinner together.

The Mad Dog

March 5, 1932 | Director: Burt Gillett

Pluto swallows a bar of soap while being bathed by Mickey and when he escapes, people assume his foaming mouth is the result of rabies. Mickey saves Pluto from Dogcatcher Pete.

Notes: The Chinese laundryman duck has long been assumed to be a reference to the phrase "Peking Duck". However, it is also likely that it was intended to be a parody of cartoonist George Herriman's Mock Duck character in his *Krazy Kat* comic strip.

Barnyard Olympics

April 15, 1932 | Director Wilfred Jackson

Several sporting competitions are all going on at once, including Mickey running, rowing, and finally participating in a cross-country bicycle race.

Notes: The cartoon was released just prior to the 1932 Summer Olympics in Los Angeles to take advantage of the publicity and excitement surrounding the event. Frank Churchill did the score.

Mickey's Revue

May 25, 1932 | Director: Wilfred Jackson

Mickey, Minnie, Horace, and Clarabelle put on another musical revue with a lot of dancing.

Notes: The cartoon has the first appearance of Dippy Dawg, who would evolve into Goofy.

Musical Farmer

July 9, 1932 | Director Wilfred Jackson

Mickey is a farmer and performs a musical number that prods one of his chickens into laying a huge egg.

Mickey in Arabia

July 18, 1932 | Director: Wilfred Jackson

Mickey and Minnie are on vacation in an Arabian city when Minnie is abducted by Sultan Pete for his harem and Mickey must rescue her with the help of his drunken camel.

Notes: Pinto Colvig did the sounds for the camel. Frank Churchill provided the score. The film was the last Mickey Mouse cartoon released by Columbia

Mickey's Nightmare

August 13, 1932 | Director: Burt Gillett

Mickey dreams he marries Minnie and there is a never-ending stream of children.

Notes: This was the first Mickey Mouse cartoon distributed by United Artists. The premise for *Mickey's Nightmare* came from the first Oswald the Lucky Rabbit cartoon, *Poor Papa* (1928). Mickey prays in this cartoon: "God bless Minnie! God bless Pluto! God bless everybody!" The song "The Wedding Party of Mickey Mouse" came out in 1931, and the song "The Wedding of Mister Mickey Mouse" would come out in 1933. Both songs were approved and authorized by the Disney Studio.

Trader Mickey

August 20, 1932 | Director: Dave Hand

When Mickey and his boatload of musical instruments are captured by cannibals, he cleverly teaches the natives how to play them rather than cooking him and Pluto.

Notes: The cartoon was a spoof of the popular MGM film *Trader Horn* (1931). It was the first Mickey short directed by Dave Hand. Pinto Colvig did his Goofy voice for the Cannibal Chief. Bert Lewis provided the score.

The Whoopee Party

September 17, 1932 | Director: Wilfred Jackson

Mickey and Minnie host a huge dance party for their friends that gets progressively wilder with even inanimate objects joining in the fun.

Notes: Another version of this cartoon exists with some restaging of the action, re-dubbing of Minnie and Clarabelle, and things like a scene with a rug under a group of dancers (no such rug exists on the official release print).

Touchdown Mickey

October 15, 1932 | Director: Wilfred Jackson

Mickey is the star quarterback of the football team, the Mickey Manglers, and leads them to victory against the Alley Cat team.

The Wayward Canary

November 12, 1932 | Director: Burt Gillett

Mickey gives Minnie a canary as a present who turns out to have several babies who escape into the house and are threatened by a cat.

Notes: The house has two framed pictures of actors Douglas Fairbanks and Mary Pickford, owners of the cartoon's distributor, United Artists. The pictures are autographed to Mickey. Purv Pullen may have provided the whistling for the canary.

The Klondike Kid

November 12, 1932 | Director: Wilfred Jackson

Mickey works as a piano player in a Yukon bar. Wanted criminal Terrible Pierre kidnaps Minnie after a gunfight in the saloon and Mickey takes to a dog sled to rescue her.

Note: The ending was inspired by Charlie Chaplin's 1925 film *The Gold Rush*, but with an original Disney twist.

Parade of the Award Nominees *SPECIAL*

November 18, 1932 | Director: Walt Disney

Intended only for the 1932 Fifth Academy Awards banquet at which Walt received a special Oscar for the creation of Mickey Mouse, this two-and-a-half-minute cartoon shot in Technicolor by the Disney Studio shows Mickey in green shorts (an accepted alternate color scheme on merchandise at the time) leading a parade of caricatures of the Best Actor and Actresses nominees for the year. It recycles some animation and background from the Silly Symphony short *Mother Goose Melodies* (1931). Disney Legend Joe Grant did the caricatures of the live-action stars. In recent re-releases, Disney has artificially brightened the cartoon so that Mickey and Minnie's original pinkish faces look white.

Mickey's Good Deed

December 17, 1932 | Director: Burt Gillett

On Christmas Eve, Mickey and Pluto are street performers in dire straits. Mickey has to sell Pluto to a rich family to get money to help out a poor single mother's large family, but the two pals are reunited happily at the end.

Notes: The cartoon was made during the Great Depression when poverty was a real issue for many in the audience. Pinto Colvig supplied the voice for the brat's rich father. The concept of down-on-their-luck street musicians who get their instruments crushed may have come from the Laurel and Hardy short *Below Zero* (1930).

1933

Building a Building
January 7, 1933 | Director: Dave Hand

Mickey is working at a construction site under the supervision of Pete when Minnie selling box lunches out of a cart drops by to visit.

Notes: Nominated for an Academy Award but lost to another Disney short, *The Three Little Pigs*. The cartoon was a remake of an Oswald the Rabbit cartoon called *Sky Scrappers* (1928).

The Mad Doctor
January 21, 1933 | Director: Dave Hand

A mad scientist kidnaps Pluto for a horrible experiment and Mickey must go to the rescue — but fortunately it is not real, just a nightmare.

Notes: At one time, the short was restricted from being shown in the United Kingdom because of its depiction of living-dead skeletons. It is the only Mickey Mouse cartoon in the public domain. The Mad Doctor character is one of the villains in the Nintendo Wii game, *Epic Mickey*.

Mickey's Pal Pluto
February 18, 1933 | Director: Burt Gillett

Pluto saves a litter of kittens from drowning. When he sees the attention Mickey lavishes on them, Pluto gets jealous but still saves the kittens again from drowning in a well at the end.

Notes: Pinto Colvig, the voice of Pluto's barks, also did the voice of Pluto's angelic half. Don Brodie spoke for the devilish Pluto. The cartoon was remade as *Lend a Paw* (1941).

Mickey's Mellerdrammer
March 18, 1933 | Director: Wilfred Jackson

Mickey and the gang perform their own low-budget melodrama based on the novel *Uncle Tom's Cabin*.

Notes: Billy Bletcher, better known as the voice of Pete, did the voice of Horace Horsecollar as Simon Legree, a character from the novel. Radio actress Elvia Allman voiced Clarabelle Cow.

Ye Olden Days
April 8, 1933 | Director: Burt Gillett

In Medieval Europe, Princess Minnie has been ordered to marry the goofy Prince of Poopoopadoo, but her heart belongs to Mickey, a traveling minstrel. After winning a fight with her suitor, Mickey wins Minnie's hand in marriage.

The Mail Pilot

May 13, 1933 | Director: Dave Hand

Mickey, a pilot carrying the U.S. mail, battles the weather and air pirate Pete, who has been robbing the mail.

Notes: The Mickey Mouse comic strip published a storyline based on this cartoon. It ran from February 27 - June 10, 1933.

Mickey's Mechanical Man

June 17, 1933 | Director: Wilfred Jackson

Mickey builds and trains a robot boxer to fight the boxing gorilla known as the Kongo Killer.

Notes: The cartoon was inspired by the "technocracy" fad of the time. It featured Leigh Harline's first score for a Mickey Mouse cartoon.

Mickey's Gala Premiere

July 1, 1933 | Director: Burt Gillett

Set at the famous Grauman's Chinese Theater, all the Hollywood movie stars come out to enjoy the premiere of Mickey's newest film, *Galloping Romance*.

Notes: On September 1, 1939, *Mickey's Gala Premiere* was the final program shown by the BBC before it ceased broadcasting during World War II. When broadcasting resumed on June 7, 1946, the first thing shown was *Mickey's Gala Premiere*. The original title card clearly says *Mickey's Gala Premier* without the additional "e", but officially Disney lists the cartoon as "Premiere".

Galloping Romance *SPECIAL*

July 1, 1933 | Director: Burt Gillett

This is the mini-cartoon within *Mickey's Gala Premiere* (1933).

Mickey is playing a xylophone and Minnie is accompanying him on a piano when Pete, wearing a sombrero. pops out of the piano and grabs Minnie. Pete throws a knife at Mickey, jumps out the window, and hops on Horace Horsecollar to make his escape. Riding his xylophone like a horse, Mickey follows and ropes Horace's tail, but Pete snips the rope. Mickey tumbles to the ground and onto the back of a turtle, firing his pistol at Pete. As Mickey goes through a river, he comes out on the other side astride an octopus with his two guns blazing.

Mickey finally ends up in a pouch of a kangaroo to continue his pursuit. From the pouch he pulls out a machine gun and eventually a cannon, whose first blast shoots Horace out from under Pete. Another blast literally goes into Pete's mouth and propels him into the branches of a tree, where newly born birds in a nest peck at his nose like a worm. Minnie proclaims, "My hero!" and rides off with Mickey in the kangaroo pouch.

All of this action is intercut with reactions from the appreciative celebrity audience who are literally rolling in the aisles while Minnie continually screams non-stop during the action.

Notes: The original title to *Mickey's Gala Premiere* had a United Artists title card since that studio was releasing the Mickey Mouse cartoons at the time. During re-releases, that card was altered to remove any mention of United Artists. However, the United Artists title card for *Galloping Romance* has always remained a United Artists title card.

Puppy Love
September 2, 1933 | Director: Wilfred Jackson

Mickey and Pluto visit their respective sweethearts, Minnie and Fifi the Pekingese, whereupon a mix-up over a box of chocolates causes heartbreak that is quickly resolved.

The Steeple Chase
September 30, 1933 | Director: Burt Gillett

Mickey is a jockey in a steeplechase race. When his horse gets drunk on a jug of moonshine hidden in his hay, Mickey costumes two stable hands as a horse and wins the race anyway.

Notes: Pinto Colvig did the voice of the Old Colonel as well as the hiccups for the drunken horse.

The Pet Store
October 28, 1933 | Director: Wilfred Jackson

Mickey gets a job at Tony's Pet Store, where a gorilla named "Beppo, the Movie Monk", inspired by a movie magazine featuring a picture of the famous King Kong on top of the Empire State Building battling planes, escapes from his cage, grabs Minnie, and climb a towering stack of boxes.

Notes: A notice sign in the window of the pet store advertises "Boy Wanted", not "Help Wanted", and Mickey grabs the sign because he is a "boy". The film *King Kong* was released earlier in the year (March 2), and around this same time *King Kong* director Merian C. Cooper was in discussion with Walt about making a full-length animated feature of *Babes in Toyland* — several years before *Snow White and the Seven Dwarfs*.

Giantland
November 25, 1933 | Director: Burt Gillett

Mickey tells the story of "Jack and the Beanstalk" to some mice children, with him playing the lead role. The story begins with Mickey climbing the beanstalk to confront the King of the Giants.

Notes: In the story conferences for this cartoon, the mice were referred to as "nephews", but they were not called such in the film or in the supplementary material. Walt referred to them as "little Mickeys" in *Screen Book* magazine (January 1934) when describing this particular short. Walt also shared that they considered having the children take a more active role in the entire short with Mickey rescuing them from the giant.

1934

Shanghaied
January 13, 1934 | Director: Burt Gillett

Mickey and Minnie are captives on Pete's pirate ship and must fight the entire scurvy crew for their freedom.

Notes: Mickey does not speak in this cartoon and Minnie only screams. Billy Bletcher voiced Pete.

Camping Out
February 17, 1934 | Director: Dave Hand

Mickey, Minnie, Horace, and Clarabelle go on a camping trip and battle a swarm of angry mosquitoes.

Playful Pluto
March 3, 1934 | Director: Burt Gillett

Pluto interrupts Mickey doing yard work, swallows a flashlight, and gets entangled in flypaper.

Notes: The cartoon is primarily a showcase for Pluto. Clips from this cartoon were used in Preston Sturges' movie *Sullivan's Travels* (1941) to show the importance of laughter. The famous flypaper sequence was storyboarded by Webb Smith and animated by Norm Ferguson and is frequently used as an outstanding example of an animated character thinking.

Gulliver Mickey
May 19, 1934 | Director: Burt Gillett

Mickey tells mice children about the time he was shipwrecked in a land of tiny people just like Gulliver from the novel *Gulliver's Travels* and how he had to battle a giant spider.

Hollywood Party *SPECIAL*

June 1, 1934

In this MGM film, many movie stars show up at Jimmy Durante's house for a shindig to celebrate his new movie. An animated Mickey Mouse crashes the party, scaring some of the women because a mouse is in the house. Durante grabs Mickey by the tail and puts him on the top of a chair. They engage in some banter, and then Durante throws Mickey by the tail onto a nearby movie screen, where he magically summons a piano and stool and begins to play the introduction to "Hot Choc-late Soldiers", a specially made Disney Technicolor short for the film.

Notes: Mickey's scenes are all in black-and-white. Mickey received a separate title card in the credits just like the popular live-action actors. For decades, the Disney sequence could not be shown because Disney had only authorized the theatrical movie rights, not television or videotape rights. In 1992, Ted Turner's company re-negotiated with Disney to obtain those rights.

Mickey's Steam Roller

June 16, 1934 | Director: Dave Hand

Mickey is a steamroller driver who flirts with Minnie as she babysits two children. When Mickey is not paying attention, the two children borrow the steamroller and create havoc.

Notes: The cartoon features the only Golden Age appearance of Mickey's two nephews, Morty and Ferdie (then sometimes spelled "Ferdy"). The nephews first appeared (with names) in the Mickey Mouse Sunday comic strip continuity entitled "Mickey's Nephews" in 1932. In the cartoon, Shirley Reed voiced one of the nephews.

Orphan's Benefit

August 11, 1934 | Director: Burt Gillett

Mickey and his friends put on a show for a bunch of unruly orphans.

Notes: This was the first cartoon where Mickey and Donald Duck appear together. It was remade in Technicolor in 1941 as *Orphans' Benefit*. The cartoon has the first official appearance of Clara Cluck.

Mickey Plays Papa

September 29, 1934 | Director: Burt Gillett

A destitute mother leaves a crying baby on Mickey's doorstep and he and Pluto try to entertain the tyke.

Notes: Marcellite Garner, the voice of Minnie Mouse, did the voice of Elmer, the baby. Frank Churchill and Bert Lewis provided the musical score.

The Dognapper

November 17, 1934 | Director: Dave Hand

Pete has stolen Minnie's dog, Fifi, and is holding her for ransom in a sawmill. Mickey and Donald are two policemen who track him down.

Notes: It has long been assumed that Clarence Nash, the voice of Donald Duck, also did the voice of Mickey in this short while Walt was in Europe on vacation.

Babes in Toyland *SPECIAL*

December 14, 1934 | Director: Gus Meins, Charles Rogers

A black-and-white live-action feature film produced by Hal Roach and released through MGM and featuring the comedy team of Laurel and Hardy. The film was loosely based on the 1903 Victor Herbert operetta of the same name. In 1948, the film was re-titled *March of the Wooden Soldiers*.

Besides characters from the Mother Goose stories, *Toyland* also includes Mickey Mouse as a resident. He harasses a cat (played by Pete Gordon in an elaborate costume) playing a fiddle by throwing a brick at him like Ignatz Mouse in George Herriman's *Krazy Kat* comic strip.

At the end of the film, Mickey takes to the air in a miniature blimp to bombard the invading Boogey Men from above with exploding bombs. When the blimp's air bag is torn by a dart, Mickey parachutes to safety.

The role of Mickey Mouse was played by a trained capuchin monkey dressed in a costume and a mask. Capuchins are among the most intelligent of monkeys and are still used in films today including *Pirates of the Caribbean: The Curse of the Black Pearl* (2003) and *Night at the Museum* (2006).

Notes: Walt was a friend of Hal Roach as well as Laurel and Hardy. No documentation has been located why Walt allowed the use of Mickey and an instrumental version of the song "Who's Afraid of the Big Bad Wolf" from the 1933 animated short *Three Little Pigs* to be used in the film. (Elmer, Willie, and Jiggs are the names of the three pigs in the movie.) It has been speculated that since Mickey was barely six years old, Walt may have seen Mickey's participation as a way to boost his visibility as well as establish Mickey's importance by having him appear in a live-action feature. Filming finished in October 1934. Some sources claim that the film was released November 30, but it was reviewed by *The New York Times* on December 13, 1934, where Mickey Mouse was mentioned as part of the cast.

Two-Gun Mickey

December 15, 1934 | Director: Ben Sharpsteen

Mickey is a cowboy hero who rescues Minnie from Pete and his gang of outlaws.

Notes: Pete switches which leg his peg leg is on twice when he jumps on the log at the end of the short.

1935

Mickey's Man Friday

January 19, 1935 | Director: Dave Hand

Mickey is shipwrecked on an island of cannibals but rescues one and names him "Friday", just like in the novel *Robinson Crusoe*. Together, they build a booby-trapped stockade to hold off an attack by the tribe and eventually escape the island.

Notes: Billy Bletcher, the voice of Pete in the Mickey cartoons, voiced Friday in this one. He also did the noises Mickey makes while wearing a mask.

The Band Concert

February 23, 1935 | Director: Wilfred Jackson

Mickey is conducting a community band on an outdoor stage and is interrupted first by Donald Duck and his flute and later by a tornado.

Notes: This is the first Mickey Mouse cartoon in three-strip Technicolor. Italian conductor Arturo Toscanini was such a fan of the cartoon that he saw it six times in the theater and invited Walt Disney to his home in Italy to discuss it. *The Band Concert* won the Venice Film Festival Golden Medal (Best Animation 1935). Disney storyman Dick Huemer animated Donald Duck in this cartoon and considered it the most perfect animated short ever made.

Mickey's Service Station

March 16, 1935 | Director: Ben Sharpsteen

Mickey, Donald, and Goofy run an automobile repair shop but run into trouble with Pete's fancy squeaking car.

Notes: This was the first short where Mickey, Donald, and Goofy work as a team.

Mickey's Kangaroo

February 23, 1935 | Director: Dave Hand

Mickey receives a crate from Australia sent by a "Leo Buring" that contains a boxing kangaroo and its baby which makes Pluto jealous.

Notes: Shortly before this cartoon was made, Walt Disney received a crate from Australia sent by Leo Buring, a pioneer in the Australian wine industry and an admirer of Walt Disney. Buring had sent Walt two wallabies that Walt temporarily housed at the Disney Studio. Officially, *Mickey's Kangaroo* was the last black-and-white Disney short released during its Golden Age. Don Brodie supplied Pluto's "internal" voice.

Mickey's Garden

July 13, 1935 | Director: Wilfred Jackson

Mickey uses insecticide to rid his garden of pests. He accidentally gets a dose himself and hallucinates that he and Pluto have shrunk down to bug size where they face dangers from the bugs he tried to kill.

Mickey's Fire Brigade

August 3, 1935 | Director: Ben Sharpsteen

Mickey, Donald, and Goofy are inept firemen responding to a hotel fire who try to rescue a hysterical Clarabelle Cow in her bathtub.

Notes: Radio actress Elvia Allman did the voice of Clarabelle.

Pluto's Judgement Day

August 31, 1935 | Director: Dave Hand

Mickey scolds Pluto for chasing a kitten and warns him that he will have a lot to answer for on Judgment Day. Pluto dreams of that time of reckoning when the cats put him on trial and he learns his lesson.

On Ice

September 28, 1935 | Director: Ben Sharpsteen

Mickey teaches Minnie to skate. Goofy tries an unusual method of ice fishing. Donald teases Pluto by putting skates on his paws.

Notes: The cartoon is one of only three Golden Age theatrical shorts that featured all five characters. The other two are *Hawaiian Holiday* (1937) and a short cameo at the end of *Pluto's Christmas Tree* (1952).

1936

Mickey's Polo Team

January 4, 1936 | Director: Dave Hand

Mickey's team of cartoon stars — Donald Duck, Goofy and the Big Bad Wolf — takes on a team of movie stars composed of Laurel and Hardy, Harpo Marx, and Charlie Chaplin in a rough-and-tumble polo match.

Notes: The cartoon was inspired by Walt Disney's love of polo. Originally, Will Rogers was to appear in the short, but his death in a plane crash resulted in his caricature being removed out of respect.

Orphan's Picnic

February 15, 1936 | Director: Ben Sharpsteen

Mickey and Donald take mice orphans out into the country for a day, but Donald is constantly frustrated at their antics in stealing food.

Mickey's Grand Opera

March 7, 1936 | Director: Wilfred Jackson

Mickey conducts an opera starring Donald Duck and Clara Cluck, while Pluto's attention is focused on a magician's hat spewing animals.

Notes: A re-creation of Donald and Clara's duet was performed by Clarence Nash and Florence Gill in the live-action studio tour segment of *The Reluctant Dragon* (1941).

Thru the Mirror

May 30, 1936 | Director: Dave Hand

Falling asleep while reading Lewis Carroll's *Through the Looking Glass*, Mickey dreams he passes through his large bedroom mirror into an anthropomorphic world where he dances with playing cards.

Notes: Legendary Donald Duck comic-book artist Carl Barks worked as an in-betweener on the scenes where Mickey dances.

Mickey's Rival

June 20, 1936 | Director: Wilfred Jackson

Minnie's former boyfriend, the overbearing but cowardly Mortimer, shows up, but it's a jealous Mickey who must rescue Minnie from an angry bull.

Moving Day

June 20, 1936 | Director: Ben Sharpsteen

Mickey and Donald are six months behind on their rent, so Sheriff Pete comes by to evict them and seize their possessions. They decide to secretly move out in a hurry with Goofy's help.

Alpine Climbers

July 25, 1936 | Director: Dave Hand

Mickey, Donald, and Pluto go climbing in the Alps, where Mickey has trouble with some eagles, Donald has troubles of his own with a goat, and Pluto falls into a snow bank.

Mickey's Circus

August 1, 1936 | Director: Ben Sharpsteen

Mickey is the ringmaster of Mickey's Circus featuring "Captain" Donald Duck and his trained seals.

Mickey's Elephant

October 10, 1936 | Director: Dave Hand

Mickey builds a house for his new pet, Bobo the Elephant, a gift from the Rajah of Gahboon, but Pluto gets jealous.

Notes: Bobo the Elephant first appeared two years earlier in a sequence of the Mickey Mouse comic strip.

1937

The Worm Turns

January 2, 1937 | Director: Ben Sharpsteen

Mickey is a chemist who perfects a serum to give courage to the meekest of creatures. He experiments with several animals before injecting Pluto so he can stand up to a dogcatcher.

Magician Mickey

February 6, 1937 | Director: Dave Hand

Mickey performs as a magician on a theater stage but is heckled by Donald Duck, who becomes the unwilling subject for Mickey's tricks.

Moose Hunters

February 20, 1937 | Director: Ben Sharpsteen

Mickey, Donald, and Goofy go hunting for moose with Donald and Goofy disguised as a female moose and Mickey as a bush.

Mickey's Amateurs

April 17, 1937 | Directors: Pinto Colvig, Walt Pfeiffer, Ed Penner

Mickey is the host of a radio amateur talent show with performers Donald Duck, Clara Cluck, Clarabelle Cow, and Goofy.

Notes: The film is a parody of the famous *Major Bowes Amateur Hour* radio show. Oddly, the directing credit is shared by three Disney storymen.

Hawaiian Holiday

September 24, 1937 | Director: Ben Sharpsteen

Mickey, Minnie, Donald, Goofy, and Pluto have fun on a Hawaiian beach.

Notes: This was the first Mickey Mouse cartoon released by RKO, and one of just three Golden Age theatrical shorts where the Fab Five appear together. It won the prize for best short subject from the International Film Exhibition in Venice, Italy. *Hawaiian Holiday* was made roughly 22 years before Hawaii became a state on August 21, 1959.

Clock Cleaners

October 15, 1937 | Director: Ben Sharpsteen

Mickey, Donald, and Goofy attempt to clean a massive, intricate clock near the top of a tall building.

Notes: Originally, the story was going to be Mickey, Donald, and Goofy as watchmakers who will fix any clock for one dollar, with Pete tricking them into fixing the huge city clock for only a dollar.

Lonesome Ghosts

December 24, 1937 | Director: Burt Gillett

Mickey, Donald, and Goofy operate the "Ajax Ghost Exterminators" and some lonely ghosts call them over to their house for some fun.

1938

Boat Builders

February 25, 1938 | Director: Ben Sharpsteen

Mickey, Donald, and Goofy build a boat, the "Queen Minnie", from a do-it-yourself kit, but it collapses after it is christened.

Mickey's Trailer

May 6, 1938 | Director: Ben Sharpsteen

Mickey, Donald, and Goofy in a disastrous road trip with a car and a trailer.

The Fox Hunt *SPECIAL*

July 29, 1938 | Director Ben Sharpsteen

During the last minute of the cartoon, when Donald thinks he has the fox by the tail in the log, Mickey in full fox hunting regalia on horseback (along with Clara Cluck, Horace Horsecollar, and Minnie Mouse in the back) stops on a bridge to cheer Donald before galloping off quickly when the fox tail turns out to be the tail of a skunk.

The Whalers

August 19, 1938 | Director: Dick Huemer

Mickey, Donald, and Goofy are a three-man whaling crew who try to handle annoying situations and then encounter a real whale.

Notes: Mickey does not talk in this cartoon. Some feel that *The Whalers*, with its water and its whale, was made to give the animators practice for the forthcoming feature *Pinocchio* (1940) where those two elements were significant.

Mickey's Parrot

September 9, 1938 | Director: Bill Roberts

A stray talking parrot finds its way into Mickey's basement. After listening to a warning on the radio, Mickey and Pluto think the noise coming from their basement is an escaped convict.

Notes: In the Disney Channel *Have a Laugh!* version of this short telecast on September 23, 2011, the gun Mickey originally had is digitally edited into a broom.

Brave Little Tailor

September 23, 1938 | Director: Bill Roberts

Based loosely on a familiar fairy tale, Mickey is a tailor mistaken for a giant killer and must save the kingdom from a rampaging giant to win the hand of Princess Minnie.

Notes: Nominated for an Academy Award as Best Animated Short, *Brave Little Tailor* lost to another Disney short, *Ferdinand the Bull*. The story was retold in a fourteen-week continuity in the Sunday Mickey Mouse comic strip that ran from August 28 to November 27, 1938. The strip was book-ended by segments showing Mickey as an actor cast by Walt Disney to play the role of a tailor in the film. Disney producer Harry Tytle took photos of Bill Tytla sitting on a stool so that Tytla could use it as a reference to animate the giant sitting on a cottage. This cartoon was one of the inspirations for the Sir Mickey's merchandise shop at the Magic Kingdom in Florida.

1939

Society Dog Show

February 3, 1939

Mickey tries to enter Pluto in a high-society dog show, but Pluto is kicked out because of his behavior. Pluto redeems himself when he rescues Fifi from a fire in the building.

Notes: This was the last cartoon before Mickey's design change, which included his "dot" eyes becoming the pupils he has today.

Mickey's Surprise Party *SPECIAL*

February 18, 1939

Minnie bakes cookies to impress Mickey but an accident in the kitchen with popcorn ruins them. Mickey and Pluto save the day by rushing to the store and purchasing a variety of Nabisco cookies, including Milk Bones for the dogs.

Notes: This five-minute commercial was made in Technicolor for the

National Biscuit Company (Nabisco) to show at their 1939 World's Fair pavilions in New York and San Francisco. In the VHS release *The Spirit of Mickey*, all the Nabisco packaging was replaced by generic products, and all of Minnie's lines referencing the names of the products were overdubbed by Russi Taylor. The cartoon is in the public domain. Mickey is featured with his new "pupil" eyes for the first time.

Walt Disney's Standard Parade for 1939! *special*

February 23, 1939

Mickey and Minnie lead the parade (with music and reused animation from the *Parade of the Award Nominees* short) of Disney characters, including Donald, Goofy, the Seven Dwarfs, the Three Little Pigs and the Big Bad Wolf, and Toby Tortoise.

Notes: This short was made for Standard Oil of California dealers to promote *Travel Tykes Weekly*, a four-page, full-color newspaper for kids with games, jokes, and drawings available only from Standard Oil gas stations. The short is in color, but there is a black-and-white, live-action segment with Walt in his office talking about the Disney Studio. The title card states *Walt Disney's Standard Parade for 1939!*, but directly underneath is copyright information for 1937.

The Pointer

July 21, 1939 | Direction: Clyde Geronimi

Mickey tries to train Pluto to be a quail hunting pointer dog, but they run into a huge, unfriendly bear who interrupts them.

Notes: The cartoon was nominated for an Academy Award but lost to another Disney cartoon, *Ugly Duckling*. It was the first general public release cartoon that showed Mickey's eyes with pupils. In addition, cels of Pluto were airbrushed to give him a more rounded, three-dimensional appearance. The animation of Mickey whistling and walking through the woods was reused in the Disneyland television episode "Tricks of Our Trade" in 1957. Pluto was omitted, and Mickey was redrawn wearing a different outfit and carrying a fishing pole instead of a shotgun. Originally, Mickey and Pluto were to be hunting deer until some people at the Disney Studio objected.

1940

Tugboat Mickey

April 26, 1940 | Director: Clyde Geronimi

Mickey is the captain of a tugboat. When he hears a distress signal, he fires up his crew of Goofy and Donald to proceed to the rescue. Unfortunately, a series of mishaps causes the boat to explode, but the distress signal turns out to be part of a radio drama.

Notes: The cartoon was the last of the "trio films" with Mickey, Donald, and Goofy.

Pluto's Dream House

August 30, 1940 | Director: Clyde Geronimi

Mickey decides to build Pluto a new house, but as they are breaking ground they find a magic lamp. Mickey uses the lamp to finish the job and take care of bathing Pluto. The lamp, however, hears snippets from the radio and misunderstands what it is supposed to do. In the end, it all turns out to be a dream.

Notes: The voice of the unseen genie in the lamp sounds like a gruff version of the black "Rochester" character from the Jack Benny show, so the cartoon is rarely seen today.

Mr. Mouse Takes a Trip

November 1, 1940 | Director: Clyde Geronimi

Mickey and Pluto go on a train trip, but since dogs are not allowed on the train, Mickey must try to hide Pluto and trick the conductor, a suspicious Pete.

Notes: Mickey and Pluto leave from a train station in Burbank, California, home of the Disney Studio, to Pomona, California, roughly a twenty-five mile trip. Live-action film footage exists of Walt Disney and Bill Bletcher at a recording session for this cartoon. It appears on the DVD *Walt Disney Treasures: Mickey Mouse in Living Color Volume Two*.

The Sorcerer's Apprentice (Fantasia)

November 13, 1940 | Director: James Algar

Based on the music of Dukas, the "Sorceror's Apprentice" segment inspired the creation of the feature film *Fantasia*.

In this classic tale, Mickey Mouse is an apprentice to the powerful sorcerer YenSid (Disney spelled backwards). Once his mentor leaves, Mickey uses the magical hat to make a broom do his chores of bringing in water from the well to fill the inside vat. As Mickey dreams, things get out of control and when he wakes the situation continues to escalate. Only the return of YenSid stems the rising tide of water and a contrite apprentice now must clean the damage in addition to his other chores.

Notes: This short cartoon cost over $125,000, three to four times the cost of a regular *Silly Symphony* short. Mickey does not talk in the short itself but only afterwards when he thanks conductor Leopold Stokowski.

1941

The Little Whirlwind

February 14, 1941 | Director: Riley Thomson

Mickey offers to clean Minnie's yard in exchange for a slice of the cake she is baking, but a little whirlwind and its much larger relative cause mischief and later total destruction.

Notes: The cartoon was the first attempt by animators to give Mickey two-toned, more three-dimensional ears. Mickey loses his tail when he dons his overalls (although Disney will later claim the tail is just tucked in to his pants). Some of the whirlwind animation was reused from the tornado in *The Band Concert* (1935). Director Thomson's name has sometimes been mistakenly spelled "Thompson" over the years. His Mickey shorts have been referred to around the Disney Studio as the "Drunk Mickeys" because of the fluidity and exaggeration of the character animation.

Cartoonist Walt Kelly, famed for his work on the comic strip *Pogo*, animated scenes of Mickey mowing with a lawnmower in mid-air and dodging various objects as they flew by, including an issue of a newspaper, the *Bridgeport Post*, where Kelly had worked as a younger man. He also animated Mickey in a bucket falling from the underside of a well and being sucked into the whirlwind on the end of a rope.

A Gentleman's Gentleman

March 28, 1941 | Director: Clyde Geronimi

Pluto behaves like Mickey's personal butler, serving him breakfast in bed and then rushing to the store to get a newspaper. However, Pluto loses the coin Mickey gave him to buy the newspaper, and hilarity ensues.

Notes: Mickey's two-tone ears are very noticeable in this short to give them the impression of three-dimensionally, but they just look odd. It must be Sunday, which is why Mickey can stay in bed, because the newspaper is huge with a front section of color comic strips including a six-panel episode of a Pluto comic strip. While Pluto never had a comic strip of his own, he did appear in a fourteen-week series in the Sunday *Silly Symphonies* newspaper strip in 1939-1940 as a test. Artist Bob Grant drew them from Hubie Karp's scripts.

Canine Caddy

May 30, 1941 | Director: Clyde Geronimi

Mickey goes golfing with Pluto as his caddy, but Pluto gets distracted by a destructive gopher.

Notes: Mickey has two-tone ears and no tail (unless it is tucked in his golf pants).

The Nifty Nineties

June 20, 1941 | Director: Riley Thomson

Taking place in the 1890s, Mickey and Minnie meet in a park, go on a date to a vaudeville show. and then experience trouble in a new-fangled "horseless carriage" automobile.

Notes: For this cartoon, *Pogo* cartoonist Walt Kelly drew storyboards and animated the scene where Mickey and Minnie tip their hats to Goofy as he rides by their old-fashioned car.

Orphans' Benefit

August 12, 1941 | Director: Riley Thomson

Mickey as the host of a theater show with Donald as a performer constantly harassed by the orphans.

Notes: The cartoon was a remake of the 1934 *Orphan's Benefit* using the same sound track and basic layout but updating the appearances of the characters. The apostrophe is now in the correct place in the title.

Lend a Paw

October 3, 1941 | Director: Clyde Geronimi

Pluto saves a kitten from drowning but gets jealous of Mickey's attention to it, and so debates about saving the kitten again when it falls into a well.

Notes: This Academy Award-winning cartoon is a remake of *Mickey's Pal Pluto* (1933) using some of the same elements but also with significant differences, such as updated appearances for Mickey and Pluto, and Pluto rescuing just one kitten instead of several as he had done in the original. Mickey must have his tail tucked in his shorts again. The opening title card stated: "This picture is dedicated to the Tailwagger Foundation in recognition of its work in lending a paw to man's animal friends."

1942

All Together *SPECIAL*

January 13, 1942 | Director: Ford Beebe

Disney made this three-minute film for the National Film Board of Canada to promote the sale of Canadian war bonds. It features a parade of marching Disney characters, with Mickey Mouse bringing up the rear on a float — in animation reused from *The Band Concert* (1935) — and conducting the band. The building that the characters parade past is the Canadian Parliament Building. This was the last of the four Canadian war bonds films made by Disney.

Mickey's Birthday Party

February 7, 1942 | Director: Riley Thomson

Minnie throws a surprise birthday party for Mickey while Goofy struggles to bake a birthday cake. Mickey is given an electric organ as a gift and uses it to perform.

Notes: The cartoon was inspired by *The Birthday Party* (1931) but with significant differences, such as the appearance of Donald Duck, Goofy, and Clara Cluck . Those characters did not exist in 1931.

Symphony Hour

March 20, 1942 | Director: Riley Thomson

Pete, a sponsor for a radio show that features classical music, hires Mickey's orchestra. The audition is wonderful but before the actual performance, Goofy drops all the instruments under an elevator. The resulting radio performance with the twisted instruments sounds like a Spike Jones concert.

Notes: The film marked the last theatrical appearance of Horace Horsecollar, Clarabelle Cow, and Clara Cluck for over 40 years until *Mickey's Christmas Carol* (1983). It was the last cartoon to feature Mickey's two-tone ears.

Out of the Frying Pan into the Firing Line *SPECIAL*

July 30, 1942 | Director: Jack King

Minnie and Pluto are taught the importance of saving bacon grease which can be turned into glycerin for cannon shells to aid the World War II effort. A framed picture of Mickey dressed as a soldier is glimpsed in Minnie's house.

Notes: This three-minute film was made for the Conservation Division of the War Production Board to illustrate the necessity of saving fat and grease.

1943

Pluto and the Armadillo

February 19, 1943 | Director: Clyde Geronimi

On a fifteen-minute re-fueling stopover in Belém, Brazil, during Mickey and Pluto's flight to Rio de Janeiro, Pluto mistakes a rolled-up armadillo for his favorite ball and takes him along for the rest of the trip.

Notes: The story was originally developed for *Saludos Amgios* (1942). It has the last appearance of Mickey's red two-button shorts until *Runaway Brain* (1995). Mickey's pith helmet covers both of his ears completely; they do not stick out like they do when he wears his other hats.

1946

Squatter's Rights
June 7, 1946 | Director: Jack Hannah

Prototype versions of Chip'n'Dale (both with black noses) take refuge for the winter in the stove in Mickey's cabin (which has a sign reading "Mickey's Hydout"). Mickey and Pluto show up for a vacation and Pluto tries to dislodge the intruders.

Notes: The cartoon was nominated for an Academy Award but lost to Tom and Jerry in *The Cat Concerto*. It was in production at the same time as *Mickey and the Beanstalk*. Jimmy MacDonald did the voice for Mickey.

1947

Mickey and the Beanstalk *SPECIAL*
September 27, 1947

Mickey, Donald, and Goofy climb a beanstalk to battle Willie the Giant and rescue the golden Singing Harp.

Notes: Originally called *The Legend of Happy Valley*, the cartoon was an adaptation of the famous Jack and the Beanstalk fairy tale, and part of the feature film *Fun and Fancy Free* (1947). It was the last time Walt Disney voiced Mickey Mouse in a theatrical cartoon. Roughly half-way through the production, Jimmy MacDonald took over as Mickey's voice. The film actually began production in 1940, but various factors including World War II delayed its completion.

When shown on the Disney weekly television show, two different endings were used. In one, Walt Disney talked to Willie the giant and told him Mickey was having a cheese souffle at the Brown Derby. In the other, Ludwig von Drake talks to Willie. This cartoon was one of the inspirations for the Sir Mickey's merchandise shop at the Magic Kingdom in Florida.

Mickey's Delayed Date
October 3, 1947 | Director: Charles Nichols

Mickey oversleeps and Minnie angrily phones to tell him that she has been waiting an hour for him to meet her for their date. In his rush out of the house, Mickey forgets the tickets and Pluto must save the day by grabbing them and racing after Mickey before he gets to the Hard Times Costume Party.

1948

Mickey Down Under
March 19, 1948 | Director: Charles Nichols

Mickey and Pluto visit Australia where Pluto has problems with a boomerang and Mickey has an encounter with an emu (which looks like an ostrich but there are no ostriches in Australia).

Notes: Toucans, bananas, and ostriches are not indigenous to Australia, and other aspects of flora and fauna in this cartoon are also incorrect.

Pluto's Purchase
July 9, 1948 | Director: Charles Nichols

Mickey sends Pluto to buy some sausages. After he buys them, Pluto must protect the sausages from Butch the Bulldog.

Mickey and the Seal
December 3, 1948 | Director: Charles Nichols

A baby seal from the zoo sneaks into Mickey's basket and finds a new temporary home in his bathtub much to the distress of Pluto.

Notes: Nominated for an Academy Award, *Mickey and the Seal* lost to the Tom and Jerry cartoon *The Little Orphan*. The film has a scene of Mickey in the bathtub completely naked except for his gloves.This short was originally intended to be a vehicle for Donald Duck but was re-done as a Mickey story.

1949

Pueblo Pluto
January 14, 1949 | Director: Charles Nichols

While on vacation at a Southwestern Indian village, Mickey goes into a souvenir store, leaving Pluto to get into trouble with a small dog and a big bone.

1950

Crazy Over Daisy *SPECIAL*
March 24, 1950 | Director: Jack Hannah

Within the first minute of the cartoon, Donald tips his hat to Mickey and Minnie driving down Main Street in a similar "horseless carriage" as that seen in the *Nifty Nineties* (1941).

1951

Plutopia
May 18, 1951 | Director: Charles Nichols

Mickey is on vacation at wonderful Camp Utopia but Pluto must stay outdoors leashed and muzzled, so the dog dreams of his own version of utopia with a cat servant.

R'coon Dawg
August 10, 1951 | Director: Charles Nichols

While hunting with Mickey, who is wearing a Davy Crockett-style coonskin cap, Pluto encounters a clever raccoon who always seems to get the upper hand.

1952

Pluto's Party
September 19, 1952 | Director: Milt Schaffer

The mice children come over to celebrate Pluto's birthday but end up being more of an annoyance to the poor pup.

Notes: This cartoon was the only one directed by Disney storyman Milt Schaffer who was also scheduled to direct the unmade Mickey cartoon, *The Talking Dog*, this same year.

Pluto's Christmas Tree
November 21, 1952 | Director: Jack Hannah

Mickey chops down a tree for Christmas not realizing it is the home of Chip'n'Dale. He accidentally brings them inside his house with the tree, and Pluto is continually thwarted in his attempts to show Mickey the truth.

Notes: The short ends with carolers Goofy, Donald, and Minnie on Mickey's front lawn singing "Deck the Halls".

How to Be a Detective *SPECIAL*
December 12, 1952

Mickey's face and name are on the back cover of the comic book Goofy is reading in the first minute of the cartoon.

1953

The Simple Things
April 18, 1953 | Director: Charles Nichols

Mickey and Pluto go fishing and confront a menacing clam and a clever hungry seagull.

Notes: This short is the last theatrical Mickey Mouse cartoon for the next thirty years.

1980

Mickey Mouse Disco *SPECIAL*
June 25, 1980

This seven-minute short includes footage from a number of classic cartoons with Mickey, Donald, and Goofy, and features a soundtrack from the 1979 Disney record album of the same name.

Notes: Basically a music video, *Mickey Mouse Disco* was often included in television compilation shows like *Mickey Mouse Tracks* and had a very brief theatrical release. The album tracks heard in the video were "Mousetrap", "Disco Mickey Mouse", "Watch Out For Goofy", "Macho Duck", and "Welcome To Rio".

1983

Mickey's Christmas Carol
October 20, 1983 | Director: Burny Mattinson

Uncle Scrooge plays Ebenezer Scrooge and Mickey his poverty-stricken clerk, Bob Crachit, in a loose adaptation of Charles Dickens' *A Christmas Carol*.

Notes: Inspired by *An Adaptation of Dickens' Christmas Carol*, a 1975 Disneyland Records Storyteller Album original musical, this film was co-written by actor Alan Young who supplied the voice of Scrooge McDuck. It was nominated for an Academy Award for Best Animated Short but lost to *Sundae in New York*. Wayne Allwine voiced Mickey Mouse for the first time theatrically, and Mark Henn animated Mickey for the first time.

1988

The Marathon *SPECIAL*
Release Date Unknown | Director: Misha Tumelya

A young boy in black silhouette goes to a line that divides the screen image in half vertically. It is like a mirror with the young boy on one side and the classic black-and-white Mickey Mouse in black silhouette on the other side. At the top of the screen is the number "1928", the year of Mickey's debut. The number clicks back to zero and then starts clicking upwards to the number 60. During this time, the young boy ages into a young man and finally an old, overweight man as he and Mickey dance and play to the music. When the ravages of age finally tire the old man, Mickey whistles for a chair. The old man sits on the chair as another young boy runs up to him. The man directs the boy back to the line where the number clicks to zero again, under the assumption that the same adventure will be repeated with this new boy and an ever-ageless Mickey.

Note: The cartoon, which ran just over two minutes, was animated by Sasha Dorogov and Alexandre Petrov. It was made in honor of Mickey's 60th birthday and presented to Roy E. Disney during his visit to Moscow's famed animation studio, Soyuzmultfilm Studios.

1989

Who Framed Roger Rabbit *special*

June 22, 1989 | Director: Richard Williams

Mickey Mouse only appears for about twenty-five seconds in a scene where detective Eddie Valiant, played by Bob Hoskins, is falling down the side of a building. Mickey is skydiving with a parachute and wears red goggles that he pulls up when he talks to Bugs Bunny and Valiant. Mickey and Bugs reappear for roughly another twenty-five seconds in the finale to comment on the death of Judge Doom and sing "Smile, Darn Ya, Smile".

Notes: Warner Bros was concerned about the use of their star characters and demanded that if Bugs Bunny appeared, he had to have exactly as much screen time as Mickey Mouse and the same number of lines. Wayne Allwine voiced Mickey, and Andreas Deja animated him. The film was produced in association with Steven Spielberg's Amblin Entertainment.

Michael and Mickey *special*

Release Date Unknown | Director: Jerry Rees

Mickey, done in CGI animation, walks into then Disney CEO Michael Eisner's office (where it is revealed that while Michael wears a Mickey Mouse watch, Mickey wears a Michael Eisner watch) to remind him they need to go to the screening room. As they walk down the hall, both live (like the evil queen from *Snow White*) and animated characters (like Roger Rabbit) stream out of offices and conference rooms to join the procession. In the screening room, the demon Chernabog sits in front of them and must be reminded that there are people behind him who want to see the screen.

Notes: The short was made at the Disney Studio in Burbank to introduce a "Coming Attractions" Disney movie reel at the end of the Backstage Tour at Disney-MGM Studios in Florida. It was shown in the Walt Disney Theater. Robert Zemeckis, who had just finished *Who Framed Roger Rabbit*, was hired to direct, but illness forced Disney to replace him. The animation was done by Mark Kausler, Steve Moore, Bruce W. Smith, David Spafford, and Frans Vischer. This two-minute clip was later shown as the opening of the television special: *Best of Disney — 50 Years of Magic* (1991).

1990

The Prince and the Pauper
October 20, 1990 | Director: George Scribner

Mickey, Donald, and Goofy help to set things right in this loose adaptation of the Mark Twain story in which a commoner and a member of royalty who look exactly alike trade places temporarily only to become embroiled in political turmoil.

Notes: Only the pauper is called Mickey; the Prince is referred to as Prince Mickey. Animator Andreas Deja did the animation for Mickey and considered the prince and the pauper as two separate characters: one who was Mickey and one who looked like Mickey but acted differently.

1991

Mickey's Big Break *SPECIAL*
Release Date Unknown | Director: Rob Minkoff

In this five-minute live-action film originally made for use at Disney-MGM Studios in Florida, a costumed Mickey Mouse struggles as an actor until he gets his big audition for Walt Disney (who is portrayed by Walt's nephew Roy E. Disney) in the final moments of the film, which includes cameos by many celebrities such as Mel Brooks, Ed Begley Jr., Angela Lansbury, and Dom DeLuise.

Notes: The film was made in 1991 as the prologue for a guest "screen test" attraction but never used. In December 1994, it was shown at the Main Street Cinema in Magic Kingdom, where it played until the Cinema closed in 1998. The film is sometimes called *Mickey's Audition*. The banner outside the Main Street Cinema read "World Premiere. Mickey's Big Break. The discovery of Hollywood's most animated star!" The banner was thirty-one inches tall and eleven feet wide.

1995

Runaway Brain

August 11, 1995 | Director: Chris Bailey

To earn enough money to take Minnie on a Hawaiian vacation, Mickey applies for a job with the sinister Dr. Frankenollie. The mad doctor switches Mickey's brain with that of his monstrous creation, Julius. Minnie is in peril until the two switch brains back again.

Notes: The film was nominated for the Academy Award for Best Animated Short but lost to *A Close Shave*. It was released in North American theatres in 1995 with *A Kid in King Arthur's Court*. Internationally, it was released a few months earlier with *A Goofy Movie*. *Runaway Brain* was later re-released in North American theatres with *George of the Jungle* in 1997.

2013

Get a Horse!

November 27 | Director: Lauren MacMullen

Mickey, Minnie, Horace Horsecollar, and Clarabelle Cow go on a musical hay wagon ride that is interrupted by Pete trying to run them off the road with his car. Mickey is thrown up against the screen, bursts through a hole, and lands in color and CGI on a 3-D stage. The characters chase each other back and forth from the stage to the screen, and in the process keep changing from full color 3-D to flat black-and-white.

Notes: The film debuted at the Annecy International Animated Film Festival on June 11. Walt Disney provided the voice of Mickey thanks to clips from his past performances as the character. Disney tried a unique marketing campaign suggesting this was a "lost, never seen" Disney short from 1928. In reality, it was newly made with a combination of hand-drawn, black-and-white 2D animation and full-color computer animation. The hand-drawn animation was supervised by Eric Goldberg and the computer animation by Adam Green.

Producer Dorothy McKim revealed:

> Our associate editor went through all the Mickey cartoons voiced by Walt, and it took her quite awhile. It was two to four months of really combing through them. And then, we'd think we had everything (for the dialog in the short) and we'd be like, "Oh, we still have to get this." We wanted to make it 100% authentic to Walt (voicing Mickey). There was one word we couldn't find. The one word was "red". We couldn't find it anywhere, so she had to build it out of syllables. That took two-and-a-half weeks.

They also utilized sound bites of Billy Bletcher as Pete and some of Marcellite Garner as Minnie from the original cartoon shorts.

After the animation was completed, the production team went back and frame-by-frame even added digital film damage to better replicate the era, including gate weave, emulsion flicker, cel paint mistakes, cut out overlay, and high contrast on individual lines.

Straight-to-Video Mickey Mouse Featurettes

Mickey's Once Upon a Christmas
November 9, 1999 | Director: Alex Mann

In this straight-to-video release with three separate segments linked through narration by actor Kelsey Grammer, Mickey and Minnie appear in an adaptation of the O. Henry story, "The Gift of the Magi". On Christmas Eve, Mickey trades his beloved harmonica for a chain for Minnie's watch, but Minnie has traded her treasured watch for a case for Mickey's harmonica.

Mickey, Donald, Goofy: The Three Musketeers
August 17, 2004 | Director: Donovan Cook

In this sixty-eight minute straight-to-video release, inspired by Alexandre Dumas' famous novel *The Three Musketeers*, Mickey, Donald, and Goofy are janitors who dream of becoming Musketeers. The villainous Pete, captain of the guards, assigns them to guard Princess Minnie, knowing their shortcomings will allow him to proceed with his evil plans to become king.

Notes: In the 1940s, Walt considered a feature film with these same three characters in the roles of Musketeers.

Mickey's Twice Upon a Christmas
November 2004 | Director: Matthew O'Callaghan

This straight-to-video sequel to *Mickey's Once Upon a Christmas* was created entirely with computer animation. Mickey appears in one of its five segments, "Mickey's Dog-Gone Christmas", in which Pluto makes a mess of things as Mickey is decorating for a Christmas party. Mickey sends Pluto to his doghouse, but Pluto runs away to the North Pole where he is adopted by Santa's reindeer. A distraught Mickey runs around town with "Lost Dog" posters and even turns for help to a department store Santa who turns out to be the real Santa. With the help of his reindeer, Santa drops Pluto off back home just in time for the party.

Television

Disneyland Television Show (1954–2008)

Mickey Mouse cartoons were a staple of the early Disney weekly television show, including the first episode, "The Disneyland Story" (October 27, 1954), which devoted half the show to "A Tribute to Mickey Mouse" with clips from *Plane Crazy*, *The Pointer*, *Lonesome Ghosts*, and "Sorcerer's Apprentice".

On that show Walt said:

> During the last few years, we've ventured into a lot of different fields. We've had the opportunity to meet and work with a lot of wonderful people. I only hope we never lose sight of one thing: that it was all started by a mouse. Now, that is why I want this part of the show to belong to Mickey, because the story of Mickey is truly the real beginning of Disneyland.

Those famous words were written not by Walt but by Jack Speirs, who wrote most of Walt's lead-ins (over three hundred of them) for the weekly television shows.

Here is a list of a few of the Mickey-centric episodes and some other episodes featuring new Mickey animation footage that aired on the Disneyland television show:

- "The Adventures of Mickey Mouse" (October 12, 1955)
- "On Vacation" (March 7 1956)
- "The Plausible Impossible" (October 31, 1956)
- "Tricks of Our Trade" (February 13, 1957)
- "Magic and Music" (March 19, 1958)
- "Four Tales of a Mouse" (April 16, 1958)
- "From All of Us to All of You" (December 19, 1958)
- "The Mickey Mouse Anniversary Show" (December 22, 1968). An edited version of this show was screened theatrically overseas in 1970. The live-action sequences were deleted and replaced by additional animated clips with new narration by Pete Renoudet.
- "Mickey's 50" (November 19, 1978) This episode ran 90 minutes.
- "Mickey's Greatest Adventures" (January 20, 1980)
- "Mickey and Donald Kidding Around" (September 24, 1983)

- "Mickey's Christmas Carol" (December 10, 1984)
- "Mickey's 60th Birthday" (November 13, 1988)
- "Mickey's Happy Valentine Special" (February 12, 1989)

First Mickey Mouse Animated Commercials (1954)

Phyllis Hurrell, Walt Disney's niece, set up a small area at the Disney Studio when she started work as the television commercial co-coordinator from 1954-1957. Using Disney animators and facilities, she produced commercials for such clients as 7-Up, Ipana Toothpaste, Mohawk Carpets, and others.

The commercials for American Motors (a sponsor both of the Disneyland weekly television show and the Circarama attraction at Disneyland) featured Disney characters hawking Nash Ramblers and the Ambassador.

Innovative artist Tom Oreb streamlined the design of the classic Disney characters for the American Motors commercials. Mickey was given a big "adult" suit and a triangular face. His iconic round ears were transformed into what looked like large floppy jungle plant leaves.

One of the more unusual American Motors commercials, featured Pluto napping by his doghouse when he is hit by an advertising flier for the 1955 Nash Ambassador and Statesman. He takes the flier to Mickey Mouse, who is relaxing in a hammock. Pluto is distracted by a cat eating out of his bowl and chases the feline through the yard and into the garage while the announcer (Bill Ewing) extols the benefits of how the car can turn and has a nice big windshield (since Pluto now has his head stuck in a fishbowl). Mickey is convinced and takes Pluto with him to go to the American Motors car dealership.

Directed by Nick Nichols and with Clarence "Ducky" Nash voicing Mickey Mouse, the commercial ran for 90 seconds and was completed on November 29, 1954.

Victor Haboush, who did background design on a number of the commercials, told animation historian Amid Amidi that when the Nash commercial aired with Mickey Mouse:

> There was a little kid that used to write Walt telling him to stay away from modern art because it's communistic. So when the commercial came on, he got a letter from this kid, a little malcontent somewhere

and he wrote, "I'm disappointed Walt. I never thought you'd succumb. What happened to you?" and Walt went crazy.

He stormed down there and outlawed us against using any of the Disney characters in commercials. I remember at the time everybody was incensed that we couldn't use them, and it basically spelled the end of the unit. [Companies] were coming for the celebrity, to be able to use Disney characters in commercials.

Another AMC commercial had Mickey conversing admiringly with his image in a mirror about the "dream" he is meeting (actually a car) and then joins Minnie Mouse who is resting comfortably in the passenger seat of a new Nash Rambler. Two talkative male mouse children in the back seat enjoy the "all season air conditioning".

Disney's official title for this ninety-second commercial, directed by Nick Nichols and completed on October 26, 1954, is "Mickey Mouse & Nephews". Ruth Clifford, who did Minnie Mouse's voice at the time, was also the voice for the nephews, "Marty and Morty" (rather than Morty and Ferdie as they were known elsewhere).

The AMC commercials were animated by regular Disney animators Jerry Hathcock (who did much of the work on all the Disney commercials), George Nicholas, and George Kreisl, with feature layouts by Tom Oreb. There are at least two other AMC commercials with Mickey that have not resurfaced yet, one with Pluto and one with Minnie. Both were completed in January 1955.

The Mickey Mouse Club (1955–1958)

In reference to an outline prepared for the Mickey Mouse Club (MMC) by its producer, Bill Walsh, in 1955, Disney historian George Grant stated:

> Realizing that the Disney name would be synonymous with cartoons, [producer] Bill Walsh assigned one quarter-hour to a short from the studio vault, while suggesting the show's opening and closing be animated to give the illusion of more cartoons than were really present.

At Walt Disney's personal request, Bill Justice and X. Atencio formed a separate unit at the Disney Studio to do the opening of the MMC. That opening, two minutes and forty seconds long, included animation and the "Mickey Mouse March", the familiar MMC song written by Jimmie Dodd: "Who's the leader of the club that's made for you and me?"

Walt paid extra to have the opening filmed in color even though it would air in black-and-white so that he might use it in the future, just as he did with many of his weekly television shows. In color, Mickey is wearing a completely red bandleader's outfit with a white feather on the front of his hat and holding a gold baton.

Mickey's introductory segment, filmed in a different outfit for each day of the week, was roughly twenty-five seconds each. The closing animation of Mickey saying good-bye was ten seconds each.

Even though sound effects man Jimmy MacDonald was voicing Mickey at the time, Walt himself stepped in and did the voice for these segments. It was the last time he would do Mickey's voice on film.

As MacDonald was preparing to record the introductions with Walt listening nearby, Walt turned to the sound crew and said, "Hey, don't forget. I do Mickey's voice, too!" MacDonald motioned for Walt to step to the microphone and Walt recorded the tracks.

Mickey's different outfits were:

- Monday: "Fun with Music Day"

  Mickey is dressed in a straw hat and striped jacket like a Main Street U.S.A. song-and-dance man (animated by Ollie Johnston).

- Tuesday: "Guest Star Day"

  Mickey is dressed in a tuxedo with white tie (animated by Ollie Johnston).

- Wednesday: "Anything Can Happen Day"

  Mickey is dressed in his "Sorcerer's Apprentice" outfit (animated by Hal King). (Mickey's robe is purple in the color version of this opening.)

- Thursday: "Circus Day"

  Mickey is dressed in a red bandleader outfit (animated by Hal King).

- Friday: "Talent Round-Up"

  Mickey is dressed as a rope-twirling cowboy (animated by John Lounsberry).

Near the last quarter of the show, different Mouseketeers would stand in front of the Mickey Mouse Treasure Mine and chant these lines to open the doors and find the name of the day's Mousekartoon:

Time to twist the mouse-ka-dial to the right and the left with a great big smile.

This is the way we get to see a Mouse-kar-toon for you and me.

Mee-ska! Moose-ka! Mouse-ke-teer! Mouse-kar-toon time now is here!

("Mousekartoon Time" words and music by Jimmie Dodd.)

The Mousekartoon segment was popular during the first season, running every day during the last quarter of the show and featuring cartoons from 1929–1936. During the second season, the cartoons were reduced to four days a week with two dozen repeats from the first season. More Donald Duck cartoons were shown, and the selection was from 1938–1948. For the third season, the cartoons were cut down to once (sometimes twice) a week, with more Pluto cartoons and the selection from 1939–1952. All were edited and broadcast in black and white.

Mickey Mouse Club authority George Grant wrote:

> The guy in charge of selecting and editing the cartoons for broadcasting was Bill Park. Editing generally consisted of removing the opening titles and credits, finding a suitable place to insert the commercial break, and a logical ending. Some cartoons consisted solely of an excerpt made from a longer animated feature, and some had parts excised for "appropriateness". Cartoons were a secondary responsibility for Park, his primary tasks being to supervise the creation of the newsreels, encyclopedia specials, and short serials.

The MMC also ran a special five-episode segment entitled "Karen in Kartoonland" where popular Mouseketeer Karen Pendleton would visit a Disney artist to learn how to draw. In the segment for February 2, 1956, she visited Bill Justice who showed her how to draw Mickey Mouse and had her model facial expressions that he then duplicated on Mickey's face.

The Disney Channel (1983–1998)

The Disney Channel broadcast several series consisting of classic Disney shorts that included many appearances of Mickey Mouse, such as *Good Morning, Mickey* (1983), *Donald Duck Presents* (1983), *Mouseterpiece Theater* (1983), *Mickey Mouse Tracks* (1992), *Donald's Quack Attack* (1992), and *The Ink and Paint Club* (1997).

Mickey Mouse Works (1999–2000)

The *Mickey Mouse Works* was a half-hour television series created to re-capture the spirit of the classic Disney shorts with newly made cartoons. The first season had 13 episodes; the second, 12. Each episode featured different shorts ranging in length from 90 seconds to 6-12 minutes. Some of the shorts were later rerun on *The House of Mouse*. The shorts with Mickey Mouse were:

1999

- "Pluto Gets the Paper: Bubble Gum" (90 seconds)
- "Pluto Gets the Paper: Spaceship" (90 seconds)
- "Mickey to the Rescue: Train Tracks" (90 seconds)
- "How to Be a Waiter"
- "Roller Coaster Painters"
- "Mickey's New Car"
- "Pluto's Penthouse Sweet"
- "Mickey's Airplane Kit"
- "Turkey Catchers"
- "Organ Donors"
- "Mickey's Mistake"
- "Donald's Valentine Dollar"
- "Pluto's Kittens"
- "Pluto vs. the Watchdog"
- "Around the World in Eighty Days"
- "Purple Pluto"
- "Sandwich Makers"
- "Mickey to the Rescue: Staircase" (90 seconds)
- "Pluto Runs Away"
- "Hansel and Gretel"
- "Mickey's Mechanical House"
- "Pluto Gets the Paper: Street Cleaner" (90 seconds)
- "Hydro Squirter"
- "Mickey's Piano Lesson"
- "Mickey to the Rescue: Cage and Cannons" (90 seconds)
- "Mickey's Remedy"
- "A Midsummer Nights Dream"
- "Mickey Tries to Cook"
- "Topsy Turvy Town"
- "The Nutcracker"
- "How to Haunt a House"
- "Pluto Gets the Paper: Vending Machine" (90 seconds)
- "Mickey Foils the Phantom Blot"
- "Daisy's Road Trip"
- "Gift of the Magi"

2000

- "Locksmiths"
- "Minnie Takes Care of Pluto"
- "Mickey's Rival Returns"
- "Mickey and the Seagull"
- "Car Washers"
- "Pluto's Seal Deal"
- "Mickey's Mixed Nuts"
- "Mickey's Mountain"
- "computer.don"
- "Donald's Halloween Scare"
- "Pluto Gets the Paper: Mortimer" (90 seconds)
- "Mickey's Mixup"
- "Mickey's Christmas Chaos"
- "Mickey's Cabin"
- "Mickey's Answering Service"
- "Pluto's Magic Paws"
- "Mickey's Big Break"

Disney's House of Mouse (2001–2003)

Disney's House of Mouse was a half-hour show produced by Disney Television Animation that had Mickey running a Toontown nightclub similar to the famous *House of Blues* with dinner and performances in an elegant setting.

The comical mishaps from operating such a venue formed the framework for newly-made cartoons, Disney classic cartoons, and some shorts from the *Mickey Mouse Works*. Fifty-two episodes were produced.

Executive producers Tony Craig and Bobs Gannaway came up with the idea of a nightclub where "characters who usually do the entertaining are being entertained on their night off". In reference to the eight-ten minutes of new animation wrapped around the cartoons, Gannaway said:

> We put the characters in a contemporary environment and modern dress to represent their day-to-day life. They are not bookends. They are part of the show. We even added sponsor parodies such as flying-safety tips presented by Peter Pan and courtesy of Dumbo Airlines.

Two films were made:

- *Mickey's Magical Christmas: Snowed in at the House of Mouse* (2001) with the Mickey cartoons *Pluto's Christmas Tree* and *Mickey's Christmas Carol*
- *Mickey's House of Villains* (2002) with the Mickey cartoons *Lonesome Ghosts* and *Mickey's Mechanical House*

Mickey is also prominently featured in these *House of Mouse* cartoons:

2001

- Hickory Dickory Mickey
- Pit Crew
- Big House Mickey
- Mickey's April Fools
- How To Be Groovy, Cool and Fly

2002

- Mickey and the Goatman
- Pinball Mickey
- Housesitters
- Babysitters
- Mickey and the Color Caper

Mickey Mouse Clubhouse (2006–2014)

Mickey Mouse Clubhouse is a computer-animated interactive series that premiered in prime time on the Disney Channel on May 5, 2006. It is the only Mickey Mouse series specifically aimed at pre-schoolers to help them learn problem-solving skills. The series was part of the *Playhouse Disney* block of programming from 2006-2011 and then became part of Disney Junior.

Mickey gathers his friends Minnie, Donald, Daisy, Goofy, and Pluto at the clubhouse and shares with them a problem. They go to the Mousekadoer, a giant Mickey-head-shaped computer that distributes the tools needed to solve the challenge. These tools are downloaded into Toodles, a small, Mickey-head-shaped flying extension of the Mousekadoer who joins them on their adventure.

Mickey Mouse (2013–)

This new series was announced in March 2013 with the first short (*No Service*) premiering on The Disney Channel on June 28. Actor Chris Diamantopoulos voices Mickey Mouse. It's created by a thirty-person team in Burbank and an animation team in Canada using Flash software called Harmony, with background done in Photoshop.

There are a total of nineteen cartoons, each running three-and-a-half minutes, with one of them seven minutes. Each cartoon finds Mickey in a different modern setting such as Santa Monica, New York, Paris, Beijing, Tokyo, Venice, and the Alps, facing a silly situation, a quick complication, and an escalation of physical and visual gags.

Emmy Award-winning artist and director Paul Rudish (*Star Wars: Clone Wars, Dexter's Laboratory, Powerpuff Girls*) is the executive producer and director. Aaron Springer (*SpongeBob SquarePants, Gravity Falls*) and Clay Morrow (*Dexter's Laboratory, The Powerpuff Girls*) are directors, and Joseph Holt (*Sym-Bionic Titan*) is the art director. The series is produced under the supervision of senior vice presidents Eric Coleman and Lisa Salamone at Disney Television Animation.

Coleman told animation historian and author Jerry Beck:

> The goal is to introduce Mickey to a new generation of kids and at the same time entertain their parents who have their memories of Mickey Mouse. Our intention is to highlight his personality and show him as the star he has always been. Making them feel contemporary doesn't mean give them an iPhone and headphones; it's the execution, the sensibility, the tone, the way they are animated, the music the movement, the timing, the editing. We wanted to make shorts that would play well globally. We have Disney Channels around the world.

The following cartoons were released by the time this book was published:

- "No Service" (Director: Paul Rudish. June 28, 2013)
- "Yodelberg" (Director: Aaron Springer. June 29, 2013)
- "Croissant de Triomphe" (Director: Paul Rudish. June 30, 2013)
- "New York Weenie" (Director: Aaron Springer. July 5, 2013)
- "Tokyo Go" (Director: Paul Rudish. July 12, 2013)
- "Stayin' Cool" (Director: Dave Wasson. July 19, 2013)
- "Gasp!" (Director: Clay Morrow. July 26, 2013)
- "Panda-monium" (Director: Aaron Springer. August 2, 2013)
- "Bad Ear Day" (Director: Chris Savino. August 16, 2013)
- "Ghoul Friend" (Director: Aaron Springer. October 4, 2013)

- "Dog Show" (Director: Dave Wasson. October 11, 2013)
- "O Sole Minnie" (Director: Paul Rudish. October 18, 2013)
- "Potatoland" (Director: Aaron Springer. November 18, 2013)
- "Sleepwalkin'" (Director: Paul Rudish. December 5, 2013)
- "Flipperboobootosis" (Director: Paul Rudish. January 3, 2014)
- "Tapped Out" (Director: Clay Morrow. January 10, 2014)
- "Third Wheel" (Director: Clay Morrow. February 14, 2014)
- "The Adorable Couple" (Director: William Reiss. March 7, 2014)
- ""Cable Car Chaos" (Director: Aaron Springer. April 11, 2014)
- "Fire Escape" (Director: Paul Rudish. April 25, 2014)
- "Eau de Minnie" (Director: Paul Rudish. May 23, 2014)
- "O Futebol Classico" (Director: Paul Rudish. June 6, 2014)
- "Down the Hatch" (Director: Paul Rudish. June 20, 2014)
- "Goofy's Grandma" (Director: Aaron Springer. July 11, 2014)
- "Captain Donald" (Director: Paul Rudish. August 8, 2014)
- "Mumbai Madness" (Director: Paul Rudish. October 2, 2014)
- "Space Walkies" (Director: Paul Rudish. November 7, 2014)
- "Mickey Monkey" (Director: Aaron Springer. November 18, 2014)
- "Clogged" (Director: Paul Rudish. December 12, 2014)
- "Goofy's First Love" (Director: Clay Morrow. January 9, 2015)
- "Doggone Biscuits" (Director: Eddie Trigueros. January 16, 2015)

The Academy of Television Arts & Sciences juried winners for the 65th Emmy Awards (2013) included two who worked on *Croissant de Triomphe*: Jenny Gase-Baker (Background Paint) and Joseph Holt (Art Direction). In the regular competitive categories, *Croissant de Triomphe* won the Emmy for Outstanding Short-format Animated Program.

"By bringing Mickey's comedic adventures to life with vitality, humor, inventiveness, and charm, the entire Disney Television Animation team of artists, animators, and directors have worked to capture the essence of what Walt Disney himself created 85 years ago," said Disney Channel's Worldwide President and Chief Creative Officer Gary Marsh.

Easter Eggs on Walt Disney Treasures

Mickey Mouse in Black and White (Volume One)

From the Disc 1 bonus features menu, highlight Mickey's cowboy hat and press "Enter" for a newsreel about the original Mickey Mouse Club in Worchester from the 1930s and a sing-along of "Minnie's Yoo Hoo".

Mickey Mouse in Living Color (Volume One)

From the Disc 1 main menu, select Mickey's head and press "Enter" to view a 2½-minute excerpt from Walt's first anthology episode, "The Disneyland Story" (1954), and his famous "It was all started by a mouse" speech.

From the Disc 2 main menu, press "Up" to highlight the "O" in the name "Mickey Mouse" at the top of the screen. Pressing "Enter" plays the short *Mickey's Surprise Party*.

Mickey Mouse in Living Color (Volume Two)

From the Disc 1 main menu, highlight the cane under Mickey and Pluto, then press "Enter" for an 11½-minute black-and-white film clip of Walt Disney and Billy Bletcher recording lines of dialogue for Mickey Mouse and Pete, respectively, for the short *Mr. Mouse Makes a Trip*.

From the Disc 1 bonus features menu, press "Down" until a musical note becomes highlighted on the right-hand side, then press "Enter" to see a 1939 promo film Walt Disney made for Standard Oil which includes a brief history of the Disney Studio and a Technicolor short featuring Disney characters on parade in support of Standard.

Mickey at the Parks

In the summer of 1964, I took our two oldest sons to California to visit Disneyland. We met Mickey Mouse. We were struck by his great, childlike presence and how he embodied so much of Walt's wise, playful spirit. Walt was so magnificently human and friendly. We still see Mickey at the parks and think of Walt.

— Former President Gerald Ford, 2003

A Mickey Mouse Park

With the success of Mickey Mouse, Walt Disney found himself flooded with requests from people wanting to come and visit the Disney Studio to meet Mickey Mouse in person. The Disney Archives has a copy of a letter from silent screen star Mary Pickford making a similar request in the early 1930s. Disney Legend Ward Kimball remembered that Walt told him:

> You know, it's a shame people come to Hollywood and find there's nothing to see. Even the people who come to this studio. What can they see? A bunch of guys bending over drawings. Wouldn't it be nice if people could come to Hollywood and see something?

Walt purchased two 1931 Austin roadsters (only 1,500 were built from 1931 through 1934) and housed them in a small garage on the Hyperion lot between the sound stage and the Comic Strip Department bungalow. Above the two doors were triangular nameplates that said "Mickey" and "Minnie".

Along the sides of the car doors was the iconic image of a smiling Mickey Mouse with outstretched hand. The small sedan Austin roadster was popular among celebrities like comedian Buster Keaton.

The cars were to serve a special purpose in addition to general transportation and for parking outside theaters to promote Mickey's films, as recounted by Pulitzer Prize-winning author Henry Pringle, who visited Walt at the Hyperion Studio and wrote about it in an article entitled "Mickey Mouse's Father" (*McCall's* August 1932):

> The best clues to Walt Disney, the creator of Mickey Mouse, are to be found in a large building of white stucco located on the outskirts of Los Angeles, just off Hollywood Boulevard. Mickey himself, his hand stretched out in welcome, is perched on top of an electric sign which announces that this is the Walt Disney Studio.

> The courtyard is divided, in California style, into little sections of green grass. There is a ping pong table in one corner, where, if it is the lunch hour, some people are playing. At the extreme right is a two-car garage: a miniature garage in which two very small sedans are kept.

> Name-plates proclaim that Mickey owns one of the cars and Minnie, his playmate and leading woman, the other... As a matter of fact, the two small automobiles are entirely serviceable and are used by the studio staff... Mickey gets bags of fan mail from children throughout the world and his picture is mailed to thousands who ask for it.

> The embarrassment arises when some small boy or girl gets into the studio. Such visits are not encouraged, for they often end in disappointment. One little girl of five, the daughter of a friend, confronted Disney one day and demanded that he produce Mickey in person.

"He's gone to the grocery for some cheese," answered Disney, a stock excuse for such crises.

"Why hasn't he taken his car?" she demanded suspiciously, pointing to the dwarfed sedan which stood in front of the garage.

Disney did some fast thinking, "Why you see," he said, "Mickey was getting fat and has been ordered to walk several miles every day. He's gone to a grocery at the other end of town. He won't be back for hours."

After the Disney Studio moved to its Burbank location, Walt developed an idea for an amusement area that would be located on an eight acre parcel of land across Riverside Drive from the Disney Studio.

In an August 31, 1948, memo to Dick Kelsey, an art director at the Disney Studio who would later be involved in designing Disneyland, Walt elaborated on his "Mickey Mouse Park" that would have included a train, a Western village, a singing waterfall, a carousel, a doll store and hospital for the sale and repair of Disney dolls, as well as small statues of the Disney characters, especially Mickey, for photo opportunities.

Karal Ann Marling, in her book *Designing Disney's Theme Parks: The Architecture of Reassurance* (Flammarion 1997), wrote:

Children from every corner of the country wrote to Walt, wanting to come to Hollywood and see the place where Mickey Mouse lived. There really wasn't much to see. But a little park, with statues of Mickey and the other characters, with picnic tables, grass, and trees. A place for all the kids who wanted to meet Mickey [was Walt's plan].

Burbank officials saw a "Mickey Mouse Park" as just another noisy, unsafe carnival that attracted unsavory people to the area, so it refused to sanction Walt's proposal. In response, Walt expanded upon his idea, purchased land in Anaheim, and built Disneyland.

In 1985, Disney Legend Ken Anderson, who had worked on the early Disneyland, recalled:

People forget that one of Walt's first ideas for Disneyland was called "Mickey Mouse Park". Mickey was always a big part of the idea.

However, when concerns arose even at the studio that Disneyland might not be a successful venture, Mickey's role in the park was kept to a minimum. In particular, Walt's brother Roy expressed that he would like Mickey's involvement minimized so the brand would not be damaged if the park failed.

As a result, the front of the park only sported nothing more than an impressive floral image of Mickey's face similar to the title card at the beginning of a Mickey animated short, with some park specific merchandise featuring the Mouse available inside.

There was no Mickey attraction, though Walt had considered putting a Mickey Mouse Clubhouse on Tom Sawyer's Island to tie in with his new television program, the *Mickey Mouse Club*.

The Mickey Mouse Club Theater (later re-named the Fantasyland Theater) in Fantasyland at Disneyland did at one time show a continuing half-hour loop of three color Mickey cartoons: *Mickey's Trailer* (1938), *Through the Mirror* (1936), and *The Band Concert* (1935).

The six screens (which were arranged in a semi-circular pattern) in the Main Street Cinema showed silent live-action movies like *The Great Train Robbery* (1903) and one animated feature, Winsor McCay's *Gertie the Dinosaur* (1914). Later, a silent version of *Steamboat Willie* (1928) was added to the mix.

In 1978, to celebrate Mickey's 50th birthday, the Cinema showed only Mickey cartoons but in black-and-white and without their soundtracks: *Steamboat Willie, Plane Crazy, The Dognapper, Traffic Trouble, The Moose Hunt,* and *Mickey's Polo Team.* Many guests assumed they were old silent cartoons.

In their book *Walt Disney Imagineering* (Hyperion 1996), Imagineers Kevin Rafferty and Bruce Gordon wrote that:

> [Mickey Mouse] lent us a hand in giving all our parks a most magical character.

At first, however, Mickey was the unseen host. A Mickey Mouse attraction would not appear in a Disney theme park until 1971 and the opening of the Magic Kingdom in Florida.

Mickey Mouse Attractions

Mickey Mouse Revue

When the Magic Kingdom opened in 1971, its signature attraction was the *Mickey Mouse Revue*, a show created primarily by Disney Legend Bill Justice featuring over eighty Audio-Animatronics Disney characters. In 1999, Justice recalled:

> [Walt Disney Imagineering] had designed some imaginative shows for the parks, but we seemed to be getting away from our heritage. What we needed was a reminder of what Walt had accomplished. I pulled out a sheet of paper and got to work. Mickey Mouse would have to be the main figure.
>
> The show we had in mind was this: Mickey Mouse would lead an orchestra of Studio characters through a medley of Disney tunes. Then on the sides of the stage and behind the orchestra, scenes from our most popular animated features would appear one by one. Mickey and his orchestra would close the performance.
>
> [Walt's brother] Roy looked the model over, then paid me the best compliment I ever had in my career: "This is the kind of show we should spend our money on." That's how the *Mickey Mouse Revue* was born.
>
> One big problem surfaced: Mickey. With 33 functions crammed into a 42-inch body, he was the most complex audio-animatronics figure to date. He also became my biggest programming challenge because I had to do extreme movements so it would appear that Mickey was keeping up with the tempo.

An eight-minute pre-show gave an overview of Mickey's animated career as well as the use of sound in animation.

On September 14, 1980, the *Mickey Mouse Revue* closed at Walt Disney World and was moved to Tokyo Disneyland, where it was an opening day attraction in April 1983 and continued to operate there until May 2009.

At the Magic Kingdom, the building that housed the *Mickey Mouse Revue* was eventually re-named the Royal Fantasyland Concert Hall and became home in 2003 to another Mickey attraction, *Mickey's PhilharMagic*.

Mickey's PhilharMagic

Mickey's PhilharMagic opened in Fantasyland at Walt Disney World's Magic Kingdom on October 3, 2003, as a 4-D attraction, meaning that in addition to a 3-D film, the show features other elements like scents, water effects, and a three-dimensional figure moving in the theater.

The twelve-minute film, written by Alex Mann and directed by George Scribner, who also directed the animated feature *Oliver and Company* (1988), recounts the misadventures of Donald Duck after he borrows Mickey Mouse's magical hat from the "Sorcerer's Apprentice". Donald is swept away into several different Disney animated feature scenarios as he tries to catch the errant hat.

Although the premise is that Mickey Mouse (voiced by Wayne Allwine) will conduct the PhilharMagic Orchestra, just as he had led several other orchestras in his short cartoons, Mickey appears only briefly at the beginning and end of the show.

Mickey's Birthdayland/ Mickey's Starland

One of the biggest complaints by guests at the Magic Kingdom was that they weren't guaranteed an opportunity to meet Mickey Mouse in person or snap a souvenir photo or get an autograph.

So, for Walt Disney World's eighteen-month promotional event celebrating Mickey Mouse's 60th birthday, a temporary area was quickly built in Fantasyland called Mickey's Birthdayland.

Creative Director Steve Hanson of Walt Disney Entertainment was the show writer and the director for this new land, the first ever added to the original Magic Kingdom (and also the smallest).

Cindy Williams (who then starred in the popular television program *Laverne & Shirley*) and First Lady Nancy Reagan were on hand to open Mickey's Birthdayland on June 18, 1988. Williams cut the ribbon officially dedicating the area, which had been built with facades indicating it was the town of Duckburg, the home of Donald Duck and his friends, according to the comic books.

(Toontown, the official home for all toons, would not exist until the release of *Who Framed Roger Rabbit* on June 22, 1988.)

Guests could enter Mickey Mouse's house to take pictures and eventually meet Mickey himself after a live stage performance of *Minnie's Surprise Party* (for Mickey Mouse).

The new land had a small playground, a petting farm, and a child-friendly roller-coaster attraction called Goofy's Barnstormer.

Mickey's Birthdayland was so popular that instead of closing it after 18 months, as had been planned, it remained open until April 22, 1990, and only closed then so it could be re-themed as Mickey's Starland, which opened on May 26, 1990. The birthday theme was no longer appropriate and it was hoped that the new version of the land could be used to promote the stars of the *Disney Afternoon* syndicated television package.

Mickey's Toontown/
Mickey's Toontown Fair

Mickey's Starland was also unbelievably popular, so Disney executives decided to re-create it for Disneyland in a more elaborate form called Mickey's Toontown.

The Imagineering storyline was that Mickey and his friends had lived in Anaheim, even before Disneyland was built, and that their presence was one of the reasons Walt had chosen Anaheim as the location for his theme park.

However, by 1993, it was time to tear down the wall that separated the town from the park and welcome guests to come and visit, so on January 24, 1993, Mickey's Toontown opened at Disneyland. As expected, it was embraced eagerly by the guests.

On October 1 1996, to mark Walt Disney World's 25th anniversary, Mickey's Starland in the Magic Kingdom became the more elaborate Mickey's Toontown Fair, inspired by Disneyland's Toontown.

Although Mickey and the gang still lived in Toontown in California, the Florida location became their vacation home. They were on vacation, in part, because it was the time of year for the big Fair, and traditionally Mickey was one of the judges. He took such pride in being a judge that he appears that way on the entrance sign and his judging outfit is hung with care in the bedroom of his home.

The centerpiece of Mickey's Toontown Fair was a chance to visit the four-room (bedroom, living room, game room, kitchen) interior of Mickey's Country House. The living room and the game room each featured a strong sports theme. The kitchen was in the midst of a disastrous remodel for a contest by Mickey's friends Donald Duck and Goofy.

Inside Mickey's bright yellow house everything is "mouse-ified", from the design of such items as checkers, chairs, and plants with the famous three-circle icon to references to Mickey's favorite food, a variety of cheeses.

Unlike his former house in Mickey's Birthdayland, the Disney Imagineers designed this house with curves and the animated "stretch and squash" architecture that echoes a major principle of Disney cartoon animation.

During construction, both Mickey and Minnie's houses provided difficulties for builders used to straight, level lines rather than "toony" curves. It was the same problem they faced when building a similar house for Mickey's Toontown at Disneyland, where the designs originated.

Mickey was never at home when guests arrived at his door because he was in the Judge's Tent next door participating in the activities of the fair.

A walk-through tour of Mickey's home not only gave guests a clever glimpse into the lifestyle of the world's most famous mouse but also showcased an endless selection of humorous details.

Mickey's bedroom had an open closet filled with the same pressed black, white, and red suits that he always wears. A drawer overflowed with the famous four-fingered white gloves. A huge pair of glasses on the bed implied that the Mouse's eyes may finally have succumbed to age. The room was filled with pictures and memorabilia that logically would be in Mickey's house, such as photos of him as a baby, posing with Santa, and as a Boy Scout.

Just outside the bedroom, by Mickey's telephone, was a stack of mail including a package from Peter Pan with the notation "use no hooks", referring to Peter's nemesis Captain Hook. A letter from Buzz Lightyear had the return address "Infinity and Beyond" and another from Ariel the Little Mermaid was sent from "Under the Sea".

The living room, recently abandoned because Mickey lost track of the time and had to rush to his appointment in the Judge's tent, showed signs that Mickey and his friends had been watching a sports competition between Duckburg University and Goofy Tech. Pennants, pompoms, and popcorn were scattered around, and the television still broadcast news of the big game.

Mickey loved sports and his game room was filled with activities and some clever, often unnoticed pieces of humor like a real rubber dart hitting a picture of Donald Duck's rear end as he is golfing. Trophies and memorabilia filled the room. A scoreboard showed that Mickey was winning at a ping pong game.

Directly across from the game room was Mickey's kitchen, completely unusable because Donald and Goofy have entered the Toontown Fair Kitchen Remodeling Competition and have left the work unfinished. There was a dangerously tipping stack of paint cans in the sink, makeshift wiring hung from the top, tools and blueprints scattered around, paint splattered on the wall and the cabinets, and more. The observant guest would see red hidden Mickeys in the wallpaper. In fact, the entire house was filled with hidden Mickeys scattered among the more obvious decorative Mickeys.

The kitchen blueprints were from the Chinny Chin Construction Company headed by general contractor Practical Pig, a reference to the Three Little Pigs, and the plans included a garbage disposal that is merely a pig under a sink, among other amusing possibilities.

On Mickey's stove there was a heating dial that indicated "volcano heat", a reference to the cartoon *Mickey's Surprise Party* (1939) where Goofy uses that setting to quickly bake Mickey's birthday cake.

Pluto's doghouse outside had bone-shaped wind chimes. The doghouse seemed a little plain and unused, but that's because Pluto probably stayed inside with Mickey most of the time. In fact, a screen over a pet gate leading to Mickey's bedroom showed the silhouette of Pluto bursting through to join his master.

While it might surprise some people that Mickey Mouse is quite the gardener, the classic short *Mickey's Garden* (1935) reveals his previous experience, especially with oversized items. Mickey's Mousekosh overalls hung outside awaiting his return from the Judge's Tent.

Mickey's cactus garden has grown into the shapes of his toon friends. His pumpkins (the "Pumpkin Pie Are Squared" variety) were huge thanks to the special growth mixture, Super Toon Plant Food, that Mickey borrowed from Minnie, who lived next door. There was also a healthy crop of large tomatoes, labeled "Hollywooden Vine Tomatoes" of the species "Maximus Ketchupicus".

After exiting Mickey's backyard garden, guests could return to Mickey's Toontown Fair through Mickey's garage or enter the Judge's Tent for a private meeting with Mickey himself. In the Judge's Tent, a video pre-show of Mickey's animated exploits entertained guests as they waited to meet the Big Cheese.

The Toontown Hysterical Film Society had set up an old sheet and projector to show Mickey's *History of the Fair*, and some of the upcoming programs advertised were *The Art of Crop Dusting* by Goofy and Minnie's film *Paint Yourself Silly*.

Like his house, Mickey's garage was filled with wonderful details such as a "Last Aid" kit (rather than a "First Aid" kit) for emergencies, Craftmouse tools, and books with clever titles like *Build a Staircase in 3 Easy Steps*, *Repairing Electrical and Bermuda Shorts*, *How to Toon Up Your Car*, *Replace Your Wheels Without Tiring*, and *The Auto-Biography of Susie the Blue Coupe — It's Not the Years, It's the Mileage*. That last book title is a reference to a Disney cartoon short, *Susie the Little Blue Coupe* (1952), which helped inspire the character designs for the Disney-Pixar film *Cars* (2006).

On an upper shelf was Mickey's mailbox from his original house in Mickey's Birthdayland. Another shelf had cans of Mohave Oil, the oil company whose tanker truck runs into trouble at Catastrophe Canyon in Disney's Hollywood Studios.

A picture can be worth a thousand words. On the wall of Mickey's garage was a framed picture of Mickey fishing with Pluto. It is from the cartoon called *The Simple Things* (1953), the last of the regular series of Mickey Mouse theatrical shorts for the next thirty years. Up above in the rafters were framed posters of some of Mickey's classic cartoons like *Mickey's Good Deed* (1932) and *Mickey's Nightmare* (1932). *Mickey's Good Deed* is the story of an impoverished Mickey and his dog Pluto, and how their friendship is put to the test at Christmastime. *Mickey's Nightmare* involves a dream where Mickey marries Minnie with a frightening outcome.

The house next door painted pink and lavender and covered with hearts was the country home of Mickey's long-time girlfriend, Minnie Mouse, and her living room was filled with framed pictures of her with Mickey.

Mickey's Toontown Fair was closed on February 11, 2011, in order to build the New Fantasyland extension. In the process, both Mickey and Minnie's houses were demolished, though different versions of them still exist at Disneyland's Mickey's Toontown.

Town Square Theater

On April 1, 2011, Town Square Theater opened on Main Street U.S.A. in the Magic Kingdom as a new meet-and-greet area for Mickey and Minnie. Officially, it is entitled Backstage Magic with Mickey Mouse, and themed as "Mickey the Magnificent" preparing to do a magic show but who takes time to meet guests in his dressing room. Tributes and references to Disney films and theme park attractions are placed throughout the theater.

Jason Grandt, WDI (Walt Disney Imagineering) Concept Designer said:

> Upon entering the lobby, guests will be faced with a beautiful tile mosaic featuring the Town Square Theater logo. The color scheme reflects that of historical theaters with a little inspiration from our master magician, Mickey Mouse.

Jon Georges, WDI Director and Senior Show Producer explained:

> You will recognize the poster style as that of turn-of-the-century magicians such as Houdini. But these posters carry Mickey's magical touch that can bring them to life and interact with you as you wait.

Town Square Theater was the first location to use FastPass for meeting Disney characters.

Fantasmic!

Fantasmic! is a complex, night-time entertainment show combining water effects, fireworks, film, music, and dozens of live performers at Disneyland, Walt Disney World, and Tokyo Disneyland. These three versions have significant differences, though the basic premise remains the same.

Fantasmic! debuted at Disneyland in 1992. Originally, the show was going to be called *Imagination*, but the Disney Company could not copyright that title so created a uniquely Disney-esque word.

The opening narration sets the story for the show:

> Welcome to *Fantasmic!* Tonight, our friend and host Mickey Mouse uses his vivid imagination to create magical imagery for all to enjoy. Nothing is more wonderful than the imagination. For, in a moment, you can experience a beautiful fantasy. Or, an exciting adventure!
>
> But beware — nothing is more powerful than the imagination. For it can also expand your greatest fears into an overwhelming nightmare. Are the powers of Mickey's incredible imagination strong enough, and bright enough, to withstand the evil forces that invade Mickey's dreams?
>
> You are about to find out. For we now invite you to join Mickey, and experience *Fantasmic!* — a journey beyond your wildest imagination...

In the end, Mickey defeats the Disney villains who have invaded his peaceful animated dreams, including the evil Maleficent who transforms herself into a massive dragon.

Mickey Mouse Attractions
Planned But Never Built

Disney Legend Ward Kimball proposed two Mickey Mouse-themed attractions that never evolved off the drawing board.

In 1976, Kimball designed an indoor dark ride called Mickey's Mad House. Using a traditional Wild Mouse Coaster similar to the Primeval Whirl in Disney's Animal Kingdom, guests would have careened madly back and forth, not able to see clearly where they were going, while they experienced the wild antics of early black-and-white Mickey Mouse animated cartoons.

In the early 1980s, a Movie Pavilion was planned for EPCOT's Future World between the Imagination Pavilion and The Land Pavilion. The new pavilion would have included a version of The Great Movie Ride, and Kimball came up with an additional dark ride for the pavilion tentatively called Mickey's Movie Land that would have allowed guests in Omnimover vehicles to glimpse a tongue-in-cheek, behind-the-scenes process of the making of a classic Mickey Mouse cartoon.

Floral Mickey

When Disneyland opened in July 1955, the first thing guests saw was the huge, smiling face of Mickey Mouse created in colorful flowers at the entrance of the park. Disney Legend Bill Evans, who supervised the landscaping of both Disneyland and Walt Disney World, claimed:

> It was the most photographed location at Disneyland. Everybody took a picture standing in front of it.

In a 1985 interview with me, Evans said:

> It was Walt's idea. Just like the face [on the title card] before every [theatrical] Mickey [Mouse] cartoon and audiences would start cheering and applaud.

Evans built a light wooden framework for the outline of the head and individual sections like the eyes, ears, and nose, and then filled in the framework with thousands of plants.

Depending upon the seasons and what bedding plants and annuals were available, or even upon the whim of the landscapers, the colors might change drastically.

Over the years, the shape of Mickey's head, as well as the individual facial elements inside of it, has changed significantly while still remaining identifiable as Mickey Mouse. For example, sometimes the mouth will be designed to be wider or larger.

Special limited-edition, "occasion-themed" variations have also appeared, such as an orange pumpkin version for Halloween. Today, it takes over 4,500 plants to make Mickey's face. The whole display can take around 7,000 plants.

Originally, the face was just called the Mickey Mouse Planter, but in recent years it has been referred to as the Floral Mickey. Evans stated that it was a "parterre", a French term for an ornamental garden that forms a distinctive pattern.

On July 11, 1955, just six days before the park opened to the public, Joe Fowler, who oversaw construction of Disneyland, sent a memo to landscaper Jack Evans, who with his brother Bill were handling Disneyland landscaping, that asked, "When are you going to plant Mickey Mouse in the entrance? Looks to me like the time is getting pretty late."

History of the Mickey Mouse Costumed Character

The first professional appearance of Mickey Mouse as a costumed character was probably the 1931 Fanchon and Marco traveling stage show, *Mickey Mouse Idea*, that premiered March 12, 1931, in Los Angeles. Popular vaudeville performer "Toots" Novelle was the man inside the mouse and even posed with and without his mouse head for photos with Walt Disney at the Disney Studio.

The next Disney-related public appearance by a costumed Mickey and Minnie was in 1937 at the premiere for *Snow White and the Seven Dwarfs* at the Carthay Circle Theater. The images of those Disney characters shocked Disney Legend Bill Justice:

> They must have been an afterthought, because they weren't anything close to the model sheets.

In some ways, the costumed characters resembled large versions of the Charlotte Clark stuffed Mickey and Minnie Mouse dolls. Those costumed characters obviously were not created by the Disney Studio because their "pie-eyes" were done incorrectly, unlike the dolls, making them appear cross-eyed.

Over the decades, homemade costumes of Mickey Mouse, as well as some limited professional versions, were used at department store and movie theater events. Those outfits had no direct input from the Disney Studio artists and were commonly pajama-style costumes (referencing the famous "footie pajamas" for children), meaning they followed the natural contours of the human body rather than replicating the proportions of the animated character.

In the late 1940s, full Mickey Mouse costumes (with pupil eyes) manufactured by Gertrude Cornell of Blairstown, New Jersey, were sold to stores, theaters, and other venues for commercial promotional use at $135 each.

The first consistent appearances of Mickey and the gang in costume began with the opening of Disneyland.

During the July 17, 1955, broadcast of *Dateline: Disneyland*, host Art Linkletter described the first parade down Main Street:

> Dumbo, Pluto and Donald Duck and all the other characters are from the Walt Disney costumes created for John Harris' *Ice Capades* which is on tour with Peter Pan right now around the United States.

Skater Donna Atwood portrayed Peter Pan, following in the stage tradition of a mature woman playing the young boy who never grew up. (The Peter Pan *Ice Capades* show began in 1956.)

In 1955, *Ice Capades* did not feature any Disney number, which may be why the costumes were available for Walt Disney to borrow for the grand opening of Disneyland. Some *Ice Capades'* performers may have been in those Disney costumes for the ABC broadcast.

In 1949, *Ice Capades*, a touring ice skating show produced by John H. Harris, partnered with the Disney Studio to showcase a lengthy segment in each year's show featuring Disney characters.

The Disney segment for the first show, *Snow White and the Seven Dwarfs*, was advertised on the back of the program book. It proved so popular that it was revived for the 1954 and 1959 shows.

Disney segments in the *Ice Capades* continued through 1966 and included short adaptations of *Alice in Wonderland*, *Cinderella*, and a salute to Disneyland itself in 1957, with improved Mickey and Minnie costumes for the performers.

Walt attended the *Ice Capades* productions, watching the Disney-inspired segments closely. He noticed that audiences accepted the costumes as the characters with no complaints.

The costumes, however, were designed to provide flexibility for the skater, and so once again, they followed the contours of the person's body with human, not cartoon, proportions. In addition, the costumes were designed to allow the greatest visibility, which explains the horrid teeth on Mickey Mouse at Disneyland's opening day, since the mesh between the spiky chompers was necessary for peripheral vision.

As with most theatrical costumes, these Disney costumes were meant to be viewed briefly at a distance under proper lighting, not inspected up close by a Disneyland guest for an extended period of time.

Disney Legend John Hench wrote:

> The walk-arounds were not originally intended to be an on-going feature of Disneyland. These first walk-arounds were very clearly costumed actors portraying the characters (not the characters themselves).

But the guests' enthusiasm even for these oddly proportioned figures persuaded Walt that the characters must become a permanent part of Disneyland.

It was impractical for Disney to keep borrowing costumes from the *Ice Capades*, so the Disney Studio Costume Shop tried to make their own based on those from the *Ice Capades* but with an improved appearance. These newer versions turned out to be extraordinarily heavy, awkward, and at times unprofessional, with flashes of real skin like a wrist or a back of the neck often visible.

The earliest costumes for the Three Little Pig characters were made with rebar and weighed more than seventy pounds each. The Seven Dwarfs looked through mesh in their hats and their arms hung limply at their sides, making it impossible for them to shake hands or sign autographs.

Disney Legend John Hench said:

Mickey's transformation from 2-D to 3-D worlds was natural, except for the design, of course. It is actually astonishing that Mickey held his identity. Making him a real, live character represented a violent shift that violated the head-to-body proportions [of the 2-D character].

After a time, we made our own costumes for the walk-around characters. Of course, we got better at it as we went along. For example, we found smaller people [to wear the costumes] who didn't distort the image so much. The first characters weren't that great, I guess.

Ron Logan, former Executive Vice-President Walt Disney Entertainment, explained:

Because height ranges for the characters had not been established, Mickey was sometimes over six feet tall! In the Fall of 1961 that all changed through the contributions of Bill Justice and John Hench who brought a higher quality design and consistency to the characters.

At Walt's personal request, a new Mickey Mouse costume was designed by John Hench. Walt wanted to cast a smaller performer as Mickey and standardize the performer's height in costume. Paul Castle (who had performed in the *Ice Capades* as Mickey and other Disney characters like Dopey for years) was personally selected by Walt to perform the role.

Disney Legend Bill Justice remembered:

When Disneyland opened, we needed characters to meet the public regularly. Everything had to be re-designed to more accurately represent the characters and stand up to the rigors of everyday use among the guests.

Walt told me, "Other places can have thrill rides and bands and trains. Only we have our characters." The costumed characters were very important to Walt. He said, "Bill, always remember we don't want to torture the people who are wearing them. Keep in mind they've got to be as comfortable as possible. Try to get the lightest weight materials and the most ventilation as possible." The first concern was always safety and the second was accuracy.

In his book *Designing Disney* (Disney Editions, 2003), Hench wrote:

To create the walk-arounds, we have to choose those physical features that convey a character's essential identity. The essential characteristics that best identify the animated film Mickey and Minnie are their large heads and ears... since no human body has the exact proportions that the animated characters have onscreen, we had to find the right degree of exaggeration that would make the walk-around heads large enough to establish the character's identity while relating well to their body size.

Many experiments were made in those early years to create an acceptable Mickey Mouse costumed character.

For example, the head was enlarged to the same size as the body to achieve a cartoonish smallness. Mickey's regular-sized black shoes were replaced with large yellow shoes and a huge red bowtie to suggest a smaller character. He was given long pants and coat sleeves to hide his skinny mouse legs and arms but still suggest them. And the last two fingers of his standard white gloves were sewn together to give the impression of three fingers and a thumb.

Disney Legend Ward Kimball said:

> People's perception of Mickey Mouse is the one they see at [Disneyland]. That's the one they meet with their children. He's got long pants. He's got extra eyebrows....more like the stuffed dolls they sell [than how he ever appeared in any cartoon].

In the early to mid-1960s, Disneyland used a core group of ten to twelve full-time character performers supervised by Marvin Marker. They performed sets in the park five days per week (Disneyland was closed on Mondays and Tuesdays, except for summers and holidays). In addition, forty part-time performers worked on weekends, holidays, and evenings.

Character training and supervision was informal at best, according to Ron Logan:

> In the early years, the characters walked around Disneyland freely, greeting guests and posing for pictures. There was no schedule shared with the guests so there was no guarantee that the guests might see them. It was all serendipity.

Bill Justice recalled the high cost of the costumes:

> In the mid-1960s, an original costume could cost ten to twelve thousand dollars and at least six months to design and build. Duplicates were around three thousand dollars each.

In 1967, Bob Jani was hired as Director of Entertainment, and soon after, Bob Phelps joined the staff from Western Costume Company as Director of Costuming. Phelps introduced such improvements as padded poles on which to put the character heads so they would not be damaged by moisture and dirt on the ground.

In the late 1960s, Jack Muhs directed some redesigns of the character costumes, and in 1971, Alex Goldstab and Fred Duffy relocated from Disneyland to Walt Disney World to establish a Disney Character Department in Florida. They hired more than two hundred character performers.

By the 1970s, character training had become more formalized, with standardized choreographed movements for specific characters, practice in reproducing an approved autograph signature, and study of the animated cartoons.

Each character had a training video. Here is a small excerpt from the 1973 training video for Mickey Mouse:

> The Disneyland-Walt Disney World Entertainment Division presents this training tape so that you who are portraying the character of

Mickey Mouse will better understand the responsibility of your job as well as the problems you might encounter. It's also our purpose to acquaint you with the personality of the character and the possibilities for animation and movement within the limits of the costume.

Mickey Mouse has a glorious history. Naturally, the best way to get to know him is to start at the beginning. Mickey made his film debut in the first Disney sound cartoon entitled *Steamboat Willie*. This cartoon made in 1928 portrayed Mickey as a mischievous but innocent young boy.

In his early days, Mickey enjoyed stirring up trouble but managed to win the hearts of millions with his boundless energy, his sense of humor and fun loving nature. *Steamboat Willie* was the beginning of a long and successful career for Mickey Mouse.

Over the past forty-five years, he has played everything from a fireman to a giant killer, from an inventor to a detective and from a cowboy to a magician. Indeed, Mickey has become an international personality and is known and loved all over the world as the single official host of Walt Disney Productions.

Our Mickey Mouse is an average young boy of no particular age, clean-living, fun-loving, bashful around girls, polite, brave, and clever. He is not a clown nor silly or dumb.

Mickey would never lose his temper or do anything dishonest or sneaky. His age will vary with the situation. When he is among children, he is always light and gay. He loves to have fun with them and possesses all the energy and curiosity of a young boy.

Among dignitaries, Mickey is extremely humble and will politely shake hands. He is the symbol of the Disney Company, of everything that Walt Disney created in the past and for everything he hoped for in the future. Mickey Mouse represents a unique era in motion pictures, art, television, animation and design.

Most importantly, this little character represents a spirit of happiness, laughter, harmony and friendship to millions of people all over the world. Undoubtedly, Mickey Mouse is the most famous of all Disney characters.

Whether you are playing Mickey in the park, at a special event, in a department store or out on the road, you should try to locate a clean, fairly spacious area in which to dress. Be sure to set your costume on a chair or table or hang it up.

As you go out to greet your audience, remember the voice of Mickey Mouse is easily recognized and children are not fooled by imitations. So, while you are in costume, the first rule is that you not talk. Mickey Mouse will invariably attract large crowds of youngsters eager for autographs, pictures or some special attention. Always keep the safety of these children in mind.

Remember you are working with a very young unpredictable audience. Children are sometimes hard to understand and may give you an extra affectionate pat on the back or even a playful punch. Patience is the key word in being a Disney character.

Most important to remember is to the children, Mickey Mouse is real. The fact that there is a person in the costume should never be revealed.

Even though the costume is limiting in some respects, try to move as naturally as possible. Mickey is a happy character and loves to dance and perform.

Basically, your goal as a Disney character is to become that character. It is your job to bring the animated Mickey Mouse to life, to give him energy, feeling, color. Couple your imagination with your good judgment and always keep the safety of the children in mind.

Remember while you are in costume, the reputation of Mickey Mouse and of Walt Disney Productions depends on you. First and most importantly, be proud of what you are doing. Without you, none of the rest of us would be needed. You are the pixie dust which keeps the spirit of Walt Disney alive.

You have an amazing power for with a mere handshake and gentle hug, you can bring a smile to a care-worn face, a sparkle to a child's eye or some long-needed joy into a tired life. You represent a spirit of laughter, harmony and friendship to millions of people all over the world. You are responsible for the unique happiness which families discover when they visit your Disney home.

Disney continued to experiment with costume improvements, but most were unsuccessful. Bill Justice said:

We kept finding lighter materials with better ventilation, especially for the heads, until the weight was down to about a fourth of the original designs.

An attempt to install a cooling unit inside the costume added greatly to its weight and its awkwardness. In addition, the devices created an ungainly bump on the side of the costume for the battery pack. Justice recalled:

Air conditioning was even built into a few [of the costumes] after getting technical advice from Kennedy Space Center. These were technological marvels. You could run in them for ten minutes and not break a sweat, even in Florida. But the young people inside didn't like the extra weight.

An attempt to include a tape recorder with pre-recorded phrases didn't anticipate the challenge of the wrong response as the next one queued for play when a guest asked a question. Also, many guests came from foreign countries where they had heard Mickey speak fluently in their native language. Justice stated:

Once we tried Mickey with a tape of standard phrases like "How are you?", "What's your name?" but this was too artificial an arrangement to be successful.

In 2010, Disney introduced an interactive Mickey Mouse head in the Disney theme parks. Mickey blinked his eyes, moved his mouth, and by 2013 was able to talk with guests as part of the Living Character Initiative.

Since 1955, a costumed Mickey Mouse has been the official host at Disney theme parks throughout the world and has brought joy to millions of guests. Whatever the outer costume, Mickey's inner spirit always shines through to brighten someone's visit.

The Man Inside the Mouse: Paul Castle

"Don't shoot the mouse," intoned the Secret Service man in a firm, terse, monotone over the radio

The Disney characters were standing in a line patiently awaiting a chance to meet the President of the United States.

Impulsively, Mickey Mouse bounded forward with his arms outstretched when he saw the chief executive. The government hidden sniper had been trained to react to any sudden, unexpected movement toward the president, but the crackling order over the radio stayed his trigger finger.

Inside the mouse was Paul Castle.

When Mickey Mouse pounded on the huge drum in "Fantasy on Parade" down Disneyland's Main Street for thousands of times, it was Paul Castle.

When Mickey Mouse cavorted publicly at the 1964 New York World's Fair, it was Paul Castle.

When Mickey Mouse rode beside Walt Disney at the 1966 Rose Parade, it was Paul Castle.

When Walt appeared in his final photo in front of the Sleeping Beauty Castle with Mickey Mouse waving, it was Paul Castle.

When Mickey Mouse received his star on the Hollywood Boulevard Walk of Fame, it was Paul Castle.

On April 23, 1965, Walt Disney, accompanied by Mickey Mouse, opened the Anaheim Stadium in California. Walt was given the first ball to throw out. He handed it to Mickey, who threw it to the catcher, Goofy. That historic pitch was made by Paul Castle.

From 1961 to 1986, when he officially retired, Castle would refer to himself as the Main Mickey, and it would be hard to argue with that designation. Of course, the Disney Company cannot give official recognition to Paul for his twenty-five years of milestones in fur because Castle was not Mickey Mouse.

He might have assisted in the portrayal of Mickey Mouse. He might have been a "friend" of Mickey Mouse, but everyone knows that Mickey Mouse is real and can magically appear at the same time at Disney theme parks worldwide, as well as at special events.

No single talented performer is Mickey Mouse, though the Mouse has had a lot of help over the years, both male and female, to meet his appearance obligations.

Most Disney fans may be unfamiliar with the name Paul Castle, who spent the last years of his life in a condominium in Edmond, Oklahoma, far from the attention of Disney fan conventions. Yet, he cast a very long shadow in Disney history, even though in actuality he was only four foot, five inches tall.

Paul E. Castle Senior was born in Cleveland, Ohio, in August 1923, the son of Richard and Anna Castle. He died peacefully in his sleep on January 23, 2010, after battling Alzheimer's for two years and losing a final bout with pneumonia. He was 86 years old.

At the age of seven, Castle entered his first ice skating competition, which eventually led him to become, many years later, an ensemble skater with three-time Olympic gold medalist Sonja Henie and her show.

He eventually had a long career with *Holiday on Ice* and the *Ice Capades*. He amazed audiences as the world's smallest barrel jumper — able to jump over fifteen feet of obstacles like barrels or suitcases.

Castle also had a movie and television career. His first movie role was in *Jungle Moon Men* (1955) with Johnny Weissmuller as the famous Jungle Jim comic strip character. Castle later appeared in such films as *Under the Rainbow* and *One Hour Photo*. In addition, Castle made good money standing in for children in movies and television shows like *Dennis the Menace*.

Castle enjoyed flying and, despite his height, he obtained his pilot's license and bought his own airplane.

In the *Ice Capades*, his specialty was performing falls and rolls in animal character costumes. Jumping through a hoop over eight prop circus wagons (each twenty-two inches high) and leaping over fifteen feet of suitcases in ice skates were hallmarks of his act. These rough-and-tumble activities led to a fractured leg and many other injuries.

Castle said:

> It was wonderful. No two ways about it. It was fantastic. But nothing like working at Disneyland as Mickey Mouse, of course. That was my primary thing.

While performing, he met his wife Alma, whom he married in 1947. In 1950, they were skating together in the *Ice Capades* as two of Cinderella's mice in a Disney-themed segment. The show had begun to feature Disney characters a year earlier in 1949 with a *Snow White and the Seven Dwarfs* segment in which Castle also performed.

The 1958 *Ice Capades* program advertises:

> PAUL CASTLE... the mighty mite! Short but mighty, small but speedy. This in very few words describes the little man of the big show. Just a little over four feet in height, he is perfectly proportioned and his smooth, solid muscles stamp him as a miniature Hercules. Made a name for himself as the champion of the Silver Skates Derby. He actually jumps one foot higher than he is tall. Born in Cleveland, he is now a resident of Long Island, New York. Married, has one daughter.

On several occasions, according to Castle, Walt Disney himself had watched him in the *Ice Capades*. Castle said:

Walt Disney saw how good I did and knew I was an amateur character because I'd first met him when I did *Snow White and the Seven Dwarfs*.

(When the Ice Capades did another version of that segment in 1958, Castle performed as Dopey.)

Although eager to work for the Disney Company, Castle balked at the minimum-wage salary offered characters because he was already making a nice sum of money in the entertainment world. But since Walt wanted a small Mickey beating a long drumstick on top of a huge drum for a new Disneyland parade, he negotiated a salary that Castle found acceptable.

"Fantasy On Parade" premiered on Saturday, December 18, 1965, 8:00 pm with Walt in attendance. The parade was retired after the 1976 holiday season but brought back in 1980.

Castle recalled:

> I did over 15,000 parades leading the band ... down the street at Disneyland. I enjoyed being Mickey, of course. He's the most famous character in the world.

> I was the Main Mouse. We did everything. Walt Disney gave me the ball when we opened the Angels stadium. [Paul kept the ball as a keepsake.] He was a wonderful man, a wonderful, wonderful man. He was the greatest.

Castle was always a little star struck and kept a scrapbook of his encounters with celebrities. For example:

> I met Muhammad Ali backstage at Disneyland one time. Well, I was in costume, primarily to take pictures with him.

During the twenty-five years that Castle worked at Disneyland, at least fifty other performers assisted him in the portrayal of Mickey Mouse. Castle, however, was the "Main Mouse" and the official greeter at Disneyland's entrance. He was also known as the "small Mickey."

His wife Alma also assisted in the portrayal of Mickey when Castle was on tour. She recalled:

> Walt said, "Alma, you're pretty good. You can fit in Paul's costume, can't you?" And I said, "Yeah, pretty close." So I got in the costume and he said, "Good, you'll be my Pinocchio."

Alma assisted in the portrayal of Pinocchio for four summers. (In the earlier costumes, it was discovered that women had greater stamina inside them than men.)

Like her husband, Alma remembered Walt Disney as a "wonderful person", and she was especially impressed that he knew both of them by their first names. She said:

> He would come up to you and he'd look in the costume and say, "Alma, is that you?" And I'd say, "Yes, Walt." He would then say, "Where's Paul?" and I'd say "On Main Street, Walt." Everyone would call him "Walt".

One time Alma was standing backstage during the filming of *Babes in Toyland* (1961) and watched a machine being blown up. She recalled:

> I said, "Oh, my goodness! Look at all that money going up." And Walt said, "All $50,000 worth." And I turned around and said, "Oh, Mr. Disney." And he said, "Just call me Walt."

Paul Castle's *Ice Capades* experience came in handy when the holiday special *Christmas at Disney* aired in 1976 with host Art Carney.

On Main Street they laid two-foot square tiles on the asphalt street from the Market House to Town Square. They then sprayed the tiles repeatedly with silicone to make them suitable for skating.

Then, using the same foam they use on airport runways, the sidewalks were foamed to resemble snow. Plastic chips thrown in front of a huge fan added to the illusion of a snow storm. One of the highlights of the special was Paul Castle costumed as Mickey skating down Main Street.

As his niece Heather Lear remembers:

> Uncle Paul and Aunt Alma would visit her brothers [my grandfather and Great Uncle John] on many occasions [they also lived in Florida for a short while as well]. They took me to Disney and Epcot a few times when they visited. I remember that for the longest time we were the same height, but then I started to tower over him as I got older.
>
> He had the mouth of a sailor, but he was a lot of fun. I remember one New Year's Eve, he had brought a mini-cannon with him and placed it on my grandmother's bench outside. He proceeded to put Palm Tree Seeds in it with a fire cracker and accidentally shot it at his brother-in-law's car which caused a few small dents. I thought it was hilarious. He did, too, but we had to run back inside as if nothing happened. I miss him.

Abby Disney, granddaughter of Roy O. Disney, recalled a following memorable experience she had as a child:

> Just outside the employee's parking lot, there was a little cafeteria outside for the employees. I looked over and saw Mickey having a cup of coffee with Snow White. His head was on the table and he was smoking a big cigar. He was very short and old and had this gravelly deep voice. He came over to my grandmother and gave her a big hug. "Edna! Edna! Glad to see ya!" That's how I remember Mickey Mouse; he's emblazoned on my brain that way.

That was Paul Castle again.

It is rumored that the number one rule for Mickey Mouse — that he never talks in costume — was made because of Castle's gruff, raspy voice (he loved smoking cigars backstage which further irritated his throat). When he tried talking with Disneyland guests, he often sounded like Baby Herman from the feature film *Who Framed Roger Rabbit* (1988) with the same rough vocabulary and inflection.

In 1985, during Disneyland's 30th anniversary, Castle said he "kind of got a little upset because they didn't use me in that parade." He explained:

> I'd been there 24 years and they let some girl do Mickey Mouse in the parade. That's the one thing I sort of feel bad about. I said, "Oh boy, I'm breaking my back out here and you don't care enough to even let me do this parade" . . . It was on national television too.

> On [Mickey's 50th birthday in 1978], Mickey got to the White House, but it wasn't me. The same year I put the star in the Walk of Fame in Hollywood they had a girl [portraying Mickey Mouse] going cross country at the time, and she met the President. That's one of the little things that used to upset me, you know, heh, heh, heh.

Castle was not the only performer who assisted in portraying Mickey Mouse during the time when Walt Disney was alive.

John Matthews was a Disneyland Cast Member who often appeared as Mickey Mouse. He told part of his story to Pat Williams, Senior Vice President of the Orlando Magic, for the book *How To Be Like Walt* (HCI 2004):

> Walt had the memory of a politician. I first met him when I was substituting for Paul Castle as Mickey. I was in the backstage area at Disneyland, and I had the Mickey suit on. It was early morning and we were going to do a photo shoot for a magazine ad. Walt saw me and said, 'You aren't Paul. Who are you?' Even with the head on, he could tell I wasn't the regular Mickey. I said, 'I'm John Matthews'. And he said, 'Well, John, you're doing a good job'.

> The next time I ran into him, I was in character as Mickey for the 'Mary Poppins' premiere at Grauman's Chinese Theater in 1964. Again, I had the complete suit on, including the Mickey head. Walt came up to me and said, 'Hi, John!' That was just amazing. He recognized me and remembered my name, even though I was in the Mickey costume.

> The following year, I was in New York for the World's Fair, working as Mickey at 'it's a small world'. There was no reason for him to even know I was there. I usually worked at Disneyland. But when he arrived, he came up to me and said, 'Hi, John!'."

However, it was Paul Castle who was best remembered by Disney Cast Members as the man inside the mouse.

What was the favorite memory of the bald, cigar smoking, sometimes foul-spoken, four-foot-five-inch-tall man who stared through the eyes of Mickey more often than anyone else before or since — and who might be one of the most photographed persons in the world and yet still remained completely unknown?

At the New Year's Day Tournament of Roses Parade on January 1, 1966, Walt was the Grand Marshal. For three hours, it was just Paul Castle as Mickey Mouse with a smiling Walt Disney about a year before Walt's death.

In January 1988, Castle told a reporter for the *Los Angeles Times*:

My most favorite time of all was with Walt Disney in the Rose Parade in 1966, the year he passed away. He was the Grand Marshal of the Rose Parade and I was in the car with him in the back seat, just Walt and I for three hours. Just Walt and I. Of all the things I've done in my lifetime, that to me was my biggest day. Walt and me, January 1, 1966.

Walt Disney World's First Friend of Mickey Mouse: Doug Parks

In the Thirties, when a young girl wrote to Walt Disney asking him how many Mickey Mouses there were since she saw Mickey in so many different places, Walt wrote back (and the letter is in the Disney Archives) that there was only one Mickey Mouse just like there is only one Santa Claus even though she might see several of his helpers at Christmas and there is only one of her.

When it comes to the Disney characters in the parks, there is only one Mickey Mouse, though he seems to get around to a lot of different places on property very quickly.

At one time, if Mickey was appearing in a parade, he would not be seen anywhere else property wide so that no child could ask, "But Mickey, aren't you supposed to be in the parade at the Magic Kingdom right now like when I saw you yesterday?"

Of course, no one person IS Mickey Mouse. In the Character department, the explanations are that a Cast Member "assists in the portrayal" of a character or is a "friend" of a character. Over the decades, many talented performers both male and female have "assisted in the portrayal" of a particular character.

Paul Castle was the "Main Mickey" at Disneyland but did not make the trip to Florida for the opening of the Magic Kingdom in 1971. Another "friend" of Mickey was needed for the dedication ceremonies and all the related media events, in addition to portraying the physical, on-site park ambassador for guests.

That "friend" was Doug Parks.

Doug Parks was born in Auburn, New York, on August 15, 1950, to Dawse and Margaret Parks, and attended Weedsport Central High School in update New York, where he was a track star and known for his agility and cheerfulness. He graduated in 1969.

His mother worked as a cashier at a New York movie theater, so Parks and his two older brothers Ralph and Lowrey spent a lot of time watching movies as children. Since his brothers played the organ and the trumpet, Parks tried playing a small guitar, but since his fingers were too tiny he switched to making 1/32 scale model cars, a hobby he maintained throughout his life.

In April 1971, Parks moved to his brother's house in Central Florida so he could apply for work at Walt Disney World, which was scheduled to open in six months. He was roughly four-foot-eight-inches tall (today, the height range for Mickey is usually between four-foot-ten and five-foot-two) and never weighed more than ninety-five pounds in his life.

"He was a little fellow," his brother Ralph recalled in a 2010 interview, but "he had a giant personality."

A story about Parks with his picture that ran in a 1971 issue of the *Orlando Sentinel* identified him as the first Mickey Mouse. He personally trained two "substitute" East Coast mice during the earliest days of Walt Disney World.

Another talented Cast Member who performed as Mickey Mouse during that same time was Marvin Weams, a black man with a visual handicap. When Weams completely lost his vision, he became a manager of the character performers at Walt Disney World.

As a friend of Mickey, Parks traveled around the country as well as to Canada and South America promoting the newest Disney theme park. His most memorable, important moment was at the dedication of Walt Disney World when Roy O. Disney motioned for Parks to join him as Disney read his speech.

Disney Legend John Hench recalled:

> Roy Disney stood facing the microphone before a crowd of guests ready to deliver the dedication speech at the opening ceremony. He suddenly turned and looked around and I heard him say quietly, "Somebody go find Mickey for me. We don't have Walt any more, and Mickey is nearest thing to Walt that we have left." Mickey appeared and Roy promptly began his speech, with Mickey standing proudly at his side.

Actually, looking at photos of the occasion, Mickey is respectfully bowing his head with his hands folded in front of him, completely aware of the importance of the occasion and the significance of Mickey's presence at that moment in time.

Parks collected Disney memorabilia and was a strong Disney fan and supporter for his entire life. His other priorities were his two cats, Lil' Darlin' and Honey Cone.

Some Cast Members and friends knew him for his sense of humor and his joking phrases of "that's all rat" or "you will always be all rat" or just plain "all rat." Sometimes he would even put on a mouse nose.

Parks developed an allergy to the material in his Mickey Mouse costume and had to move on to other roles during his thirty-nine years working at Walt Disney World. He was a sort of "secret shopper" sent to visit the resort hotels and write reports. Toward the end of his career, he worked at the Disney Reservation Center, making reservations and helping schedule trips for guests.

When Doug Parks passed away from cancer on August 29, 2010, two weeks after his 60th birthday, the Disney Company would not admit that Parks was the first Mickey Mouse to avoid spoiling the magic as well as the headline that Mickey Mouse was dead, but did confirm he was an entertainment Cast Member in the early 1970s.

Walt Disney Resort President Meg Crofton wrote in a letter to his family:

For four decades, Walt Disney World was a better place thanks to Doug and his contributions. He was an important part of our business of making dreams come true.

His brother Ralph remembered:

Often they would refer to Douglas as the mayor of Disney.

According to his wishes, Doug Parks was cremated, but the magical memories he created, especially as Mickey's first East Coast friend, are still an inspiration to Mickey's other friends today.

Mickey Mouse Ears

From the opening of Disneyland, theme park exclusive Mickey Mouse merchandise was sold that ranged from a flip book of Cowboy Mickey twirling a lariat to a lenticular flicker button with the image of Mickey's face replacing the statement "I Like Disneyland" to flashlights to postcards (including the Jumbo Mickey Mouse 8x10 postcard with Mickey in an artist beret drawing the word "Disneyland") to pennants to imprinted ball-point pens in silver or gold (with an image of Mickey and the word "Disneyland") and more... all costing under a dollar each.

But the most popular item was the famous black skull cap/beanie with round ears that became a necessity for most youngsters after the 1955 debut of the original Mouseketeers, who wore them daily on their television show.

The head gear was designed for the show by Disney storyman Roy O. Williams, the "Big Mooseketeer", who based them on a gag in an early Mickey Mouse cartoon, *The Karnival Kid* (1929), where Mickey tips his ears like a hat to Minnie Mouse.

Oswald the Rabbit had done the exact same gag in *Sleigh Bells* (July 1928) about a year earlier. In that cartoon, Oswald tips his ears to Sadie, a cute female cat who was his girlfriend and who in this cartoon has fallen on the ice as she learns how to skate.

Although Williams came up with the rough design, someone still had to physically make the original ears to fit on a person's head. That man was Chuck Keehne of the renowned Western Costume Company in Hollywood.

As Disney expanded into television and more live-action productions, it became important to have a Wardrobe Department. Keehne was hired in April 1955 to set up such a department. His first assignment was to create costumes for the *Mickey Mouse Club* show that was due to start filming just a few weeks later.

George Grant, a *Mickey Mouse Club* authority, wrote:

> According to Chuck's daughter, Bill Walsh, Hal Adelquist, Roy Williams, and Chuck worked together on this. The early versions were too large and looked ungainly, nor would they stay on when the kids danced or moved quickly.

> Eventually Chuck and his team devised small hand-crafted caps with wire-reinforced felt ears and rubber-bands that fit under the chin to hold them on, each one tailored to an individual Mouseketeer.

> They were time-consuming to make, and were a far cry in quality from the caps eventually marketed to viewers and Disneyland visitors. Each cap contained $20 worth of high-quality felt, and cost an

additional $5 to make, a considerable sum in those days, especially when multiplied by two dozen Mouseketeers.

The thread for the simple "M" logo used in the first season was actually orange, not red, so that it would show up better on monochrome television screens.

To the usual problems in costuming actors were added the additional difficulties that these were kids, who often grew out of their clothes from month to month, and had a propensity for "losing" the detested ears. A $50 fine slowed down the rate of missing ears.

In her autobiography *A Dream Is a Wish Your Heart Makes* (Hyperion 1994) original Mouseketeer Annette Funicello wrote:

Being kids, some of us were a bit careless with our ears, leaving them lying about or just forgetting where we put them. In short order, I managed to lose three pairs of ears, and the cost of each was deducted from my pay. It was a hard lesson, but one we all learned quickly and well. After a while, no one ever set his or her ears down, not even for a second. We either wore or carried our precious ears with us everywhere we went, and I do mean everywhere.

The original ears sold at Disneyland (for sixty-nine cents each) were made by the Benay-Albee Novelty Company of Maspeth, New York, from felt and two plastic ear shapes. At first, they had an "M" on the front, but Walt quickly changed it to just the famous image of Mickey's face encircled in red so the hat could be trademarked. In the red circle were the names "Disneyland" and "Mickey Mouse".

In honor of the *Mickey Mouse Club* show's 50th anniversary, Walt Disney Collectibles and Master Replicas produced a special limited edition replica of one of the original pairs of ears used on the television show. An actual pair from the Walt Disney Archives was carefully studied and painstakingly copied to create this special collectible.

Gradually, the design and material of the ears changed, but the famous silhouette did not. A Minnie Mouse version with a red bow was introduced, and Disneyland also offered guests the option to have their names embroidered on the back of the ears The embroidery, at first, was free, and it was done on a sewing machine by a Cast Member who had to turn the hat inside out and write the name in script backwards. Today, the embroidery is done by automated machine and not for free.

In the last decade, many styles of mouse ears have been introduced in many colors and images, including light-up versions.

In May 2008, the Gag Factory souvenir shop, located in Disneyland's Toon Town, began selling completely customizable ears. Guests could choose from a variety of colors for the dome and the ears as well as choose from among different patches.

The only photo of Walt Disney wearing mouse ears appeared in the December 1, 1956, issue of the *Saturday Evening Post*. Walt had told photographer Gene Lester that he'd pose that way "over my dead body", but Lester got Walt's grandson Christopher (wearing a Mickey Mouse Club t-shirt) to put the hat on Grandpa's head during a bedtime story reading, and then quickly took the shot. Walt was wearing the Disneyland hat with the big "M".

Mickey Mouse Topiary

The first Disneyland topiaries, created by landscaper Bill Evans, appeared in 1963. They consisted of roughly two dozen generic animals, some of which would be moved to the area in front of "it's a small world" when it opened in May 1966.

When Walt Disney World opened in 1971, most of the topiaries (with a handful of exceptions) were generic creatures not linked to any specific Disney film.

When Disney finally developed a Mickey Mouse topiary, it was due to the innovation of using steel frames wrapped with chicken wire and then stuffed with unmilled sphagnum moss.

In this process, small plants or "plugs" are then planted into the sphagnum and require daily watering, often from an internal irrigation system. Because the plants in these sphagnum figures are rooted into the frame itself, they do not require any type of container — just a metal stand to keep them upright.

Consequently, the plants are easily moved from one location to another, they are adaptable for use as stage decorations or for special occasions, and they can quickly be created in days rather than years.

The steel frames are reused and modified. For example, when a Flower and Garden Festival display called for Mickey Mouse in cookout mode, the basic Mickey Mouse frame was altered to raise his arm and add a fork. That led to recalculations of how much the arm would weigh — dry and wet — and if the structure could handle it.

Partners Statue

Disney Legend Blaine Gibson sculpted what is known as the *Partners* statue of Walt Disney holding Mickey Mouse's hand originally for the Hubs in Disneyland and Walt Disney World.

Several different compositions were considered.

One featured a young Mickey running ahead and pulling Walt along. It was rejected because it seemed awkward for Mickey to be dragging Walt forward.

Another featured Walt with the rolled-up blueprints of Epcot in his right hand and using them to point forward. Yet another had Walt giving an open-handed wave while Mickey held a small black globe with two mouse ears.

One image under serious consideration had Mickey holding a one-scoop ice cream cone. It was rejected because Disney felt it made Mickey look immature and that it might be misinterpreted as supporting a particular sponsor like Nestle or Carnation.

The size for Mickey Mouse in proportion to Walt Disney was chosen based on a brief moment from the animated short *The Pointer* (1939). As animator Frank Thomas recalled:

> When he recorded the voice [for Mickey], [Walt] couldn't help but feel like Mickey and he added all these little gestures that were spontaneous with him. At one point [where Mickey was talking to a huge bear], he put out his hand like this [to indicate that Mickey was about 3 feet tall], it was the only time we knew how big Walt thought Mickey was.

Imagineer Marty Sklar remembered his amazement at Gibson and Imagineer John Hench spending hours to discuss exactly how Walt's five-fingered hand should hold Mickey's four-fingered hand. Their decision was to base it on the one time that an animated Mickey held the hand of a real person: in *Fantasia* (1940), Mickey shakes the hand of conductor Leopold Stokowski at the end of the "Sorcerer's Apprentice" sequence.

As Blaine Gibson said in May 1992:

> I don't think of Mickey as a real mouse. When I sculpt Mickey, I think of him as a young boy.

The *Partners* statue was unveiled at Disneyland on November 18, 1993. At the ceremony, Gibson told the press:

> Many people asked me what Walt might be saying as he stood there with Mickey, and the expression I tried to capture was Walt saying to Mickey, "Look what we've accomplished together", because truly they were very much a team through it all.

In June 1995, another *Partners* statue was installed in the Hub of Walt Disney World's Magic Kingdom. Tokyo Disneyland also has a *Partners* statue as does the Walt Disney Studios Park in Paris and the courtyard of Team Disney in Burbank, California.

Hidden Mickey

A Hidden Mickey is usually an image of the tri-circled silhouette of Mickey's head "hidden" at a Disney venue like a theme park, a restaurant, or a cruise ship. It might be found in a swirl on a piece of furniture or in an arrangement of rocks and plants or in a wallpaper or carpet pattern or in some other unusual grouping.

Some Hidden Mickeys are much cleverer like Mickey's foot peeking out beneath the movie poster for *Public Enemy* (1930) in the gangster scene of *The Great Movie Ride* attraction in Disney's Hollywood Studios.

The first Hidden Mickey appeared in Disneyland's 1955 Rocket to the Moon attraction (designed by Imagineer John Hench) where the rapidly diminishing spaceport in the bottom viewport has a remarkable resemblance to Mickey's head.

Officially, Hidden Mickeys originated at Epcot Center in 1982. The secret was revealed in the December 1991 issue of *Disney News* magazine by Imagineer David Fisher:

> So you think you know your Disney trivia, huh? When EPCOT Center opened at Walt Disney World in 1982, a conscious decision was made to give the new Theme Park a distinctly separate identity from the older, more familiar Magic Kingdom. One of the ways this was done was to purposely keep all references to the Disney characters out of the new Park.

> Leave it to the devious denizens of Walt Disney Imagineering to work the familiar ears or silhouette into just about anything they could during those early, no-Mouse days of EPCOT Center.

> Tributes to Mickey Mouse do not begin and end in EPCOT Center. Disney's forever-fresh-faced star is hidden in many places around Walt Disney World.

Actually, Cast Members had been alerted to the practice two years earlier by fellow Cast Members Arlen Miller and Bob Weir in their "Hidden Disney" article for the November 30, 1989, edition of the Walt Disney World weekly, Cast Member-only newspaper, *Eyes and Ears*.

There is no official, complete listing of Hidden Mickeys since they are done in impromptu fashion and areas at the parks are constantly changing.

More significantly, Disney Imagineers do not want to encourage guests' fascination with the phenomenon because they feel trying to find Hidden Mickeys distracted guests from being immersed in the full Disney experience.

Mickey Mouse Balloons

The colorful helium balloons with three bubbles that resemble Mickey Mouse's head are nearly as popular as mouse ears. These latex balloons came in red, blue, yellow, green, and pink with an image of Mickey's face imprinted on the largest bubble when they were first introduced at Disneyland in 1956.

Nat Lewis Balloon Company, a Disneyland park lessee at the time, handled sales. (Rubio Arts currently handles the balloon concession.) The Mickey balloons originally cost thirty-five cents and some guests would shout at the sellers, "I can buy a whole bag of balloons for thirty-five cents. You should be giving those balloons free to the kids."

Lewis took six of his "Disneyland Balloon Boys" to Walt Disney World for the grand opening in 1971 during which 50,000 balloons were released as part of the ceremonies.

From 1961-1965, the Mickey balloons had black ears. The machinery to create these balloons no longer exists, so for the feature film *Saving Mr. Banks* (2013), over 750 balloons had to be individually hand-dipped to match those from the film's time period.

Foil balloons became popular in the early 1990s.

The Mickey head balloon in a clear round bubble latex balloon, known as the "glasshouse", was introduced in 1999. Creators Henry Unger and Treb Heining (one of Nate Lewis's original balloon boys, who started selling Mickey Mouse balloons at Disneyland at the age of 15 in 1969) invented it specifically to be sold in Disney theme parks, where they remain a favorite today.

Heining was also responsible for the LED device that can be put in a Mickey Mouse balloon to make it light up at the touch of a switch placed near the knot. It took him years of waiting for the technology to develop so that he could fit the little bulb inside and keep it glowing for 48 hours without melting the balloon.

Speaking of the Mouse

Bringing smiles to the faces of children of all nationalities, Mickey Mouse is an ambassador of goodwill and a peacemaker who speaks the universal language of friendship. I thank Mickey for all he has done to spread laughter and love and to unite the world as one human family.

— Jimmy Carter
Former U.S. President (1988)

In this chapter are individual quotes relating to the life and career of Mickey Mouse in several different categories.

Walt Disney and Mickey Mouse

Overland Monthly, October 1933:

> "Walt is Mickey. If Mickey is good, it is because Walt is good. Every characteristic of Mickey's from the lift of his eye-brow to his delightful swagger is Walt's own. Mickey is not a mouse; he is Walt Disney."

Lillian Disney, Walt's wife. *McCall's* magazine, 1953:

> "Father (Walt) is no mouse. Walt was the first voice of Mickey Mouse. Because of that, and because Walt can seem shy and retiring with people he doesn't know, and because Roy has been heard to complain that Walt has no more money sense than Mickey Mouse, the myth has grown up that Mickey Mouse is a projection of Walt's real personality. I can assure you it isn't true. No matter how hard the rest of us squeal, Walt goes ahead and does what he wants to do."

Jimmy MacDonald, Disney sound effects man and one of the voices of Mickey Mouse:

> "It is no easy matter to get color into such an unnatural, limited voice, but Walt managed. No one else could capture the gulping, ingenuous, half-brave quality."

Bob Thomas, author of *Walt Disney: An American Original*:

> "Both Walt and Mickey had an adventurous spirit, a sense of rectitude, an admitted lack of sophistication, a boyish ambition to excel... The Disney animators recognized this unstated similarity, and when drawing the Mouse often kept in mind — subconsciously, at least — the characteristics of Walt."

An anonymous Disney animator talking to gossip columnist Hedda Hopper in 1939:

> "Sometimes when you go into his (Walt's) office expecting to meet Mickey Mouse, you find Donald Duck instead."

Cosmopolitan magazine, 1934:

> "Mickey Mouse's papa is not overly fond of mice. He jumps out of their way, and doesn't go looking for them."

Disney Legend Eric Larson, one of Disney's "Nine Old Men", in 1978:

> "Walt was aware of the power he had through the mouse. He kept strict control always of what Mickey did. The mouse was more than a money-making vehicle to him. He loved the character."

🐭 American film critic John Tibbetts:

> "Walt's rise from barnyard to city respectability was rapid and something of a blueprint for American enterprise. Mickey's rise was no less precipitous and no less determined. They both made fun of city slickers at first and distrusted the rascals all their lives... but they were nonetheless bent on leaving the farm."

🐭 Disney Legend Ward Kimball, one of Disney's fabled "Nine Old Men". "City Hall" refers to Walt Disney himself:

> "Mickey Mouse was untouchable. If you made any changes you really had to clear them with 'City Hall' as they say."

🐭 Disney Legend John Hench:

> "Mickey was definitely Walt's alter-ego Like Mickey, Walt was optimistic — he certainly had enormous faith in himself, and, of course, Mickey has enormous faith in himself — he takes on giants and whatnot. Mickey seemed like a live person. We knew how he'd act under a given circumstance — there'd be some surprises, but we knew basically how he'd behave."

🐭 Roy E. Disney, Walt's nephew:

> "Mickey really is Walt in a lot of ways. I'm not sure it had occurred to me earlier so strongly, but Mickey has all those nice impulses Walt had, the kind of gut-level nice guy he was."

🐭 Disney Legend Ollie Johnston, one of Disney's "Nine Old Men":

> "Nobody but Walt could do the Mouse. He was the only guy who felt how to handle Mickey. After 'The Sorcerer's Apprentice,' there really wasn't a good Mickey. Then they started drawing him in a different way, with different proportions. But the drawing wasn't the problem -- it was that they just didn't have the right things for him to do."

🐭 Disney Legend Frank Thomas, one of Disney's "Nine Old Men":

> "Mickey was Walt, and Walt was Mickey. Mickey reached his height in the days when Walt did the voice in that awful falsetto. When Walt started making features, Mickey was neglected."

🐭 Disney Legend Ollie Johnston, one of Disney's "Nine Old Men".

> "I never felt that Mickey was part of me, the way other characters I've drawn were — like Pinocchio, or Thumper in *Bambi*. I always felt Walt's presence very strongly when I worked with him. Mickey reflected Walt's boyhood personality and did a lot of things Walt had wanted to do himself---rescuing princesses, beating up bullies, putting on variety shows."

🐭 Disney Legend Ollie Johnston, one of Disney's "Nine Old Men":

"It was simply impossible for the storymen to conceive of Mickey stories or their resolutions without Walt's lead. A musical revue or the simple gags for a funny chase were easy enough, but the pictures with heart and real comedy that touched the audience were another matter. The magic was Walt."

🐭 Disney Legend Frank Thomas, one of Disney's "Nine Old Men":

"Ub Iwerks was responsible for the drawing of Mickey, but it was Walt Disney who supplied the soul. The amazing mouse was indeed Walt's alter ego, echoing the personality traits, mores, outlook on life, and dreams of his boss. He acted out Walt's fantasies in a remarkably personal way. Whether the fantasy grew from activities recalled from his childhood, or from imagined occurrences of pure fiction, it was not simply the adventures themselves that reflected Walt's imagination.

"The fantasy was in the way Mickey reacted to his predicaments, how he tried to extricate himself from a situation he could not control, never giving up and eventually finding a clever solution. This was Walt's way."

🐭 Record producer Dick Schory:

"Within a year of his creation, (Mickey) could do something no other mouse had ever done before. He could talk. People would often sit through a feature twice to see Mickey again. Walt often said, 'There's a lot of the Mouse in me!'"

🐭 Disney Legend John Hench, 1978:

"Mickey was, and is, something of Walt's. He came to stand for Walt and Walt Disney Productions and for all of our achievements. And now he is pointing our way to the future."

🐭 Roy E. Disney, nephew of Walt Disney:

"Walt was the voice of Mickey right from the start and he gave Mickey a kind of youthful, innocent bravado that somehow resonated with the dreams and aspirations of a world suffering from the Great Depression. Mickey is remarkable for many reasons, not the least of which is the lightning like spread of his popularity around the world after his 1928 debut."

🐭 Writer Irving Wallace, *Collier's* magazine, April 9, 1949:

"Is Mickey a man or a mouse? Those who write about him, who write for him, ballyhoo him, dress him, think for him and live by him, treat him as a full-fledged member in good standing of the run-down human race. Though the men who make Mickey always refer to him as the Mouse, it is their policy never to treat him as one. To them, he is a very real person.

"For years, Mickey Mouse pictures have been minus mousetraps, cheese gags or cat villains. Disney animators think he's a lot like Walt Disney. 'The same soulful eyes,' they say, 'the same beaky face, the same trick of falling into pantomime when at a loss for words'."

🐭 Bob Thomas, author of *Walt Disney: An American Original*:

"For those first Mickey Mouse cartoons, (Walt and Ub Iwerks) sat in the inner office of the tiny (Hyperion) studio. Ub drew sketches of the action and Walt typed the dialogue and action at the side of the sketches, using three fingers on the keyboard."

🐭 Disney Legend Ollie Johnston, one of Disney's "Nine Old Men":

"All the time I was there, before we got into things like *Snow White* (1937), I always thought of Walt being part of Mickey and vice versa. The ideas that he put into Mickey were so important and made the personality."

🐭 Disney Legend John Hench:

"I've always seen Mickey as a dynamic, busy fellow, looking with exuberance toward the next pioneering achievement. Perhaps that is one of the ways he is closest to Walt."

🐭 Disney Legend Frank Thomas, one of Disney's "Nine Old Men":

"(The cartoon *The Pointer*) was the high point in the development of Mickey's personality and Walt's finest portrayal of Mickey's voice. It has very little actual story and few gags but is built almost entirely on personality. In fact, it represents the peak of Walt's feeling for Mickey and has dialog development that is so specific for this character that it never would fit Donald or Goofy or anyone but Mickey."

🐭 Disney Legend John Hench:

"After a while, I noticed that there was something about Mickey that made him seem to be a real presence around the studio. He was like someone you knew intimately. It was almost as if we lived with him. I felt that I knew how Mickey would react to almost any situation. To many of us at the studio, it was obvious that Mickey's personality was born out of Walt's innate talent for storytelling and his understanding of human nature."

🐭 Disney Legend Ward Kimball, *L.A. Times WEST* magazine, 1968:
> "Your writer quoted Mr. Richard Schickel to the effect that 'Walt Disney couldn't even draw Mickey Mouse!' I can't imagine where Mr. Schickel got such information... Many of Walt's friends and associates will tell you that he not only could but, on hundreds of occasions, did draw Mickey."

Animating Mickey

🐭 Disney Legend John Hench, *Crimmers* magazine, Winter 1975:
> "Concerning Mickey Mouse... He is made out of a series of circles. He is not a static thing but very dynamic in the way the circles fall together. He has been accepted all over the world, and there is obviously no problem of people responding to this set of circles... So Mickey has made his way while a contemporary known as Felix the Cat didn't get anywhere. He had points all over him, like a cactus. He has practically disappeared while we couldn't get rid of Mickey if we tried. We haven't made a film with him in years, but he persists."

🐭 Disney Legend Marc Davis, one of Disney's "Nine Old Men":
> "I feel that (Mickey's) circles come out of the quality of moving on the screen without jiggling, whereas with a straight line, or anything with corners, you get a stroboscopic effect."

🐭 Disney Legend Ward Kimball, one of Disney's "Nine Old Men":
> "Drawing Mickey consistently was to use a circle the size of a silver dollar for the close-up shots, a fifty cent piece for medium close-ups, a quarter for medium shots, a nickel for medium long-shots and a dime for long shots. The head and fanny sections were made with the same size circle and connected with two lines."

🐭 Disney Legend Les Clark, one of Disney's "Nine Old Men", who was considered a Mickey Mouse specialist:
> "Using dimes and quarters for (drawing) Mickey's head was like moving a cut-out across the screen."

🐭 Disney Legend Frank Thomas, one of Disney's "Nine Old Men", 1993:
> "The early Mickey was all circles. We used nickels and dimes and quarters to draw the body, head and ears."

🐭 Disney Legend Ward Kimball, one of Disney's "Nine Old Men":
> "In the middle to late 1930, Mickey became very pliable. This pliability was best demonstrated in *Thru the Mirror* (1936) in

which Mickey shrinks to four inches and then grows to hit his head on the ceiling."

🐭 Disney Legend Frank Thomas, one of Disney's "Nine Old Men":

"It was very important to get the right proportions: how far down the ears were on the head, how the ears related to the nose to balance the face. Some animators made Mickey's ears too small, too high or too separated. As a result, the audience felt that something was wrong, though they didn't know what."

🐭 Disney Legend Ward Kimball, one of Walt's "Nine Old Men":

"In terms of reality, Mickey does not have believable construction. No matter which way he turns, the ears remain the same. He can make a 360-degree turn, and the ears will float in the same position. They're always round like bowling balls."

🐭 Animator Glen Keane:

"Mickey takes a leap forward whenever an animator makes him his own and isn't afraid of flexing the design a little to personalize him. The worst thing for animators is to be afraid of Mickey, so they don't put something of themselves into him. If you approach him too reverently, you end up with a lifeless, stiff icon, instead of a real flesh-and-blood character."

🐭 Disney Legend Ward Kimball, one of Disney's "Nine Old Men", 1975:

"If you were a top animator at Disney, you would work on the *Silly Symphonies* because they were the artistic cartoons. Mickey Mouse was the potboiler. That sounds funny because Mickey is such a camp hero now. But the *Silly Symphonies* were in color and the 'Mickeys' were in black and white. The *Symphonies* had a little more money spent on them. Also, we didn't grind them out like the 'Mickeys'."

🐭 Disney Legend Frank Thomas, one of Disney's "Nine Old Men":

"It was considered a great honor to work on a Mickey short. He was our star. Then Walt got too busy, and he was the only one to come up with the ideas."

🐭 Animator Andreas Deja who animated Mickey in *The Prince and the Pauper* (1990):

"The hardest thing about animating Mickey... is that the whole world knows him and how he behaves. You really have to go back and study the old shorts to find out what these characters are all about. It's not just how he looks or moves, but what is in his soul that makes him so incredibly appealing. Mickey Mouse represents the world of animation… and I think every animator at one time or another would love to draw him."

Animator Mark Henn, who animated Mickey in *Mickey's Christmas Carol* (1983):

"Mickey is a character with difficult proportions to render. And if you don't do it really well, if his nose is too big, or his ears are off, it jumps out at you. Mickey is very easy to draw… badly."

Animator Andreas Deja who animated Mickey in *Runaway Brain* (1995):

"I have always wanted to draw him (Mickey) and I think any animator, at one point or another, would have loved to do Mickey because he symbolizes the world of animation. It's no small potatoes to animate Mickey. Everyone knows him, people know how he moves, how he acts, so you have to abide by this reality and study the old short films closely in order to figure out Mickey's true personality."

Mickey's Personality

Lillian Disney, Walt's wife, *McCalls* magazine, February 1953:

"At this late date, I have no idea whether (Mickey) is a better name than "Mortimer". Nobody will ever know. I only feel a special affinity to Mickey because I helped name him. And besides, Mickey taught me a lot about what it was going to be like married to Walt Disney."

Disney Legend Ward Kimball, one of Disney's "Nine Old Men", *Sky* magazine, July 1988:

"Mickey became an international success practically overnight because, in his early films, he relied on sight gags for the majority of his laughs — much like Laurel and Hardy, Buster Keaton, and especially Charlie Chaplin. Whether people were watching in Hong Kong, Paris or Cairo, they didn't need to follow any dialogue. They could simply laugh at what was happening on screen."

Writer Henry Pringle. *McCalls* magazine, August 1932:

"(Walt) Disney insists solemnly, it is not at all true that Mickey is devoid of temperament. There are frequent days when he will not dance as he is supposed to dance. Hours are spent in the sound-proof recording room during which no progress is made. Mickey can be elusive and obstinate."

🐭 Disney Legend Ward Kimball, one of Disney's "Nine Old Men", 1975:

"Mickey was a great character in the early days when the plots were very, very simple. Most of Mickey's antics were based on playing musical instruments or tap dancing or doing something like the Charleston with Minnie. Our dilemma became one of trying to find new, logical material for Mickey, more sophisticated material, if you will.

"Mickey was really an abstraction. He wasn't based on anything that was remotely real. That's what killed him. Writing for Mickey became very difficult. Mickey began to be relegated to roles that were Boy Scoutish in nature. And then we just couldn't fit him into anything — so we finally discarded him. Mickey just faded away."

🐭 Writer Peter Ericsson, 1949:

"Mickey himself was indispensable (when he was with the rest of the Disney gang)... Not the most interesting or even likeable figure of the lot, he was always the pole of normality round which all else revolved in apparent lunacy."

🐭 Disney Legend Ub Iwerks, who designed and animated the original Mickey Mouse:

"Mickey was based on the character of (actor) Douglas Fairbanks Sr. He was the superhero of his day, always winning, gallant, and swashbuckling. Mickey's action was in that vein. He was never intended to be a sissy. He was always an adventurous character. I thought of him in that respect, and I had him do naturally the sort of thing Doug Fairbanks would do."

🐭 Animator and director Don Bluth:

"(Mickey) is an American institution, like Fred Astaire, Ginger Rogers and Judy Garland. He's been so popular because of his personality which is similar to Charlie Chaplin's Little Tramp — the innocent little fool the world crushes. People like him because he believes that things will work out."

🐭 Novelist Irving Wallace:

"Mickey is just one of those guys who never gets older. He is a miracle. He is of a special planet where we never grow old, or achy, a perfect place without politicians and poverty — that is the world of Mickey Mouse."

🐭 Nationally syndicated columnist Bob Greene:

"Mickey Mouse is the quintessential symbol of innocence.

Subliminally, he represents a lot of things we've lost. He represents how things used to be simple and fun and free of darkness."

🐭 Roy E. Disney, Walt's nephew:

"I sort of grew up with Mickey Mouse. He's so popular because he's such a nice little guy — feisty but not pushy. He has a basic goodness, a niceness — well, a likable friendliness. It gets translated without words."

🐭 Disney Legend Frank Thomas, one of Walt's "Nine Old Men":

"The gag man could put in gags, but Walt was the only one who could say, 'Hey, you're not using this guy right'. He would act out what he was talking about. He got everybody laughing, and he kept going. Mickey's personality was from out of Walt's past."

🐭 Writer Alva Johnston, *Woman's Home Companion*, July 1934:

"Mickey Mouse is not a foreigner in any part of the world. Mickey's public extends to and beyond the frontiers of civilization. He has, for example, an Eskimo following in Alaska... he was recently created a citizen of France at a carnival in Granville."

🐭 Animator and director Ralph Bakshi:

"Mickey Mouse's popularity is due to the integrity of how he was animated. He is a very beautifully designed character. That's what keeps him alive. Walt loved him and that shows."

🐭 Wayne Allwine, one of the official voice performers of Mickey Mouse:

"The tendency to make (Mickey) too nice has limited him. But he's an actor, and he's capable of doing whatever he's given to do — provided it's kept in the context of what Mickey would and wouldn't do. I've had people ask to hear him swear, but I'd never do that — he's too special. I think the character is still as Walt envisioned him: forever young and forever optimistic. Walt has always been very much alive in Mickey Mouse."

🐭 Cartoonist Roman Arambula who drew the Sunday *Mickey Mouse* comic strip:

"Mickey is not just one personality — he couldn't be, because he's been done by so many artists. As an artist, I have to be myself, so the Mickey I draw is my Mickey."

🐭 Disney Legend Frank Thomas, one of Disney's "Nine Old Men":

"In the beginning, Mickey was a different character in each picture, but all the Mickeys had something of Chaplin in them."

🐭 Animator Mark Henn, who animated Mickey in *Mickey's Christmas Carol* (1983):

"There are definitely limits to the character. He's a hero. He represents all the good things in people. Just to say he's a good guy who would never hurt a fly is too extreme. I like to think of him as the kind of person who's good at whatever he does."

🐭 Character analysis from "How to Draw Mickey Mouse: Walt Disney Character Model Guide", Disneyland Art Corner, 1955:

"Mickey is the natural leader and the smartest of the Disney crew. He is cheerful, sensitive, warmhearted, and generally likes people. He is brave and will fight against impossible odds, if he knows he's in the right. He is shy in front of crowds, yet always puts on a good show."

🐭 Disney Legend Ward Kimball to author Richard Shale in 1976:

"He was the one character in our cast that was not believable. Because when you saw Donald Duck, you accepted him as a duck. He walked like a duck. He was two feet high. Pluto was a real dog. Goofy you accepted him as a man. He might have had those ears, but he was a man. But what are you going to do with a mouse that's three feet high, where his ears just float?

"They don't turn in perspective. (He) has this funny black and white division (on his face), has garden hose legs... and this is what happened to Mickey. He finally just became a symbol because he's three feet high and he's a mouse."

🐭 Disney Legend Frank Thomas, one of Disney's "Nine Old Men":

"(Mickey Mouse) was more of an actor placed in funny situations than a comedian. He was like any of us somehow inadvertently getting ourselves into awkward situations or becoming the victim of misunderstanding. These were areas where Walt could give his best suggestions in story and acting."

🐭 Disney Legend Ward Kimball at the Mouse Club convention 1982:

"Something's happened to the Mouse through the middle years. You know, he started out without shoes or gloves. Then he got red pants. His face got rounder. They added eyebrows, and now, most youngsters know him as a cute youngster with a bowtie of all things. He's become a sissy!"

🐭 Jimmy MacDonald, one of the voices of Mickey Mouse, *North Carolina Times-News*, October 23, 1982:

"People still love Mickey. Maybe the children love him most but adults love him, too. Walt always reminded us that it was the adults who took the children to the movies. I like being Mickey. He was a nice character, sort of a family man. You could count on him. He was dependable. He was also brave and honest, a leader in a way."

Disney producer Harry Tytle:

"We always considered Mickey a 'boy scout' character and therefore limited the fixes he got into. Mickey had always been 'top mouse' so to keep him alive, we put him in Pluto stories at the opening and ending, but released the short subject under the Mickey Mouse banner."

Disney Legend Ollie Johnston, one of Disney's "Nine Old Men":

"Almost from the start, Walt had thought of his cartoon characters as being definite personalities. Mickey Mouse was shy and chivalrous, courageous and compassionate, and had a deep sense of right and wrong. You could not have him throw a tantrum like Donald Duck and expect anyone to laugh."

Unnamed Disney story writer in 1949:

"Mickey is limited today because of the public idealization has turned him into a Boy Scout. Every time we put him into a trick, a temper, a joke, thousands of people would belabor us with nasty letters. So we can whip out three Donald Duck stories in the time it takes us to work out one for the Mouse."

Fortune magazine, November 1934:

"Mickey Mouse is an international hero, better known than Roosevelt or Hitler, a part of the folklore of the world. It takes more than humor to achieve such renown. It takes a quality real and simple enough to cut deep into the emotions of people everywhere... Mickey Mouse was Disney's own creation, the braggart, precarious master of a world taken whole from the rustic conditions of Disney's childhood... Mickey Mouse was good plebian name for a mouse of the people.

"The Mickey Mouse personality has a very real existence. It gives him an entrée into home both royal and obscure where neither Garbo nor Noel Coward could ever enter. Charms and tokens and medals bearing his image are carried in more far places than ever carried the likeness of an emperor."

Playwright Arthur Miller 1933:

"Mickey is 'Everyman', battling for life and love...he is honest, decent, a good sportsman...Mickey has little weaknesses but there is no question which side he is on. He is little David who slays Goliath. He is that most popular, because more universally conceivable, hero — the little man who shuts his eyes and pastes the big bully in the jaw."

Disney Legend Marc Davis, one of Disney's "Nine Old Men":

"(Mickey Mouse) was one of the greatest folk characters of all time...I don't think you can name any character that represents the last fifty years better than Mickey...He's a completely symbolical guy."

Animator Floyd Norman, writer on the *Mickey Mouse* comic strip:

"Mickey Mouse is not really a funny guy. He is, however, a great character, and can be wonderful in stories... I saw Mickey Mouse as a cartoon version of George Lucas' Indiana Jones. Come to think of it -- maybe that's where George got the idea in the first place. Mickey Mouse was always the scrappy little guy who never gives up. The Mickey adventure stories (in the newspaper comic strips) were a joy, and now I knew why Floyd Gottfredson (artist for the Mickey Mouse comic strip for 45 years) must have loved his job so much."

Press Sheet to theater managers entitled "Columbia Pictures Presents Mickey Mouse" (1931):

"Mickey, a moral young mouse, never sings in his bathtub unless the more delicate portions of his sinuous torso are concealed by a flock of rich, creamy suds."

Animator and historian John Canemaker:

"I think of Mickey as an actor, a jolly, cheerful symbol that embodies the American spirit of optimism, can-do energy and versatility."

Disney Legend John Hench, *Crimmers* magazine, Winter 1975:

"(Mickey's) personality was a strong point. But it was a consistent statement — his personality and this form said the same thing."

Disney Legend Marc Davis, *Crimmers* magazine, Winter 1975:

"Mickey, as he grew up, became the straight man, the average guy, and the average guy is never as interesting as the flamboyant character (like Donald Duck). Yet, he has lived all this time, and is perhaps one of the greatest folk characters of all time."

🐭 Storyman Ted Sears, 1939 lecture at the Disney Studio:

> "The public's affection for him (Mickey) grew when he encountered difficulties and acted under pressure... When he works in difficulty, the laughs reach their peak with each little snag or each event. They depend largely on Mickey's expressions, his attitude, his position, his state of mind, and the drawing style chosen to express things."

🐭 Disney animator Andreas Deja:

> "The first time I saw Mickey Mouse animated was on an old black and white TV set in Germany. I was about five, and I didn't want it to end. I love his shape and his personality. There's a positiveness that I admire. He's about using your brain, and having a sense of humor on top of it. We need more of that in our lives."

🐭 Storyman Ted Sears, 1939 lecture at the Disney Studio:

> "Mickey is at his best when he sets out to do some particular thing and continues with deadly determination in spite of the fact that one annoyance after another, or some serious menace, tries to impede his progress... Mickey can still be entertaining when things are running smoothly. Mickey is seldom funny in a chase picture, as his character and expressions are usually lost."

Mickey's Voice

🐭 Composer Carl Stalling talking to Disney historian Michael Barrier about doing Mickey's voice in *Wild Waves* (1929):

> "They couldn't decide whether they wanted (Mickey) to speak or not... Walt probably told me to try it. All of the animators were taking a shot at it."

🐭 Jimmy MacDonald, one of the official voices for Mickey Mouse, *Washington Post* April 24, 1982:

> "It's pretty simple, just a plain falsetto. You can't make any sustained speeches because it's all a monotone and it gets dull to listen to."

🐭 Wayne Allwine, one of the official voices of Mickey Mouse:

> "Jimmy (MacDonald) said to me (when I took over doing Mickey's voice), 'Just remember, kid, you're only filling in for the boss'. And that's the way he treated Mickey for years and years. I'm just filling in for the boss, too. Mickey's the star."

🐭 Russi Taylor, the official voice of Minnie Mouse:

> "We (Russi and her husband Wayne Allwine, the official voice of

Mickey) were doing an interview on a Puerto Rican radio station. People could hardly speak English and Wayne starts playing on his ukulele the chords to a song about the Puerto Rican flag. And Mickey sang. They hunted us down the next day and asked us to please come and do it again because they'd gotten so many people calling wanting to hear Mickey Mouse sing the song again."

Wayne Allwine, one of the official voices of Mickey Mouse:

"It's like being Santa. Somebody's handed you a national icon to preserve the quality and heart Walt put into it (the voice of Mickey Mouse). Walt always knew our business was really to seed memories for the future."

Disney Legend Frank Thomas, one of Disney's "Nine Old Men":

"Mickey's acting (in *Steamboat Willie*) shows Walt's great interest in personality. In the 1920s, emotions were shown in a very elemental way."

Wayne Allwine, one of the official voices of Mickey Mouse:

"I've been privileged to voice Mickey for 25 years, but he's not just a voice to me. He has so much life and spirit, and to be part of the good Mickey does in others' lives is a gift. You can't work with Mickey without it changing you. I'm a better person for having done his voice."

Memories of Mickey

Roy E. Disney, nephew of Walt Disney:

"My favorite Disney character is Mickey Mouse. Firstly, he's really my older brother (or more accurately, my older cousin) having come into the world less than two years before my birth. Secondly, he's the one who started the whole thing, and thirdly, and most importantly, he's simply a lovable character."

Magician David Copperfield:

"Mickey is magical. He looks great from every angle. He even looks good on a wristwatch. He's loved everywhere he goes. He's proof that an idea can be so pure, so specific yet universal that it can transcend every barrier and last forever."

Bridgeport Connecticut Herald, September 29, 1935:

"At the age of seven, Mickey Mouse puts to shame all the child prodigies that have ever warmed fond parents' hearts. Mickey Mouse has had more honors showered upon him than many an international hero."

🐭 Disney Legend John Hench, 2000:

"The attraction to Mickey is almost primitive. Kids who scream bloody murder when their parents put them on Santa's lap will run up to Mickey and wrap their arms around his legs."

🐭 Disney Legend Ward Kimball, one of Disney's "Nine Old Men", 1978:

"Mickey seems to have an attraction for kids from the day they are born."

🐭 Disney Legend Frank Thomas, one of Disney's "Nine Old Men":

"We always drew Minnie with real broad, feminine gestures. Most of the time, she was modest, shy and girlish. I think Minnie reflected Walt's idea of what a girl ought to be. He was kind of mystified by women, you know."

🐭 Actress Hayley Mills:

"Mickey Mouse was part of my childhood and he is part of my children's childhood. He's a wonderful link to your past and to the future. He's an experience we all share."

🐭 Director Burny Mattinson who brought Mickey back to the theatrical screen after thirty years with *Mickey's Christmas Carol* (1983).

"People would constantly ask me 'When are they going to bring back Mickey and the gang?' Finally, I realized that 'they' was me. My wife told me to stop talking and start doing."

🐭 *Motion Picture Daily*, 1930:

"When you say it is up to the Disney Mickey Mouse standard, there is nothing left to be said."

🐭 Actor Fess Parker who portrayed Davy Crockett, *Remember* magazine, April 1995:

"Absolutely amazing it all came from one little cartoon scratched on one piece of paper... and the sense of storytelling."

🐭 Disney Legend Marc Davis, *Crimmers* magazine, Winter 1975:

"There are many, many factors (for Mickey's success). One is the particular time he was born in. It was certainly a case of the right place at the right time. In 1929, there was The Crash... Here was this little character who the things he did were things people could laugh at... twenty-five cents worth of entertainment."

🐭 Writer Edwin C. Hill, *Boston American*, April 8, 1933:

"Perhaps Mickey's celebrity is not so amazing, after all, when one remembers that he came to us at the time the country needed him most — the beginning of the Depression. He has helped us laugh away our troubles, forget our creditors and keep our chins up."

🐭 Disney artist Willie Ito, renowned for his Mickey Mouse collection:

"During World War II, when I was about eight, my family and I were sent to a Japanese internment camp. I had some Mickey Mouse comic books with me. I drew from those comic books, using pages of old Sears catalogs. Mickey was always with me throughout those camp years. He gave me a sense of still being connected. He fed my imagination and gave me a goal."

🐭 Actor Fess Parker:

"I was very young when I first saw Mickey in *Steamboat Willie* and what an impression he made on me. When I was in grade school, my most prized possession was a yellow slicker with Mickey's picture on it."

🐭 Animator and author Floyd Norman, a Disney Legend:

"Writing (the last six years of the Mickey Mouse comic strip) was not always fun because I was well aware I was no longer dealing with the feisty little character Walt had created. Mickey was now Disney's corporate symbol with all the baggage that came with that image. I can't tell you how many times I found myself in hot water with Disney's legal people because of my gags. One organization thought the Disney company was taking a jab at satellite companies, because I had Goofy using a satellite dish as a bird bath."

🐭 Animation producer Joe Barbera of Hanna-Barbera:

"What about Mickey Mouse? Disney tried very hard to make him a star. But Mickey Mouse is more of a symbol than a real character."

🐭 *Motion Picture Herald*, February 23, 1931:

"Mickey is not to drink, smoke, or tease the stock in the barnyard... Mickey has been spanked... doing what everyone approves (which means) very little of anything."

🐭 Disney Legend John Hench:

"I have always been mystified with the power of Mickey Mouse, how he can go everywhere in the world, never to be questioned or suspected of being an American export. It is mostly a matter of déjà vu, apparently, because people seem to recognize something about him."

🐭 Former U.S. President Jimmy Carter, 1988:

"Nowadays, most people on Earth are young enough to remember Mickey Mouse as a delightful part of their childhood. Among children in foreign countries, Mickey is usually seen as an American friend who can speak their language perfectly and who always presents his native land in an admirable way."

🐭 Actress Julie Andrews:

"I am always filled with joy at how readily Mickey's presence is embraced. His persona transcends all barriers, and we need more like him in this world."

🐭 Astronaut Buzz Aldrin, the second person to walk on the moon:

"Mickey transcends being just a character. He's a symbol of the magnitude of the entire Disney dynasty. That Disney has been able to keep the integrity of its legend, Mickey, throughout all these generations is a real achievement."

🐭 Disney artist Willie Ito, retired Director of Disney Consumer Products International Creative, 1997:

"We've grown up with Mickey and his particular personality. In his black and white days, he was a mischievous little boy. Then he grew up to be the guy next door — adventurous and slightly mischievous, but a right fellow, never out to hurt anyone and never cruel... He's a wholesome character and we try never to show him in a military uniform."

🐭 Official Walt Disney Imagineering statement on "Hidden Mickeys":

"We will neither confirm nor deny the existence of so-called 'Hidden Mickeys' in any of our parks, resorts, or cruise ships. If they do exist, the very fact that they are hidden means we, as the official creative design and development division of Walt Disney Parks and Resorts, are unaware of them."

🐭 Business Manager of Fleischer Studio, Sam Buchwald, *New York Times*, February 13, 1936:

"An interesting thing about it [the animation industry] is the way that the familiar cartoon characters rise, have their day of great popularity, and then wane just as real stars do. Although Disney doesn't say much about it, his lovable Mickey, greatest animated character of all time, is definitely on the way out."

Final Word: Walt Disney on Mickey Mouse

"Whenever I see Mickey Mouse, I have to cry. Because he reminds me so much of Walt."

—Lillian Disney
Walt Disney's widow (1974)

Scattered throughout the text of this book are many quotes by Walt Disney about his thoughts and feelings on Mickey Mouse. Walt was constantly asked his opinions and insights about his most famous character in almost every interview he gave for over thirty years. In this section are some of those direct remarks that don't generally appear elsewhere in this book.

Physical Appearance

- "He had to be simple. We had to push out seven hundred feet of film every two weeks so we couldn't have a character who was tough to draw. His head was a circle with an oblong circle for a snout. The ears were also circles so they could be drawn the same, no matter how he turned his head. His body was like a pear and he had a long tail. His legs were pipe stems and we stuck them in big shoes.

  "We didn't want him to have mouse hands, because he was supposed to be more human. So we gave him gloves. Five fingers looked like too much on such a little figure, so we took away one. That was just one less finger to animate. To provide a little detail, we gave him the two-button pants. There was no mouse hair or any other frills that would slow down animation. That made it tougher for the cartoonists to give him character." Interview with Bob Thomas. 1957.

- "And it is certainly gratifying that the public which first welcomed him two decades ago, as well as their children, have not permitted us, even if we had wished to, to change him in any manner or degree, other than a few minor revisions of his physical appearance. In a sense he was never young. In the same sense, he never grows old in our eyes. All we can do is give him things to overcome in his own, rather stubborn way, in his cartoon universe."

- "Mickey's thirty years old now. He's a little better constructed mouse than he ever was. He's improved with age." Tony Thomas interview. 1959.

- "However, Mickey is a kind-hearted little fellow. He does the impossible but he never expects the impossible from us who work for him." *Screen Book* magazine. January 1934

Man or Mouse

- "Mickey Mouse was never anything like a mouse, no more than Donald Duck was ever a duck." Walt talking to Disney producer Harry Tytle.

- "I often find myself surprised at what has been said about our redoubtable little Mickey, who was never really a mouse nor yet wholly a man—although always recognizably human, I hope." *University of the Air* broadcast. July 9, 1948.

- "He is very real to me and to those fellow-workers of mine who guide his impish footsteps on the screen. We never think of him as a mouse. Nor as a drawing. He is always human. When we are first discussing the script of a new picture, we actually go through the scene ourselves. It is just as if we are planning scenes for a living star."

"Mickey's a very busy young star — and the only one in Hollywood who isn't paid! I often regret that it is impossible to reward him in some way for all the fun he has given to the world." *Film Pictorial* magazine. September 30, 1933.

- "He is not a little mouse. He only looks like one." *Overland Monthly*. October 1933.

- "I write their roles — Mickey and Donald — as if they were live beings, independent of their creator. I believe in them as creatures endowed with reason, they are often touching. They are not static, they evolve with time the way a child grows... When people laugh at Mickey, it's because of his humanity and that is the secret of his popularity."

- "When I bought my camera (a Victor 16mm to shoot home movies), I intended to use it entirely for my own pleasure. But Mickey Mouse intervened. He always does! Ever since I first drew him, he has become more and more real, and like a real child." *American Cinematographer* magazine. March 1932.

Mickey's Voice

- "I was trying to find somebody to be the mouse voice. I kept going through this routine: I'd try different guys and I'd say, 'No, it's more like this. It's more like this.' And the guys said, 'Well, Walt, why don't you do it?' So I did."

- "It (Walt being the voice of Mickey Mouse) started from the necessity of saving expenses and doing everything we could ourselves. Naturally, however, it has grown to be a pleasure. And when you hear him talk today, you hear me talk as well. Not that I talk like Mickey all the time!" *News of the World*. 1934.

- "He still speaks for me and I still speak for him."

- "He's a shy little feller, so I've provided the voice. I use a falsetto. His voice changed after I had my tonsils out. It became a little deeper. But no one noticed it. I kind of like it better. Sometimes I'm sorry I started the voice. It takes a lot of time and I feel silly doing The Mouse in front of the sound crew. But I'm sentimental about him, I guess, and it wouldn't be the same if anyone else did the speaking."

- "Mickey still speaks in my own falsetto-pitched voice, as he has from the first. In the early days, I did the voice of most of the other characters too. It was not financially feasible to hire people for such assignments. In *Steamboat Willie*, in addition to speaking for Mickey, I also supplied a few sound effects for Minnie, his girl friend, and for the parrot." *Who's Who in Hollywood*. Vol. 1, No. 3 April-June 1948.

Birth of Mickey

- "It seems like yesterday that Mickey Mouse first romped across our drawing board. He was born of a desire to move ahead in this great entertainment industry. He symbolized for us the breaking of a chain with the past and the beginning of a new career."

- "I got the idea, I suppose, when I was working in an office in Kansas City. The girls used to put their lunches in wire waste baskets and everyday the mice would scamper around in them after crumbs. I got interested and began collecting a family in an old box. They became very tame and by the time I was ready to turn them loose, they were so friendly, they just sat there on the floor looking at me." *Minneapolis Star* newspaper. 1933.

- "About keeping a pet mouse. Yes, I had (a pet mouse) during my grade school days in Kansas City. He was a gentle little field mouse. I kept him in my pocket on a string leash. Whenever things seemed to get a bit dull between classes, I would let him rove about on his leash under the seats to get laughs from the other kids. And he got laughs until the teacher rather sharply disagreed with my sense of extracurricular activities and made me keep the little beastie home.
  "Perhaps it was the fond memory of him... and of others of his clan who used to pick up lunch crumbs in our first cartoon studio, the family garage, that came to mind when we needed so desperately to find a new character to survive... Mickey Mouse's country forefathers, you might say."

- "Mickey Mouse, to me, is the symbol of independence. He was a means to an end. He popped out of my mind onto a drawing pad on a train ride from Manhattan to Hollywood at a time when business fortunes of my brother Roy and myself were at lowest ebb and disaster seemed right around the corner.
  "Born of necessity, the little fellow literally freed us of immediate worry. He provided the means for expanding our organization and for extending the medium of cartoon animation towards new entertainment levels."

- "So I was all alone and had nothing. Mrs. Disney and I were coming back from New York on the train and I had to have something... I can't tell them I've lost Oswald... so, I had this mouse in the back of my head... because a mouse is sort of a sympathetic character in spite of the fact that everybody's frightened of a mouse... including myself."

Mickey's Personality

- "Sometimes I've tried to figure out why Mickey appealed to the whole word. Everybody's tried to figure it out. So far as I know, nobody has. He's a pretty nice fellow who never does anybody any harm, who gets into scrapes through no fault of his own, but always manages to come up grinning. Why Mickey's even been faithful to one girl, Minnie, all his life. Mickey is so simple and uncomplicated, so easy to understand that you can't help liking him."

- "All we ever intended for him, or expected of him was that he should continue to make people everywhere chuckle with him and at him. We didn't burden him with any social symbolism. We made him no mouth piece for frustration or harsh satire. Mickey was simply a little personality assigned to the purpose of laughter."

- "Mickey isn't funny in a situation of that sort. I think people think of Mickey as a cute character --he is a cute character -- and he should be more likable in everything he does. I have always kind of compared Mickey to Harold Lloyd -- he has to have situations (or) he isn't funny... I'd rather not make Mickey (films) if we don't get the right idea for him...These things with the Duck are always funny, but if you try to pull those with Mickey, it seems like someone trying to be funny." Walt Disney's comments in a story meeting about the never-completed short, *Mountain Carvers*, held on August 8, 1939.

- "Back in those days, when I was making nothing but the Mickey (cartoons), I always thought of him as a personality. There were things that he would do and there were things that he just couldn't do. I would think of it this way, 'Now this is something that Mickey could do'. So we always thought of him as a personality. But it reached a point... I never thought of him as a mouse... we thought of him more as a little boy... Early in the Mickey Mouse series, he started out as a little boy in effect... I always thought of Mickey as a little fellow.
  "And Mickey had to have certain types of situations and things... he was only good for certain types of situations and things... he was only good for certain things. I compared him to Harold Lloyd. Mickey in himself wasn't funny. He was cute. So the situation had to make Mickey funny. Now when the Duck came along, the Duck was just the opposite. He was comic within himself. He supplied something that we just couldn't do with Mickey. (Mickey) was what I called a situation comic, and the Duck was the comic." *LOOK* magazine. January 1964.

- "The Mouse's private life isn't especially colorful. He's never been the type that would go in for swimming pools and night clubs, more the simple country boy at heart. Lives on a quiet residential street, has occasional dates with his girl friend, Minnie, doesn't drink or smoke, likes the movies and band concerts, things like that." *New York Times Magazine.* September 21, 1947.

- "He has appeared in more pictures than any flesh and blood star. He was the first cartoon character to express personality and to be constantly kept in character. I thought of him from the first as a distinct individual not just a cartoon type or symbol going through comedy routine. I kept him away from stock symbols and situations. We exposed him in close-ups.
  "Instead of speeding the cartoons, as was then the fashion, we were not afraid to slow down the tempo and let Mickey emote. We allowed audiences to get acquainted with him. To recognize him as a personage, motivated by character instead of situations." *University of the Air* broadcast. July 9, 1948.

- "He is never mean or ugly. He never lies nor cheats nor steals. He is a clean, happy, little fellow who loves life and folks. He never takes advantage of the weak and we see to it that nothing ever happens that will cure his faith in the transcendent destiny of one Mickey Mouse or his convictions that the world is just a big apple pie. Our animators and gag men having rescued Mickey from every conceivable predicament, the young fellow knows not fear save when he sees a friend in danger." *Overland Monthly.* October 1933.

- "When, on occasions, as boys will, the lad (Mickey) becomes too cocky and struts vaingloriously before admiring Minnie, Fate in the gag department kicks him from the rear and rolls him ignobly in the dust of gentle ridicule. Sex is just another word to Mickey, and the story of the traveling salesman of no more interest than the ladies' lingerie department." *Overland Monthly.* October 1933.

- "Of course, sound had a very considerable effect on our treatment of Mickey Mouse. It gave his character a new dimension. It rounded him into complete life-likeness. We kept him loveable although ludicrous in his blundering heroics. And that's the way he's remained despite any outside influences. He's grown into a consistent, predictable character to whom we could assign only the kind of role and antics which were correct for his reputation." *University of the Air.* July 9, 1948.

- "Mickey soon reached the stage where we had to be very careful about what we permitted him to do. Mickey could never be a rat. He had become a hero in the eyes of his audiences, especially the youngsters. Mickey could do no wrong." *Who's Who in Hollywood.* Vol. 1, No. 3 April-June 1948.

- "We learned after hard lessons, too, that the public wants its heroes. In some of the pictures we tried to let other animals steal the honors from Mickey. There was an immediate reaction against this. Mickey has to be the whole thing, especially in the matter of brains. No one must outdo him." *American* magazine. March 1931.

- "Mickey's decline is due to his heroic nature. He has become such a legendary character that we can't joke around with him anymore. He is surrounded by as many taboos as a hero in a Western. He doesn't drink, doesn't smoke, isn't violent... He is such an institution that we are limited in what we can make him do. Mickey always has to be nice, eternally adorable. What are you going to do with a leading role like that?" *Collier's* magazine. April 9, 1949.

- "Mickey first subsidized our *Silly Symphony* series. From there he sustained other ventures, plugging along as our bread-and-butter hero. He was the studio prodigy and pet. And we treated him accordingly." *Who's Who in Hollywood*. Vol. 1, No. 3 April-June 1948.

The Mickey Audience

- "The Mickey audience... it has no racial, national, political, religious or social differences or affiliations. The Mickey audience is made up of parts of people, of that deathless, precious, ageless absolutely primitive remnant of something, in a very world-wracked human being which makes us play with children's toys and laugh without self-consciousness at silly things and sing in bathtubs, and dream and believe that our babies are uniquely beautiful. You know... the Mickey in us." *Overland Monthly*. October 1933.

Quick Quotes

- "As long as there's a Disney Studio, there'll be Mickey Mouse cartoons. I can't live without them."

- "Girls bored me. They still do. I love Mickey Mouse more than any woman I've ever known."

- "He was born full-grown but he wasn't fully developed. That took a lot of time, twenty years so far. He'll probably keep on developing."

- "After 120 pictures, it's only natural for (my animation staff) to get a little tired of The Mouse. It's tough to come up with new ideas, to keep him fresh and at the same time in character. The Duck's a lot easier. You can do anything with him." 1948.

- "In fact, there's hardly any evidence of the Mouse or anything around the place. I've lived with it too much, and I just did not want to live with it at home. I tried to set up my home as something apart."

- "Mickey enabled me to go ahead and do the things I had in mind and the things I foresaw as a natural trend of film fantasy. He spelled production liberation for us."

- "All we planned or expected was that the audience everywhere would laugh with him or at him for pleasure."

- "If our gang ever put Mickey in a situation less wholesome than sunshine, Mickey would take Minnie by the hand and move to some other studio." *Overland Monthly*. October 1933.

- "The life and ventures of Mickey Mouse have been closely bound up with my own personal and professional life. It is understandable that I should have sentimental attachment for the little personage who played so big a part in the course of Disney Productions and who has been so happily accepted as an amusing friend wherever films are shown around the world. He expresses himself for me and I speak for him." *Who's Who in Hollywood*. Vol. 1, No. 3 April-June 1948.

- "But what they forget is that The Mouse hasn't made a picture since the war. He was in one short released in '42. Five years off the screen and he still rates third! Is there any star in Hollywood with a public that loyal?" Walt Disney commenting on a 1947 Gallup Audience Research Institute poll that the public's preference by audience members under the age of thirty was first for Donald Duck, second for Bugs Bunny and Mickey Mouse was third. That same poll showed that Mickey was second after Donald Duck for audiences over the age of thirty. Interview for Tony Thomas "Voices from the Hollywood Past". 1959.

- "Naturally, I am pleased with his continued popularity here and abroad; with the esteem he has won as an entertainment name among youngsters and grownups; with the honors he's brought our studio... These are tributes beyond all words of appreciation. The psychoanalysts have probed him. Wise men of critical inclination have pondered him. Columnists have kidded him. Admirers have saluted him in extraordinary terms." *University of the Air*. July 9, 1948.

- "To be honest about the matter, when our gang goes into a huddle and comes out with a new Mickey Mouse story, we will not have worried one bit as to whether the picture will make the children better men and women, or whether it will conform with the enlightened theories of child psychology." *Overland Monthly*. October 1933.

- "It is not our job to teach, implant morals or improve anything except our pictures. If Mickey has a bit of practical philosophy to offer the younger generation, it is to keep on trying. That's what we do who make animated cartoons. In the United States, there are fifty million children enrolled in Mickey Mouse Clubs. It is our hope and ambition to keep on trying so that the hundred million children of these fifty million children will have the Mickey in them released and nourished by better cartoons than we make today." *Overland Monthly*. October 1933.

- "Perhaps it is one of the many paradoxes of the picture business that a star who has taken the screen by storm should receive no salary for his services, and should have been made not born. His exploits have brought in many thousands of dollars, though the star himself is just something out of an inkpot." 1934.

- "Mickey and I are firm friends. We have weathered the storms together. I have tried to give him a soul and a 'keep kissable' disposition." *Windsor* magazine. January 1934.

- "Mickey's been my passport to everything I've wanted to do. When I felt I should branch out a little — I wanted to try pure beauty in cartoons. I wanted to try animating great music. I had a lot of ideas — but all the exhibitors wanted was Mickey. Okay, I gave them Mickey, but they had to take my Silly (Symphonies)". *The New York Times*. 1953.

- "By laughing at Mickey's antics and Donald's mishaps, youngsters learn to laugh at their own troubles. The period of their lives when they can live in a world peopled by fairy tale characters is all too short." January 21, 1951.

- "Mickey was the beginning. Because of his popularity, we were able to go on and attempt the things that were to make animation a real art. It was an art that was subsidized by the public's acceptance of what we were doing."

- "In this Mickey Mouse-minded world, Mickey is an international symbol of good will."

- "Fancy being remembered for the invention of a mouse!"

- "I guess you all know this little fellow here. It's an old partnership. Mickey and I started out that first time many, many years ago. We've had a lot of our dreams come true." *Disneyland* weekly television show. October 1954.

- "I was stumped one day when a little boy asked, 'Do you draw Mickey Mouse?' I had to admit I do not draw anymore. 'Then you think up the jokes and ideas?' 'No,' I said. 'I don't do that.' Finally he looked at me and said, 'Mr. Disney, just what do you do?'"

Selected Bibliography

Hundreds of books, personal interviews, magazine and newspaper articles, and other sources, including films and videos, were utilized in locating and verifying information that appears in this book.

Some of those references are identified within the text itself. Here is an additional short selected bibliography:

Bailey, Adrian: *Walt Disney's World of Fantasy* (Everest House 1982)

Bain, David and Bruce Harris, eds.: *Mickey Mouse: Fifty Happy Years* (Harmony Books 1978)

Barrier, Michael: *Animated Man - A Life of Walt Disney* (University of California Press 2007)

Barrier, Michael: *Building a Better Mouse: Fifty Years of Animation* (Library of Congress catalog 1978)

Cotter, Bill: *The Wonderful World of Disney Television: A Complete History* (Hyperion 1997)

Culhane, John: *Walt Disney's Fantasia* (Harry N. Abrams 1983)

Disney Miller, Diane and Pete Martin: *The Story of Walt Disney* (Holt 1957)

Farber, R. H.: *Time To Rewind: A Guide to Collecting Disneyana Ingersoll Wrist Watches 1933-1939* (Farber 2004)

Feild, Robert D.: *The Art of Walt Disney* (Collins 1947)

Finch, Christopher: *The Art of Walt Disney — From Mickey Mouse to the Magic Kingdom* (Harry N. Abrams, Inc. 1973)

Gerstein, David: *Walt Disney's Mickey and the Gang* (Gemstone Publishing 2005)

Gerstein, David and Gary Groth: *Walt Disney's Mickey Mouse by Floyd Gottfredson Volumes 1-4* and *Color Sundays: Walt Disney's Mickey Mouse* (Fantagraphics Books 2011-2013)

Ghez, Didier ed: *Walt's People Volumes 1-13* (Theme Park Press, 2005-2013)

Grant, John: *Encyclopedia of Walt Disney's Animated Characters* (Hyperion 1998)

Green, Amy Boothe and Howard E. Green: *Remembering Walt: Favorite*

Memories of Walt Disney (Disney Editions 1999)

Hamilton, Bruce: *Walt Disney's Mickey Mouse in Color* (Pantheon Books 1988)

Heide, Robert and John Gilman: *Cartoon Collectibles* (Dolphin Book, 1983)

Heide, Robert and John Gilman: *Disneyana: Classic Collectibles 1928-1958* (Hyperion 1994)

Heide, Robert and John Gilman: *The Mickey Mouse Watch: From the Beginning of Time* (Hyperion 1997)

Heide, Robert and John Gilman, Monique Peterson, Patrick White: *Mickey Mouse: The Evolution, The Legend, The Phenomenon!* (Disney Editions 2001)

Hench, John with Peggy Van Pelt: *Designing Disney* (Disney Editions 2003)

Holliss, Richard and Brian Sibley: *Walt Disney's Mickey Mouse: His Life and Times* (Harper & Row 1986)

Holliss, Richard and Brian Sibley: *The Disney Studio Story* (Crown 1988)

Iwerks, Leslie and John Kenworthy: *The Hand Behind the Mouse* (Disney Editions 1996)

Jackson, Kathy Merlock: *Walt Disney: A Bio-Bibliography* (Greenwood Press 1993)

Justice, Bill: *Justice for Disney* (Tomart Publications 1992)

Keller, Keith: *The Mickey Mouse Club Scrapbook* (Grosset & Dunlap 1975)

Korkis, Jim: *The Vault of Walt Volumes 1-2* (Theme Park Press 2012-2013)

Korkis, Jim and John Cawley: *Cartoon Confidential* (Malibu Graphics 1991)

Korkis, Jim and John Cawley: *The Encyclopedia of Cartoon Superstars* (Pioneer Books 1990)

Korkis, Jim and John Cawley: *How to Create Animation* (Pioneer Books 1990)

Lambert, Pierre: *Mickey Mouse* (Hyperion 1998)

Lesjak, David: *Toons At War* (Lesjak 2000)

Maltin, Leonard: *The Disney Films* (Disney Editions 2000)

Maltin, Leonard: *Of Mice and Magic* (Plume 1987)

Munsey, Cecil: *Disneyana* (Hawthorn Books Inc. 1974)

Rawls, Walton: *Disney Dons Dogtags* (Abbeville 1992)

Santoli, Lorraine: *The Official Mickey Mouse Club Book* (Hyperion 1995)

Shale, Richard: *Donald Duck Joins Up* (UMI Research Press 1982)

Shine, Bernard C.: *Mickey Mouse Memorabilia: The Vintage Years 1928-1938* (Harry N. Abrams 1986)

Smith, Dave: *Disney A to Z: The Updated Official Encyclopedia* (Disney Editions 2006)

Solomon, Charles: *The Disney That Never Was* (Hyperion 1995)

Taylor, Deems: *Walt Disney's Fantasia* (Simon and Schuster 1940)

Thomas, Bob: *Walt Disney: An American Original* (Disney Editions 1994)

Thomas, Bob: *The Art of Animation* (Simon & Schuster 1958)

Thomas, Frank; Johnston Ollie: *Disney Animation: The Illusion of Life* (Disney Editions 1995)

Thomas, Frank; Johnston Ollie: *Too Funny For Words* (Abbeville Press 1987)

Tieman, Robert: *The Mickey Mouse Treasures* (Disney Editions 2007)

Tietyen, David: *The Musical World of Walt Disney* (Hal Leonard Publishing Corporation 1990

Tytle, Harry: *One of Walt's Boys* (ASAP Publishing 1997)

Williams, Pat: *How to Be Like Walt* (HCI 2004)

Acknowledgments

I take this opportunity to acknowledge not only the people who directly helped me with this book but those who have inspired or supported me over the years and deserve to see their name printed prominently in a Disney-related book.

The names are purposely not in alphabetical order so that you have to read them all or at least most of them.

This book would not have been possible without the skills and encouragement of Bob McLain and Theme Park Press. Many thanks for a professional forum to share these stories with so many others.

Thanks to my brothers, Michael and Chris, and their families, including their children Amber, Keith, Autumn and Story, who never really understood what their uncle does or why he does it. Also, my three grand-nieces Skylar, Shea, and Sidnee, who have already at a very young age fallen in love with Mickey Mouse. Uncle Jim loves you all very much.

Many thanks to Didier Ghez, Adrienne Vincent-Phoenix, Lou Mongello, Jim Hill, Werner Weiss, Jim Fanning, Greg Ehrbar, Michael Lyons, Michael Barrier, Paul Anderson, Dave Smith, Kim Eggink, Wade Sampson, John Cawley, Sam Gennawey, Deb Wills, Cathy Perrone, Jerry Johnson, Henry Hardt, Gary and Anita Schaengold, Russell Schroder;

Marion Quarmby, Sarah Tabac, Tom and Marina Stern, Jerry and Liz Edwards, Marie Schilly, Lonnie Hicks, Michael "Shawn" and Laurel Slater, Kirk Bowman, Jeff Kurtti, Ryan N. March, Brad Anderson, George Grant, David Gerstein, Kaye Bundey, Brian Sibley;

Todd James Pierce, Betty Bjerrum, Jerry Beck, Michael Sporn, Leonard Maltin, Robin Cadwallender, John Culhane, Scott Wolf, Pete Martin, Bill Cotter, Steve Vagnini, John Canemaker, Mark Kausler, Keith Scott;

Dr. Mark Round, Dave Mruz, Tracy M. Barnes, Sarah Pate, Tamysen Hall, Evlyn Gould, Tom Heintjes, Bruce Gordon, David Mumford, Randy Bright, Jack and Leon Janzen, Malcolm and Mary Joseph (and their children Melissa, Megan, Rachel, Nicole, Richard);

Tim Foster, Arlen Miller, Floyd Norman, David Lesjak, Howard Kalov, Dana Gabbard, Margaret Kerry, Howard Green, Bob Thomas, Heather Sweeney, Don Peri, Bill Iadonisi.

My late parents, John and Barbara Korkis, who encouraged me to write and perform. Even with a very tight budget with no room for extravagances, they still took my brothers and me repeatedly to Disneyland and allowed us to watch cartoons and read comic books because it made us happy. I miss them every day. They always smiled when they saw Mickey Mouse.

And, sadly, some people whom I have foolishly forgotten for the moment. Their kindness and generosity, like the other names listed here, have lightened my journey through life and made this book possible. I hope all of you, both acknowledged and temporarily missing, live happily ever after.

About the Author

Jim Korkis is an internationally respected Disney historian who has written hundreds of articles about all things Disney for over three decades. He is also an award winning teacher, professional actor and magician, and author of several books.

Jim grew up in Glendale, California, right next to Burbank, the home of the Disney Studios.

As a teenager, Jim got a chance to meet the Disney animators and Imagineers who lived nearby and began writing about them for local newspapers. Over the decades, Jim pursued a teaching career as well as a performing career but was still active in writing about Disney for various magazines.

In 1995, he relocated to Orlando, Florida, to take care of his ailing parents. He got a job doing magic and making balloon animals for guests at Pleasure Island. Within a month, he was moved over to the Magic Kingdom, where he "assisted in the portrayal of" Prospector Pat in Frontierland as well as Merlin the Magician in Fantasyland for the Sword in the Stone ceremony.

In 1996, he became a full-time, salaried animation instructor at the Disney Institute where he taught every animation class, including several that only he taught. He also instructed classes on animation history and improvisational acting techniques for the interns at Disney Feature Animation Florida. As the Disney Institute re-organized, Jim joined Disney Adult Discoveries, the group who researched, wrote, and facilitated backstage tours and programs for Disney guests and Disneyana conventions.

Eventually, Jim moved to Epcot where he was a Coordinator with the College and International Programs and then a Coordinator for the EPCOT Disney Learning Center. During his time at EPCOT, Jim researched, wrote, and facilitated over two hundred different presentations on Disney history for Disney Cast Members and for such Disney corporate clients as Feld Entertainment, Kodak, Blue Cross, Toys "R" Us, and Military Sales.

Jim was the off-camera announcer for the syndicated television series *Secrets of the Animal Kingdom*, wrote articles for Disney publications like *Disney Adventures*, *Disney Files* (DVC), *Sketches*, *Disney Insider*, *Mickey Monitor* and others.

He worked on special projects such as writing text for WDW trading cards, as an on-camera host for the 100 Years of Magic vacation planning video, and as a facilitator with the Disney Crew puppet show. His countless other credits include assisting the Disney Cruise Line, WDW Travel Company, Imagineering, and the Disney Design Group with Disney historical material. As a result, Jim was the recipient of the prestigious Disney award, Partners in Excellence, in 2004.

Jim is not currently an employee of the Disney Company.

To read more stories by Jim Korkis about Disney history, please purchase his other books, all available from Theme Park Press, and make sure to visit the websites that feature his stories about Disney history:

- www.MousePlanet.com
- www.AllEars.net
- www.Yesterland.com
- www.CartoonResearch.com
- www.WDWRadio.com

About the Publisher

Theme Park Press is the largest independent publisher of Disney and Disney-related pop culture books in the world.

Established in November 2012 by Bob McLain, Theme Park Press has released best-selling print and digital books about such topics as Disney films and animation, the Disney theme parks, Disney historical and cultural studies, park touring guides, autobiographies, fiction, and more.

For our complete catalog and a list of forthcoming titles, please visit:

ThemeParkPress.com

or contact the publisher at: ben@themeparkpress.com

. . . .

Theme Park Press Newsletter

For a free, occasional email newsletter to keep you posted on new book releases, new author signings, and other events, as well as contests and exclusive excerpts and supplemental content, send email to:

theband@themeparkpress.com

or sign up at www.themeparkpress.com

. . . .

Index

More Books from Theme Park Press

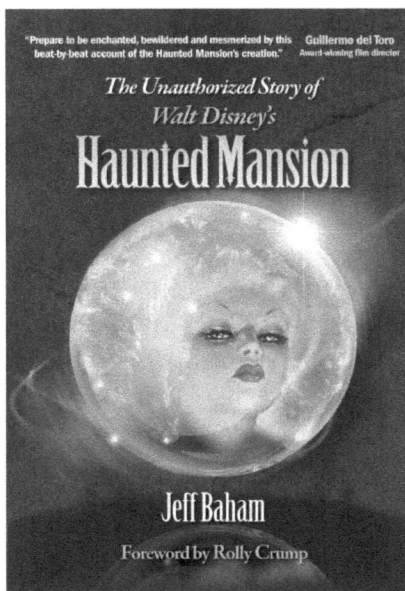

More Books from Theme Park Press

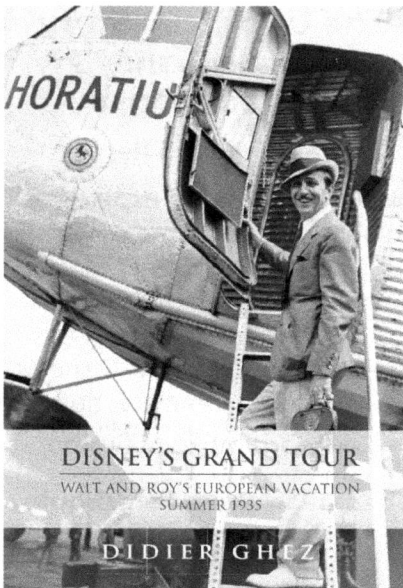

More Books from Theme Park Press

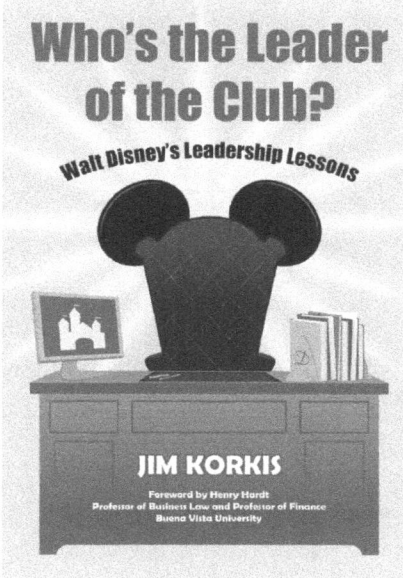

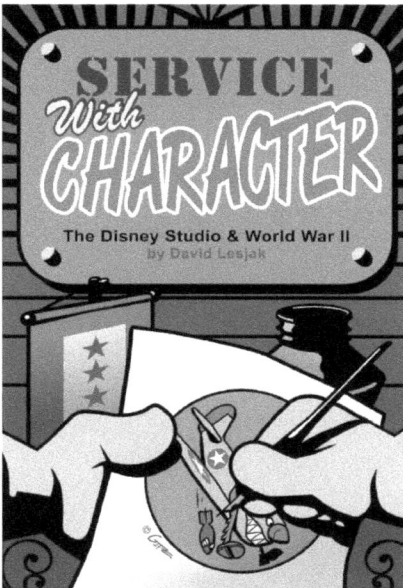

Discover our many other popular titles at:

www.ThemeParkPress.com

Milton Keynes UK
Ingram Content Group UK Ltd.
UKHW030745121124
451094UK00013B/961